ALL THE JOURNEY THROUGH

C.M. BLACKSTOCK

All the Journey Through

UNIVERSITY OF TORONTO PRESS
Toronto Buffalo London

© University of Toronto Press Incorporated 1997
Toronto Buffalo London
Printed in Canada
ISBN 0-8020-0966-2

Printed on acid-free paper

Canadian Cataloguing in Publication Data

Blackstock, C. M.
   All the journey through

   ISBN 0-8020-0966-2

   1. Blackstock family.   2. Blackstock, C. M. – Family.
   3. Gibbs family.   4. Gooderham family.   5. Canada –
   History – 19th century.   6. Canada – Social life and
   customs – 19th century.*   7. British – Canada – History –
   19th century.   I. Title.

   FC25.B57 1997   971'.009'9   C96-931846-4
   F1005.B53 1997

University of Toronto Press acknowledges the assistance
to its publishing program of the Canada Council
and the Ontario Arts Council.

'How wisely is the future hidden from our view. Could I have seen all that was before me when you came into the world, I should have sunk into the earth at the prospect before me; so we find it, bitter and sweet – sweet and bitter all the journey through – and much mercy mingled in the cup we have to drink.'

Caroline Gibbs to her daughter Caroline Collins, December 31st, 1867

CONTENTS

Acknowledgments ix
Genealogies xi

All the Journey Through 1

*Portraits and photographs follow
pages 82 and 198.*

ACKNOWLEDGMENTS

I AM INDEBTED to Major Henri McKenzie Masson for kindly permitting me to see the 'Papers Relative to the Seigniory of Terrebonne.' I am indebted also to the late Professor J.S. Will for the loan of several letters, to Felicity Leung (National Historic Sites, Parks Canada) for her research on mills and milling in Canada, to André Lalonde for information on colonization companies in his PhD thesis (Laval University, 1969), to the Reverend Glenn Lucas (retired Archivist, United Church Archives) for guiding me through the history of the Methodist Church, to Ruth Wilson (Assistant Chief Archivist, United Church Archives), to Dr Neil Semple (Victoria University), to Professor Michael Bliss (University of Toronto) for encouraging me in this project, to my friends Rachel Grover and Larry Pfaff for their advice over a long period, and to Gerald Hallowell and Kenneth Lewis, editors, for their patience and kindness.

From archivists and librarians, I received unfailing assistance. I am indebted in particular to the United Church Archives, and also to the National Archives of Canada for giving me permission to quote from the correspondence of Sir John A. Macdonald (Manuscript Group 26A) and Sir Wilfrid Laurier (Manuscript Group 26G); the Archives nationales du Québec, Montreal; the Archives of Ontario; the University of Toronto Robarts Library and the Thomas Fisher Rare Book Library; the Guildhall Library, London; the Public Record Office, London; the Devon Record Office, Exeter; and the Public Library, Jersey, C.I.

July 1996

BLACKSTOCK

- Moses m. ? (1793–1873)
  - George BLACKSTOCK m. ?
    - William m. Jane Chambers
      - William Schenck (1824–1905) m. Mary Hodge *Gibbs* (1827–1909)
        - Thomas Gibbs (Tom) (1851–1906) m. Harriet Victoria *Gooderham* (Hattie) (1855–1951)
          - William (Billy)
          - Thomas (Tommie)
          - Elizabeth (Lizzie)
          - Gibbs
          - Barbara
          - George
          - Harriet (Hat)
          - Dorothy (Dot)
        - Amelia Eliza (Millie) (1854–1936?)
        - George Tate (1856–1921) m. Emma Moulton Fraser
          - 3 children
        - Caroline Jane (Carrie) (1860–1919) m. (1) Donald Downey (2) Charles Duer
          - Jackie (adopted)
        - Mary Elizabeth (May) (1863–1924) m. Herbert McKeggie

GIBBS

Philip GIBBS (1759–1835) m. **Mary Nicholson** (1769?–1838)

Children:
- **Philip, Jr** (1793–1868)
- **Thomas** (1796–1871) m. **Caroline *Tate* Gillard** (1795–1873)
- **Mary** (d. 1825) m. **Silvanus Gillard**
  - Carrie m. W.R. Dixon
- **Cathrine**
- **Joseph** (d. 1826)
- **Elizabeth** m. ? Blake
- **Benjamin** (d. 1868)
- **John** (d. 1866)

Children of Thomas and Caroline:
- Caroline m. Joseph Collins (b. 1819)
- Thomas Nicholson (T.N.) m. Almira Ash (1821–83)
- William Henry m. Frances Colton (1823–1902)
- Sarah Ketland m. James *Gooderham* (1825–1906)   (d.1879)
- Mary Hodge m. William Schenck *Blackstock* (1827–1909)   (1824–1905)
- Amelia m. James Lobb
  (Their daughter is Cousin Marion)
- Emily m. Erastus B. Holt (d. 1876)

GOODERHAM

William GOODERHAM m. (1) ? Rodman
(1790–1881)   (2) Harriet Herring

- (2) William, Jr (1824–89)
- James (1825–79)
  m.
  Sarah Ketland *Gibbs* (1825–1906)
- George (1830–1905)
  m.
  Harriet Dean
  - Harriet Victoria (Hattie) (1855–1951)
    m.
    Thomas Gibbs *Blackstock* (Tom) (1851–1906)
  - + 11 other children
- + 11 other children

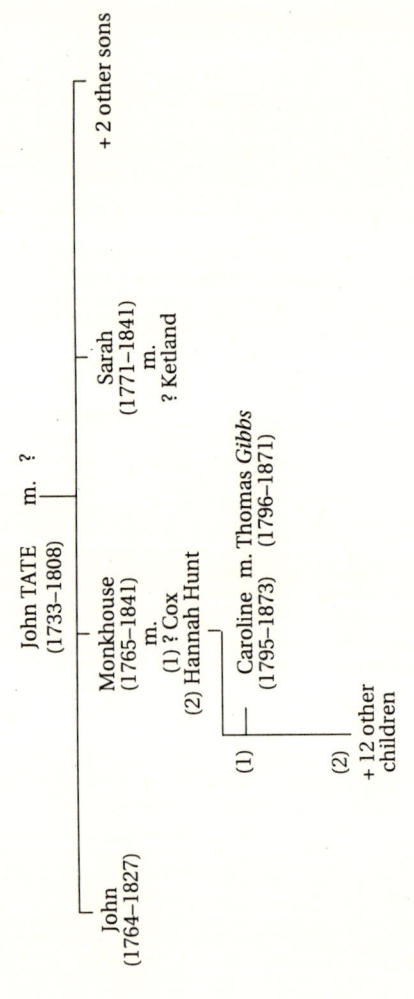

ALL THE JOURNEY THROUGH

CHAPTER ONE

*G*REAT-GRANDFATHER, a Methodist minister, used to say that the early settler was the real hero of Canada for he made possible all that was done afterwards; statesmen, businessmen, professional men, writers, all owed everything to him. Until he had accomplished the immense task of clearing the forests, there could be no nation; he was the true founder of the land as the explorers, soldiers, and administrators, in spite of their great contribution, never were. But, then, Great-Grandfather Blackstock was descended from pioneers.

If by the end of the nineteenth century cities flourished where forests had once stood and the early settlers' descendants tackled vastly different problems, they were not so far removed in time as to forget their origins and their history. They knew who they were; not for them the crises of identity that have beset later Canadians. They were proud of their country, but this was the heyday of empire and they felt themselves also to be part of a great and what seemed to them indestructible Empire. For this reason their outlook was transatlantic, unlike that of all other nations in the Western hemisphere, and if they chose to live abroad, they did not consider themselves to be expatriates as their neighbours in the United States tended to do. They were heirs to a great past; history for them did not begin with Columbus. Still, they were North Americans and the pioneer experience of their forbears had changed them forever from the peoples of Britain and Europe.

This point of view was not universal, but it characterized a large part of the population and it was our inheritance. It was how we, who were born after the First World War and who belonged to old Toronto and its conservative ways, viewed the world, while in a terrible way the war had already destroyed the old Canada, although no one knew it, and for its ravages on our parents' generation, to which the memorials in towns and villages everywhere proudly and mournfully still attest, the country grieved in brooding silence throughout our childhood.

Our family was fortunate; they returned almost unscathed from Armageddon, but my father's closest friends were all killed and within a few years two of his cousins, who had fought overseas, committed suicide – facts discreetly hidden for half a century. The awful presence of that war threw its shadow over our lives; our parents never spoke of it, a subject never to be mentioned until the Second World War, though even now, almost eighty years later, there is printed in our memories the haunted look of sadness on their faces every Armistice Day. Gone is the absolute stillness of those two-minute silences when no one stirred, and no longer do men remove their hats, clasping them to the chest and half-turning in salute when they pass a war memorial, nor do women bow their heads. How often we heard the words that went ringing down our young years: 'Oh, he was killed in the War.' And yet the dead were remembered and stories about them in happier times often made us rock with laughter; we felt we knew them and so they were part of our world.

Thus, our childhood began in the shadows of the Great War, but it was a happy time all the same. Eventually, however, Father isolated himself, Cassandra-like, from his contemporaries, for after Hitler crossed into the Rhineland to occupy the de-militarized zone, Father, like Churchill, prophesied repeatedly and insistently that war was coming, which no one wished to hear. This filled us with apprehension, and from early days the appeasers were well known to us by name, their reputations shredded at the dining-room table along, at times, with that of Mackenzie King. When the Second World War began, so that the years between the wars seemed only an interlude, brothers and cousins joined the thousands who went overseas to fight, as had Father's generation; there was never any doubt then that what happened to France and Britain mattered to Canada and that we were part of that civilization.

But I have not struck the proper note in this tale of nineteenth-century Canada. It is without hero or heroine, although there would be no tale to tell had it not been for my Grandfather Blackstock's sister, my Great-Aunt Millie. But she seemed, when I knew her, to be exceedingly odd. Memory sees her still, in the late 1920s or early 1930s, the last surviving member of Grandfather's family, with her green felt cloche hat worn both indoors and out of doors, beneath which protruded a mass of fine white curls. This was surmised, quite incorrectly, to be a wig. Chatelaine at this point to a number of cats and almost blind, she permitted no one to enter her house on Homewood Avenue, where visitors were left standing on the doorstep, whatever the inclemency of the weather, while her green-capped head appeared out of a third-floor window to engage them in conversation. Passers-by looked up in astonishment. I can still hear her crisp voice echoing down the street.

When the end came, the house presented a scene of arrested animation; everywhere months of letters and parcels lay unopened; a pyramid of rolled newspapers, just as the paper boy had flung them on the doorstep, mounted on the dining-room table; and there were the cats. But she had tied up and labelled the many bundles of letters that spanned more than a century, and on them she had written, 'Destroy everything,' having spent the last years of her life reading and rereading them, withdrawing as she did so into a past crowded with family long dead. This is the story that came out of the letters.

I am a fifth-generation Canadian with English and Scottish ancestors, the latter stopping in Ireland for half a century on their way here, but above all I am a member of a large family; none in the subcontinent of Asia could have been more extended than ours. In summertime at Longwood, scene of idyllic childhood as vanished childhood tends to be if one is lucky, for us perfect freedom reigned, unlike the many rules that hedged in city life. Here, we were all together at our Grandmother Blackstock's house at Lake Simcoe, parents, children, aunts, uncles, cousins, nannies, servants, and here our grandmother held gentle sway.

She was born Harriet Victoria Gooderham in 1855, known to her family as Hattie, and she married our Grandfather Blackstock. Nothing perhaps could more clearly distinguish this grandmother's upbringing from mine than the fact that her own mother, although in very comfortable, indeed wealthy, circumstances, deemed it necessary in the 1860s to instruct her in the cutting up of the whole pig after its butchering. A more formal education came from the Toronto Model School, which she attended with her brothers, and this was followed by Miss Dashwood & Mrs Neville's select establishment and finally, at seventeen, a five- or six-month tour of Britain and the Continent in the company of several aunts and uncles; the long stay in Paris just two years after the siege of the Franco-Prussian War made our grandmother's tales of its inhabitants' terrible privations alarmingly real in our childhood.

But to return to Longwood, remembered for its happy times, its laughter and its repartee, we were self-satisfied and self-contained; it was later that the disadvantages became apparent to me. In winter the family convened twice weekly at this grandmother's house in Toronto, 79 Prince Arthur Avenue, for Sunday afternoon teas and Wednesday night dinners, to which last as children we were not invited. For the occasional guest this mass scene of relations must have presented a formidable challenge and possibilities also of *ennui*. Indeed, the cohesive band of family so visibly present everywhere in the house attracted and repelled me at the same time, and if the memory of '79' can still evoke in me a longing for its vanished world, where even then a door opened into the further past, the past also stifled and repressed so that I longed to free myself from its shackles and from the omnipresence of so many relations.

The grandmother of whom I have been speaking was the best of listeners, generous in thought and deed: we loved her. I did not know then that she had iron in the soul, that she was the product of Victorian conventions from which she never wavered. It was a surprise to discover that my aunts, her daughters, or at least three of them, were not allowed to go to school, had to remain at home under a governess, were cut off from their contemporaries, dressed in outmoded fashions, and, circumscribed in every way, discouraged from entering university or thinking of professions; the proper place was home and family. Her views, though seldom expressed, held sway long after the aunts had grown up.

In the early 1920s, one of Father's sisters, my Aunt Barbara, concealed from her mother the fact that the leading suffragettes Emmeline and Christabel Pankhurst, whom she had known in England, had invited her to sit on the platform with them when they visited Toronto, a city they found most congenial, and while our aunt did sit on the platform she was afraid that the news would reach home before she had time to scoop up the newspapers. Our grandmother had strong views on politics, but as far as I know she never voted in her life, holding that this was not woman's proper role.

For all her gentleness, her word was law, and the aunts, when young, complained that no amount of reasoning or argument on their part prevailed. 'Because I say so' was the inevitable reply to their 'why?' but this was a side I never saw. I never saw her ruffled, never angry, her voice always low and gentle, her smile ready to welcome children and strangers. Few people ever knew of her many generous actions; only recently I learned that when the Home Bank failed in Toronto in 1923, although she had no connection with it, she reimbursed several of its unhappy depositors, one of whom was her own gardener. It was not fair, she said, that they should suffer.

She was always fearful that some accident might befall us children, but she herself had been a tomboy in her childhood, fond of jumping recklessly from pile to pile along the docks that fronted her grandfather's mill and distillery, Gooderham & Worts, down by the city's waterfront. The child is not always father to the man; I could not recognize my grandmother in this guise. During the American Civil War, her father had a farm in summertime in Maine (I think the exchange was in Canada's favour then) and the Union soldiers used to call her 'Little Garibaldi,' an epithet of which

I think she was a little proud, as dressed in a bright red skirt she would run to the gate at the end of the lane and watch them pass.

However I look at her now, from memory or what came out of letters written long ago by those who knew and loved her, it is her generous heart that lives on. She was a Victorian who shunned the ostentation and shallowness of the Edwardian Age. All who knew her loved her and if I say that she was quiet and retiring, that is not altogether true. Someone observed she had no need to talk because her daughters, my aunts, did all the talking and indeed they were loquacious.

We, her grandchildren, were, I often think, the last Victorians in the city. When young we attended a small private school conducted by the aunts' retired governess and run on ancient precepts, where endless copperplate transcriptions in last century's copybooks produced an outmoded hand and where *Little Arthur's History of England*, already out of date in its own land, reigned unchallenged. Only recently have I been able to see these early years clearly; facts and incidents long suppressed have jumped out of the past, whose reconstruction ebbs and flows.

Growing up in the midst of so many cousins, aunts, and uncles, I could never have imagined then the nuclear family of today or indeed its broken homes. One took for granted the closeness of family relationships; it enveloped us children. Therefore, it was doubly disturbing later on to learn that there had been in my grandmother's life cause for anxiety and sorrow or that she had unwittingly brought trouble on my father. I was grown up when he died, but only then did I begin to understand him. He had seldom mentioned his older brother Billy, cause of the anxiety and sorrow, but in the last months of his life and seriously ill Father sat with head in hands saying to me over and over again: 'Billy ruined my life.' This enigmatic statement my aunts to some extent corroborated, unfolding in bursts of confidence a story long hidden from me. But whatever part Billy played in his life, Father, who was the kindest of men and acknowledged by all to be clever, even very clever, had seemed to me at times to be the author of his own misfortunes.

Father had had to forgo much of the freedom of youth, made to carry an impossible burden that older men might have shirked. His thraldom began on his sixteenth birthday when, our grandfather being terminally ill, our grandmother entailed this elder brother (Billy was almost eight years older) on him, sending them on a summer tour of Ireland with incongruous instructions for Father to keep Billy, whose failing was alcohol, out of pubs; she prayed that a cure might miraculously take effect. It did not and thereafter Father's role as watch and ward began. For years he had to remain close to home in a bondage that later reached out to England, where, after university, Father went to pursue further studies in chemistry, for Billy also took up residence there, placing once more on Father the cares and burdens from which he must have thought he had escaped.

By the time Father returned home after the War, which the family spent in England, for they had been touring the Continent when it broke out, and during which he had been shunted into munitions in the unromantic and unheroic backwaters of Birmingham, his brother's failing was quite out of control. Father, now feeling the stress of long-concentrated war work (in a building that from the carelessness of British workers threatened to go up with a bang at a moment's notice, for they insisted on bringing in forbidden matches), found himself once more in charge of his brother when he was himself at the point of exhaustion and he suffered a minor nervous breakdown, the possibility of any repetition of which must have been constantly present in my English mother's mind.

Father lived ever afterwards in a cocoon of protection, and my mother was to consider it her role to devote herself and us to this end. Later she had something to say about the solitude enforced upon her in her first year in a country to which she was a stranger. Silence and subterfuge were the order of the day as my grandmother marshalled the family to conceal the canker eating at its heart. But, as my mother said, far and wide the facts were known.

Poor Billy, more sinned against than sinning, the seeds of his failure had been sown long ago in the 1880s when parental plans for his advancement in life, the best education that wealth could provide, appeared to him to be inexplicable punishment. At eight years of age, together with a cousin and an uncle who was one year younger than himself (both of them on his mother's side of the family), he left Toronto for a preparatory school in England. This was in 1889, when business relating to the distillery belonging to his mother's family required the frequent presence in London of his father and his Grandfather Gooderham.

The rest of the family soon followed in a transatlantic migration that lasted for two years. The women and children rusticated quietly in Devon while, travelling like shuttlecocks back and forth across the Atlantic, the men dined at London clubs and at the houses of financiers and leading politicians. Billy wrote to his father, 'Carus Pater, spero te esse bene ...' and ended his letters with such postscripts in English as: 'I can't really stay any longer in England, I am getting homesick.' Not, as he carefully explained, for Longwood in Devon, once the house of Sir Hudson Lowe, Governor of St Helena, and their temporary home in England, but for Canada, to which they all finally returned in the summer of 1891.

The superiority of an English education outweighed all objections or any parental misgivings, and young Billy's destiny was once more England. He almost broke down when saying good-bye to his father in New York in the autumn of that year, but nothing was so hard to bear as parting from his father's father, the Reverend W.S. Blackstock, who accompanied him overseas. Hand in hand, they walked for nearly three hours from the station to the school, as the child tried to suppress his tears: 'I had to sit down on the bank by the roadside with him,' his grandfather related, 'to prolong the time and to enable him to recover strength for the last trying moment.'

Billy proceeded eventually to Harrow, to which he became reconciled although he could write: 'My belly longeth for the flesh pots of Egypt and for the good staying dinners of home,' and to this last he returned during the long school holidays. In time, Harrow produced quite unforeseen results for, however good an education it delivered, he came home at eighteen an alcoholic, and Harrow had also unfitted him for Canadian life and for the hurly-burly of business, for which he was destined; sensitive, gentle, literary, and artistic, he could not and did not fit into the life that lay before him. With an adequate income there was no need to put his hand to a business plough, but a venture in this direction, an agency importing Wolseley cars, ended in a large bankruptcy, the payment of which affected family fortunes. His partner in this unhappy affair, a Gooderham cousin, immediately committed suicide, his young daughter discovering him in a river of blood. Some years later, in 1920, Billy's life was to end also in suicide, a fact to be concealed from us but once again known by most of the town. The distillery, source of much of the family's wealth, had exacted its revenge in the manner of Greek tragedy.

Another experiment with English schooling had more fortunate results in Father's family. His elder sister Lizzie, insisting that she had learned nothing at any of the schools she had attended in either Toronto or Ottawa, which may or may not have been true, but, more to the point, longing for freedom, begged to go to school in England. She set sail at sixteen, in 1901, to the overwhelming approval of her grandmother, the wife of the Reverend W.S. Blackstock, who never ceased to regret her own lack of opportunity:

'No such offer was thought of for girls in those days,' she told Lizzie's father with reference to her own upbringing. 'You were wise in sending her as I have no doubt it will be of immense advantage to her.'

Lizzie's younger sisters enjoyed no such latitude, and the iron hand in their mother's velvet glove ruled in mid-Victorian fashion, denying them even the opportunity to make friends with other children, because in 1887 their four-year-old brother, little Tommie, whom they had never known, had died of diphtheria caught at a children's party from a child whose parents were not of our family's immediate circle. Henceforth, all strangers were to be rendered suspect, and safety lay in associating only with relations or very close friends.

The size of our Grandmother Blackstock's family, the Gooderhams, merely reinforced this isolation from the rest of the town, and later on the mourning that followed upon Grandfather Blackstock's death in 1906 came as a relief to her, or at least so Father maintained, since it removed all necessity to concern herself with fashion or society. Family substituted for society, and these Gooderhams had many laudable virtues: integrity, generosity, and a strong social conscience. Nor would they permit any of their benefactions to the city to bear their name; wealth and philanthropy were usually synonymous in Toronto the Good.

We knew more about this family than our Grandfather Blackstock's because they appeared omnipresent in our lives, everything about them being on a massive scale ever since their arrival in 1832 in York, when, so it is said, they deposited over the counter the largest sum the cashiers at the Bank of Upper Canada had as yet seen. In Montreal the cholera epidemic had orphaned eleven children who had crossed on the same vessel; William Gooderham gathered them up, brought them to York, and in a sense adopted them, a deed that was a forerunner of his many charitable works.

The planning and execution of his migration was an earnest of the family's solid cautious progress about to unfold in Toronto, as York soon became. He met with immediate success in the business world. The family were not, however, marked by any sense of adventure in other spheres, or so I thought. Travel for them, according to my Aunt Barbara, meant the annual move to Toronto Island, and although tradition claimed descent from Guthrun, King of the Danes – Father said that could mean owner of more than one pig – they had little of the Viking left in them and seemed to me, when I reached an age to make my own observations, to be weighed down by their sense of duty and decorum.

Wisely perhaps and with their habitual reticence, the Gooderhams left no letters, memorials, or written documents of any kind behind them, and so they will not speak here with their own voices, nor will we see much of them in this account. But their influence, even in our childhood, was pervasive. For all their wealth, they were modest and shunned publicity; they were also exceedingly conventional in contrast, I felt, with the unconventional Blackstocks, and although I could not have expressed it in such terms, in Father, the aunts, and uncles could be seen opposing traits that stemmed from these two very dissimilar ancestral roots.

William Gooderham, our great-great-grandfather, epitomized conservatism, and 'to each his own' was his guiding principle, as a member of one branch of our family said during the 1860s. On another occasion, the same relation said: 'Old Mr G. is like this – every man to his profession, therefore what the doctors said must be right.' He had acquiesced in the amputation of his daughter's finger when others stated that the doctors, muddling cause and circumstance, had confused a rabid dog nowhere near the scene of the crime with the perfectly innocent and healthy cat that had scratched the unfortunate girl; the finger, soon to be chopped off, had long since healed and the cat flourished.

One member of that branch of our family levelled a caustic accusation at our great-great-grandfather in spite of all his good works. Because of the former's connection by marriage with the Gooderhams and the latter's ownership of two railways, in 1872 the Prime Minister sent T.N. Gibbs, a member of Parliament, to Toronto soliciting funds to finance the Pacific Railway, which was to be the road to ruin in all its ramifications for the Conservative Party. He approached Old William's partner, James Worts, with the offer of directorships, only to report to Ottawa on December 11th: '... If assured half a million as the result he w^d not enter into it. His ideas are and his partner's the same, that wealth is only of service so long as it can be made to minister to the comfort &

ease of its possessor. Any other obligation than those of self & family are ignored. They seem to have a natural aversion to have anything to do with matters not under their own immediate control.'

By 1880, at the end of his long life, Old William still lived close to the city's eastern limits, where he had first settled in 1832, his sons and daughters nearby on Trinity, Mill, and Palace Streets, the houses, mill, and distillery within the strongly evangelical parish of Trinity Church, of which he was warden and chief benefactor. Staunch Church of England and early in life probably coming under the influence of the Clapham Sect, he practised its precepts in daily living, held family prayers twice daily, and observed a strict Sabbath. Neither coachman nor horses worked on that day for any reason whatever.

The rising middle class to which Old William belonged had begun to merge with the earlier aristocracy, if such they could be called, but the Gooderham network, so closely bound by blood and trade, was a Family Compact in itself. Old William's advice to his sons is said to have been: 'Stick together boys.' His death in 1881 left his remaining seven sons and five daughters comfortably prosperous, and the funeral in that heyday of funerals was enormous; the Mayor and Corporation, the Board of Trade, all the judges, the Masonic fraternity, and the York Pioneers formed a procession, headed at their own request by the employees of distillery and mill and followed by one hundred and twenty-seven carriages.

Father's older sister, Lizzie, could just recall Old William's second house, built in 1860, replacing the earlier one. It too was on Trinity Street with great spreading verandah, large garden, and a many-mirrored ballroom, pale green and gold. In that year, 1860, his daughter-in-law Sarah had informed her relations in Oshawa that the house was the most splendid she had ever seen: 'So convenient, hot and cold soft water to be had anytime day or night by just turning a tap ... a fire-place in every room in the house, the marble slabs of each cost two hundred dollars and at the opening they had a party of fifty couples.' But just about this time, a Gooderham servant waiting at table on the assembled guests suddenly threw off her apron and declared she would not stay one minute longer; she preferred to live at the Asylum, where twenty girls slept to a room.

In the same year, this daughter-in-law and her husband, James Gooderham, his parents, his brothers, and their wives, all rising in the social scale, attended a ball given by the City in honour of the Prince of Wales; and while this great event took place in all its splendour, at the other end of the social spectrum thieves broke into James's store attached to his house in Meadowvale and stole some cloth. James showed ability, rose rapidly in the business world, and soon became a philanthropist, so that at his death, which occurred two years before his father's, his was said to be one of the largest funerals Toronto had yet seen.

Sarah failed to inherit her husband's share of Old William's estate, for without a doubt the latter reasoned that his son James had wealth enough already and, being childless, he and Sarah would leave everything to the Methodist Church, of which they were members. The Wesleyan Methodist Church in Canada had made inroads into the Gooderham connection, and it had ordained James a year or two before his marriage to Sarah, which took place in 1850. A throat ailment then robbed him of the one indispensable qualification for a preacher, the ability to preach, and turned him instead into a miller and storekeeper at one of his father's several mills about Toronto.

James atoned for his association with the family distillery by a lifetime of hard work as layman in a church that moved its ministers frequently and therefore depended largely on such help. He saw to the building of several churches. His untimely end occurred in May of 1879 as one day he waited with the official party on the platform at the opening up of ten new miles of track for the Credit Valley Railway, which he, as director, had helped to build. The locomotive ran into the platform and carried him off, leaving Sarah well-to-do and free to devote herself to Methodism and the cause of women. In this guise, she will reappear.

Conversion to Methodism led several of Old William's sons to avoid the distillery; they preferred to run their father's country mills that dealt in flour and grain, but the inescapable fact remains, the country mills fed the distillery; on the other hand, the Church of England sons stuck to the distillery and the town, and such (fortunately for us) was our Great-Grandfather Gooderham, George, the third son. In 1842 when Old William sent another son, William, Jr, at eighteen to Rochester as apprentice to a business associate, whatever it achieved in the line of trade, it also effected a conversion to Methodism, and as a result William, Jr, began a lifelong involvement in the social movements of his day. The family, with some unease, saw him marching up Yonge Street to the sound of brass bands bent on temperance or conversion; he regularly visited condemned men in their cells to comfort them on the last night before their execution; and his generosity funded many causes.

Later he supported the newly arrived Salvation Army at a time when its notoriety from noisy parades and bands disturbed and distressed good city folk, especially on Sabbath; but it reached those sinners and needy whom the churches had failed to touch. In 1883 when the town of Lindsay locked up the Salvation Army band in jail because rows had broken out between it and local Roman Catholics, William, Jr, received the news by telegraph, lost no time in commandeering a locomotive from the Toronto & Nipissing Railway, a family line of which he was managing director, drove it himself at top speed to Lindsay, roused the magistrate at four in the morning, paid the band's bail, and secured its release.

By the end of the nineteenth century, the Gooderhams had long since established themselves in trade and commerce in an impregnable position, their distillery one of the largest in the Empire, their banking, insurance, and trust companies flourishing. A good deal else besides lay under their control, and after Grandfather Blackstock's death in 1906, Father, his brothers, and sisters were all swept into the orbit of this large Gooderham connection both by proximity and sheer weight of numbers. Seldom were they to be out of mourning for one or other of these innumerable maternal relations.

When the mourners gathered to follow Grandfather Blackstock's bier to the grave, the house on Prince Arthur Avenue stopped half suspended in time; little in it was ever altered afterwards, which might be taken as our grandmother's tribute to Grandfather, its builder, or as a sign of her own indifference to changing tastes. Built in the closing years of the 1880s, it had been a gift from her father and it had also marked the beginning of Grandfather Blackstock's success in the business world, his arrival in the ranks of the city's leading men. Nearby, Bloor Street was sand and gravel laid on a bed of cedar blocks, and the Taddle Creek wended its way past a half rural scene to be met by the fashionable world of St George Street as it began to take shape.

At the same time his father-in-law, George Gooderham, built a house for himself next door. Both were in the Italianate, romanesque style that came to Toronto via Chicago. Red brick surmounted massive red square-hewn masonry, the gleam of copper sparkled on the deep red tiled roofs, wrought iron fences hedged the lawns, and no effort was spared to make both houses compare with the finest in town, indestructible and unchanging bastions built to outlast eternity, enclosing a private world. Workmen came from Italy to mould the ceilings. Stone that came in ballast from Caithness formed the sidewalks of half a city block.

A doge's chair stood in the front hall of '79,' a witness to Grandfather Blackstock's abiding love for Italy, which manifested itself everywhere as one entered the house; in the hall, the walls and carpet wore a deep Venetian red and led into the burst of gold and putty that flooded the Italian-empire drawing-room. The house straddled the Victorian and Edwardian years. Coal burned in the front-hall grate, wood in other fireplaces, and a giant furnace fed the radiators. A gentle gloom filled the velvet-curtained music room, while the palm-treed den, enticingly dark and mysterious to children, harboured spears, assegais, and numerous mementos of distant journeys – to British Columbia, to Palestine, up the Nile, to India and Burma, and year after year to England, Scotland, and Europe.

Moose and buffalo skulls peered over the bookcases that lined the library walls, and in the hall the great buffalo head, said to be the largest on record, stood guard, a gift from the Dominion Government when the bull died in a fight, for Grandfather, and several other men, had presented a small herd in an early effort to save the breed. In our childhood in the 1920s the nursery at '79' still had its old-fashioned furniture and toys and a portrait of that Tommie who had died long ago, in the 1880s, and yet was our childhood friend. On the third floor, one of the tower corners of the large billiard room where Grandfather had entertained his many friends still contained a perfect Victorian dolls' house that had entranced us as children.

In the dining-room the ancestral portraits stared at each other and at us. Old William Gooderham gazed down upon us from an elaborate and gilded frame, his elderly face afloat in a nebula of white beard; beside him and similarly encased in a gold-encrusted setting his elderly bespectacled wife, her cap swirling with many-hued ribbons, kept watch on us too. Instantly we knew they were worthy and rich. Equally we suspected they were not of the first rank in the colony that became their home, lacking the aura of belonging to the Loyalists or the cachet of arriving as administrators or leading members of the military or even the professions, but coming from what our Aunt Barbara called 'good yeoman stock.' She reminded us from time to time that the Cathedral would not at first have invited the men to be wardens or even sidesmen. Stout middle-class citizens, they were intent on trade.

As befitted a Methodist minister, a more modest but still handsome frame held the portrait of the Reverend W.S. Blackstock, who began this tale and whose descent from pioneers was a point in his favour, or so I thought. He sported a grey bush of beard, about which Old Cousin Marion, who was the only one of Grandfather's cousins I ever knew and who died at the age of a hundred and two, said of earlier days: 'He would insist on kissing us girls with that black beard. We did not like it one bit.' Beside him but separated by the frames sat his wife, our Great-Grandmother Blackstock, who retained still in old age traces of early good looks, made no concessions to frivolous ribbons or light-hearted smile, and appeared fully conscious of her role as wife and helpmate to a minister.

Above the dining-room mantelpiece hung the portrait of Grandfather himself, Thomas Gibbs Blackstock. His presence lingered in the house in the many reminders of his love for Italy, in the numerous late-nineteenth-century Dutch watercolours so highly recommended by the art dealers of Chicago or Detroit when he might have collected the Impressionists, in the works of local artists, in the library with its glut of musty law books, its moose and buffalo skulls; for he had loved to hunt, indeed was a crack shot, in his teens winning trophies at the Dominion Rifle Match at La Prairie. On one of his father's many circuits, the Indians had taught him as a boy how to shoot; they had made him a blood brother and given him the name 'the one who can read the moss on the trees,' which I suppose means he knew where he was going. Later in life, with Indians as his friends and guides, escaping the pressure and uncertainties of his mining empire, he found his greatest happiness in canoeing down the rivers of British Columbia.

'Tom is always so level-headed,' his father said. This quality must have appealed to his father-in-law, for by the end of the eighties George Gooderham had made him his business manager, a position which, in addition to his ever-expanding law practice, was to involve Tom (as our grandfather was usually called) in work related to the distillery, the building of the King Edward Hotel, mining in British Columbia, and numerous other Gooderham projects and companies.

George Gooderham had taken Old William's place as head of the distillery, succeeded him as president of the Bank of Toronto, was director of innumerable firms, and steadily engaged in founding other businesses. His vitality dispels some of the aura of dullness with which I had hitherto cloaked all these relations; I had not known of William, Jr's, tub-thumping nor of George's two avocations, racing and sailing, the Jockey Club and his yacht, the *Oriole*. Old photographs still conjure up this large schooner ploughing through stormy seas, while others show it gliding through gentler ones, with host and guests sporting nautical attire, lulled on calm summer evenings by the strains of the small orchestra hired for such occasions; the rosters of the invited include governor-general, prime minister, distinguished visitors. The restrictions of his parsonage youth far behind him, George's son-in-law Tom followed suit on his motor yacht, the *Cleopatra*. He too entertained prime minister, distinguished visitors.

CHAPTER TWO

*O*UR GRANDMOTHER was quiet and undemonstrative; our grandfather was gregarious, full of life, idolized by his children – 'as Father would have said' or 'that is what Father used to say' giving weight to many an observation. As a small boy, my father wrote to him: 'Please come home soon for all the kids are missing you'; so much of his time passed in business trips abroad or at Rossland in British Columbia. The mining boom had begun. Vague memories recall to mind now the few elderly men we knew in our childhood, his contemporaries at the turn of the century; they said he had contributed to the making of Canada. It did not dawn on us that he could be classed with Robber Barons, if indeed we had as yet ever heard the term, nor that mining would ever be called rape of the earth.

It was borne in upon me even as a child that unlike his eccentric brother, and to a certain extent his sisters, Grandfather Blackstock was eminently sane;

in return, he was known to his sisters as 'Poor Tom,' while his brilliant and neurotic brother was always 'Dear George.' But in July of 1906, at Tom's death, the newspapers carried long columns on his life, the *Globe* naming him a brilliant lawyer, a foremost financier, and a captain of industry: 'Toronto loses a prominent and patriotic citizen and the country a man who was well known and highly honored.' The *Mail & Empire* said: 'He was perhaps as loyal a Torontonian as the city has ever possessed and all his ambitions were centred on making this city one of the greatest on the Continent.'

It was, however, in mining that Tom (our Grandfather Blackstock) made his name. Business had altered in Toronto in the mid-nineties; a new and adventurous group of young men came to the fore; the Laurier government breathed optimism; and the industrialized countries of Europe required Canada's raw materials at an ever increasing rate. George Gooderham considered developing Ontario's Sudbury mines, which at the time were American-controlled, but experts advised against the purchase just, in fact, as Mond's nickel-refining process was about to be made known. He turned his attention to the mining of ore in British Columbia, made feasible by the development of advanced mining and smelting techniques and an extension of the railways; the Canadian Pacific had reached Vancouver in 1885. All through the Kootenay, from the Boundary country to the Slocan, it was to be a race as to whether these mines would belong to American or English companies for, by and large, Canadians lacked capital; there was no wealth in Canada comparable to New York's and London's.

The year 1894 had seen large-scale mining in Rossland by English and American companies, and two years later Tom went there with a group of mining engineers who were to assess the situation for his father-in-law. This led to the acquisition at the cost of one hundred and sixty thousand pounds, or seven hundred thousand dollars, of the War Eagle Mine by a group of Toronto capitalists to form the War Eagle Consolidated Mining Company, with George Gooderham, president, and T.G. Blackstock, vice-president, followed by a list of other names as directors. It was the first large Canadian venture in mining.

When in 1897 the Centre Star Mine was added, the name 'Gooderham-Blackstock Syndicate' appears, and in Toronto at '79' two new carriage horses, bought for a spanking new Victoria, were named War Eagle and Centre Star. With interests in the Iron Mask and a two-thirds interest in the large St Eugene Mine at Moyie, East Kootenay, to form with other purchases the St Eugene Consolidated Mining Co. Ltd, the Syndicate soon had more money invested in the Kootenay than anyone else. Here was not just opportunity and reward for investors, but national pride and sovereignty; these ventures were Canadian-owned. But the happy mood evaporated. The previous owners of the War Eagle had indulged in some questionable promotion tactics on the London market, and the stock continued to escalate, which only made Tom nervous. There was a difference between trading in stock and investing capital as he had done: 'Many people will rue mining,' he said, a sentiment that was to be his own. By October of 1898, the mine's stock still rose.

The immediate and pressing problem of inadequate smelting facilities and the settling of freight and smelter rates hung fire for two years, which made the mines' owners despair, until agreement could be reached between the owner of the Trail smelter and the C.P.R., and smelting at the lowest possible rate was the more necessary since Rossland ore was not high grade and required specialized treatment, a serious problem that bedevilled all its mines. The Syndicate made an early and unsuccessful offer to buy the smelter with a view to enlarging it, but the C.P.R. appears to have had a prior claim. The ensuing delay forced mine owners to turn elsewhere for facilities; they also complained loudly of the prevailing cost of the C.P.R. freight rates.

The railway had already begun in 1890 its policy of buying up local lines of communication by rail, ship, and road, but by 1898 matters had still not been settled, so that Tom wrote to the Prime Minister on January 7th: 'What does it profit the B.C. miner that the Government spend millions on branch lines in B.C. when American roads and smelters without state or federal aid will offer us better terms than our own state aided enterprises?' The C.P.R., however, had its own problems, servicing long unprofitable lines in agricultural communities. Meanwhile, in the mining cities of Butte, Montana, and Spokane, Washington, where large fortunes had been made, smelters, refineries, and rail facilities awaited expectantly the ore of British Columbia.

The country between Rossland and the border remained as wild and remote as in the days over thirty years earlier when Erastus B. Holt, the husband of Tom's Aunt Em, had made his way down the Columbia to the mines at Big Bend, and the area was still being surveyed by the Geological Survey of Canada in 1897 when Tom journeyed down to the Boundary River country: 'a difficult country to get into as it requires from 65 to 100 miles of staging,' he said. He made many trips into Montana: 'Butte is a heated feverish life, where everyone is seeking to grab something and get out.' Everyone found it a violent town, compared with which one American visitor to Rossland and Moyie noted with amazement that a mine manager in British Columbia, unarmed and alone, could safely transport all his miners' pay in a gig on long lonely roads.

It was soon apparent that dependence on the larger smelters and refineries in the United States made the mines a prey to the now menacing activities of the American Smelting and Refining Company, which amalgamated with the Guggenheims in 1901. Together with American railway interests and by means of a high tariff and price setting, they were forcing Canadian mines into long contracts and out of their traditional European markets with the ultimate aim, at least this is what Tom maintained, of so weakening them that they could be easily taken over.

One problem after another beset the mining industry. The price of silver fell shortly after the purchase of the mines; the War Eagle required extensive renovation; the rush to the Klondike in 1898 diverted attention from British Columbia; forest fires devastated Rossland. More serious by far were labour troubles and the fear of strikes spreading from the mines of Montana, Colorado, and Idaho, where much worse conditions of work prevailed, although in British Columbia certain mines had appallingly long hours.

Owners claimed that much of the trouble had been fomented south of the border and looked upon it as foreign interference; the Syndicate said its mines had good working conditions. But when the eight-hour day became law in the province in 1899, howls of protest arose from many mine managers, possibly from the Syndicate too, and throughout the province the Silver-Lead Mines Association of British Columbia promptly reduced miners' pay, and this of course resulted in strikes. More unrest and work stoppages reduced output in 1901. Finally, in that year, the ruination by the notorious Whitaker Wright of his own shareholders in his British American Corporation affected adversely all mines.

Tom said: 'The fact remains the mines have been a complete disappointment to all ... It is small consolation to know that the whole mining district of B.C. seems to be in the same plight, that my mining interests are not worth today what I owe against them.' The long struggle against the odds was taking its toll, and his father thought him near exhaustion. His mother said: 'Dr. Caven told me after he left that his heart caused the greatest anxiety ... Poor fellow, it will be the hardest lesson he has ever had to learn to be a laggard.'

Nevertheless, the mines were in better shape and he had seen to the solving of a number of problems, including the concentrating of lower grades of ore. Better rates of treatment in Canada and better facilities had averted the threat of the American Smelting and Refining Company; the C.P.R. had built a lead refinery, and the Dominion Government offered a bounty on lead, for all of which Tom, more perhaps than anyone, had long and persistently fought to the detriment of his health. Then he fell ill from typhoid, which led to nephritis, and nephritis led to blindness; bedridden and blind for the last years of his life, he died in the summer of 1906 at fifty-four years of age.

The newspapers said he had never regained his great wealth of the nineties. Most of it must have gone down the mines: the War Eagle and its subsidiary, the Rossland Power Company, the Centre Star and the St Eugene. All of these the C.P.R. quickly took over amalgamating them with its Canadian Smelting Works to form the Canadian Consolidated Mines Ltd. In time it added the West Kootenay Power and Light Co. and the Le Roi and Sullivan mines to form Cominco, the largest non-ferrous metallurgical plant in the world.

Tom's life typifies in some ways the American dream, the burst of energy that brought so many young men of humble origins to fame as the nineteenth century progressed, and 79 Prince Arthur Avenue, where he lay dying in 1906, presents a very different scene from the Methodist parsonage of his youth from which he had run away at fifteen in order to relieve his parents of the burden of keeping him.

That was in the year 1867, the year after the Fenian Raids, the year of Confederation, the year that his mother's brother defeated George Brown at the polls, the year his father was still minister on the Drummondville circuit in what is now Niagara Falls.

Every year or so the Methodist Church sent its shepherds to new flocks, and Conference, arbiter of fate, had appointed the Reverend William Schenck Blackstock, always referred to as Mr B. by his wife and her relations, to Drummondville after three lean years at L'Orignal on the Ottawa River. Even with the most careful domestic management, the new circuit failed to support them. Reduced to the barest of necessities and struggling to survive, Mr B. told his wife to put her trust in God: 'I do not wonder that you feel in contrasting our humble circumstances with those of friends who appear to have made no more earnest exertion than we have done, but I am sure you feel reproved as I have often done when you think of our Father's love and care and especially when you think all His perfections are pledged to provide for us. Have faith, all is there.' But poverty continued to tighten its grip at the parsonage.

'Dear Mama,' ran the note that their son Tom left on his mother's pincushion, 'ere you find this in all probability I shall be far from here. I leave because I think you are not able to support me. Yours truly, Thomas Gibbs Blackstock. P.S. I will write soon.' And when a letter reached his mother a few weeks later, she had replied: 'At first I felt as if I could not live without knowing how you were and where you were and certainly should have sunk under the feeling of loneliness that was occasioned by your absence were it not for the assurance I had that God would hear my prayer and afford you His protection.' His younger brother and sisters missed him but thought he had gone to visit relatives; his father had wept bitterly.

In this tale it is Tom's father, much buffeted by the exigencies of his calling and yet steadfastly pursuing a heavenly course, who leads off in the procession of men and women walking with ever quickening pace down the nineteenth century's path, for he alone at the final chapter of his life looks back to forgotten days in the backwoods and leaves a record of that world. In the beginning was the forest. But I have omitted to mention that before him in the forest in earlier generations were his parents, grandparents, and the minister's great-uncle, Moses Blackstock.

Moses had the distinction, an important one according to our Aunt Barbara, who seemed to know about such things, of being the first preacher on the back line. It was hammered into me when young that he delivered the first sermon ever heard in the Township of Cavan, which lay in the Newcastle District of Upper Canada. He traversed on foot great stretches of primeval forest to bring the Gospel message to the settlers, making his way in winter storms through miles of snow so deep that no horse was of use; the forests were dense and deserted, the roads non-existent or appalling. In contrast with our wealthy Gooderham ancestors, Uncle Moses rose up before me as an evangelical patron saint, until other evidence corrected this distortion of truth. He was something of an agitator.

Moses, who was Scots-Irish by descent, had attended a college of some sort in Dublin. There, one day in 1811, he chanced upon the celebrated Gideon Ouseley seated on horseback, strangely apparelled and preaching. This set in train in domino fashion Moses's sudden conversion to Methodism and his own success in converting his hitherto Presbyterian father on their farm in Ballyjamesduff. A temporary hitch seems to have been his father's rage; he had turned Moses out of the house only to repent and run after him. He too turned Methodist as did all the family. Seven years later, when the Napoleonic Wars ceased, they and a concourse of relations left for Upper Canada in an exodus like that of the Gooderham side of our family, anxious to depart from an Ireland that had been torn by violence and insurrection, arriving in Cavan Township just as the back line of settlement on the north shore of Lake Ontario opened up.

Although Colonel Talbot had already placed numbers of families on his huge tracts along the north shore of Lake Erie, 1818 is still several years ahead of John Galt and the Canada Company or Peter Robinson, who in 1824 settled Irish immigrants in the region of present-day Peterborough. A few years earlier, Lord Bathurst had proposed that Highland settlers be brought out to Upper Canada with free passage and free rations, but most state aid was indirect. Self-supporting farmers, Moses and his relations were not classed amongst the poor. In this second migration and now as Wesleyan Methodists, they depended only upon themselves; in an earlier leap, they had arrived in mid-eighteenth-century Ireland from Scotland under the banner of Lord Farnham and were, at that time, solidly Presbyterian. Sectarian differences of all shades were to be of the essence in their new home.

By order of His Excellency the Lieutenant-Governor, dated at York on September 11th, 1818, and upon providing evidence of having taken the oath of allegiance, Moses took up his hundred-acre lot in Cavan Township by location ticket and began, as did other pioneers, the laborious clearing of the trees and turning his crown grant of land into a farm, while his unsung heroine of a wife would look forward to the bearing in time of fourteen children. Armed with his licence to preach and with the period of instruction already under his belt, Moses started off as local preacher but not as ordained minister. Promoted to deacon, on foot and unpaid, he soon covered the vast distances of the Smith's Creek circuit.

On these distant shores, he had moved immediately into the maze of rivalry and discord that marred the field of Gospel endeavour, for the British Wesleyan Methodist Church had sent him out as a missionary to the tidal wave of British settlers after the War of 1812 and the Wesleyans ran headlong into unseemly conflict with the well-entrenched Methodist Episcopal Church of the United States, which much earlier had followed the Loyalists and now ministered deeper and deeper in the woods of Upper Canada. Wesleyans remained closer to their Anglican roots and tended, however uncharitably, to look down on these American-trained preachers, some of whom without much or any evidence remained under a cloud, their loyalty in the recent war with the United States suspect. This air of superiority characterized some of our family.

In this spiritual minefield, Moses threw off his first allegiance to the Wesleyans and joined the Ryanites, whose leader, Henry Ryan, had entered the country at the turn of the century under the auspices of the American church and now led an independent Canadian body, not perhaps the choicest company, for although some saw Henry as an old-time preacher with a solid reputation, others viewed him as an unprincipled rabble-rouser.

Disturbances broke out on the Rice Lake circuit, which had been carved out of Smith Creek and was the scene of Moses's operations. 'Religion is at a low ebb on the circuit,' wrote one exasperated itinerant, laying the blame squarely upon the shoulders of the disputatious local Scots-Irish such as our ancestors, but especially did he castigate Moses, whom he accused of stirring up most of the trouble and causing a large number to secede from the main body of Methodism: 'Too much confidence has been placed in him and everything that he has either seen or heard is now published to the world. Yet, I doubt not but the poor little man will one day see his folly and be more astonished at his own conduct.' Moses reacted by espousing increasingly radical views, joining in 1835 the democratic New Connexion Conference (of Wesleyan origins), which held there should be no distinction between clergy and laity.

Against this background of spiritual divisiveness and the political unrest that led to the Rebellion, the British Wesleyan Methodist Church and most of the Methodist Episcopal Church in Canada (the remainder forming yet another group) endeavoured to meet the challenge by united action in 1833 under the banner of a new name, the Wesleyan Methodist Church in Canada, only to fall briefly apart again between 1840 and 1847. In 1840 and in a *volte-face*, Moses joined the new union, and in spite of his history of defections and volatility he received a friendly welcome as a fully ordained minister in the Wesleyan Methodist Church in Canada, his reputation, influence, and respectability restored. Here in microcosm and in the woods is all the religious and political turmoil that exercised our forbears in the last century until a general accommodation could be found.

Moses's tale ends on a pleasantly contradictory note; when ill health in 1856 brought superannuation after forty-two years of preaching, he followed a son to Indiana, where the sale of his crown grant in what had been Upper Canada enabled him to buy land near Lafayette. There he found a spiritual home in the Methodist Episcopal Church, the last of his shiftings from one branch to the other of Methodism. The land rose sharply in value, and he who had steadfastly preached the rewards of Heaven found himself at last possessor of earthly riches.

The early preachers of his stamp seem to have had remarkable powers of persuasion, for these messengers of the Gospel found a ready welcome in the remoter areas of Upper Canada; there were few other diversions. Still, the shouts and hymns, emotion and enthusiasm, of Methodist services provoked stinging sarcasm from the better-educated and more sophisticated inhabitants of towns, and members of the Church of England were by no means backward in their criticisms. But these men faced toil and weariness, covering immense distances and at times encountering danger. They broke the monotony of pioneer life and kept the settlers in the forests in touch with what might be called civilization. Here, however, the backwoods in no way compared with the isolation of the American frontier.

As a child our great-grandfather, the Reverend W.S. Blackstock (Tom's father), sat spellbound when one of these early preachers paid a visit to the forest clearing: 'I have sat upon a stool eight or ten inches high at the fireside in a farmer's house, and like Felix when he heard Paul I have trembled while he reasoned of righteousness, temperance and judgment to come ...' And making no reference to any of the charges of ignorance or uncouthness that might be laid against these men, he spoke of them with respect: 'They had an experience of the salvation of God ... It was their spiritual vitality which gave them the power by which they conquered.' Surely Methodism was a mighty force in those days, and all through the century it exerted a powerful influence as, in its various guises, it moved towards greater unity, dissolving and reshaping itself like a chemical compound in an alchemist's globe.

The pioneer background, as I have already made clear, formed this great-grandfather, whose own father (nephew of Moses) appears to have provided the material necessities of life without otherwise leaving his mark. He had arrived in New York directly from Ireland in 1816, two years before his relations set foot in Upper Canada, and a few years later married a young woman from Monmouth County, New Jersey. He too was an early resident of Cavan, where he applied for a lot in 1822, and he divided his time between clearing it and working on the first Welland Canal then under construction, crossing and recrossing the border, as has been our history from the beginning. The canal lay a stone's throw from Black Rock, New York, where his son, our great-grandfather, was born on October 3rd, 1824.

The father's beginnings in the backwoods are no more illustrious than Moses's, for in that year he so annoyed his neighbours in Cavan by dumping slashing on, and thus blocking up, the concession road, the settlers' lifeline to the outside world, that they petitioned the Surveyor General at York: 'This fellow deserves chastising.' In the hope that his location ticket would expire in his long absences at the canal, they already had in mind as a replacement a young man with first-rate connections and character to take over this particular grant. They were to be disappointed for he held on to his grant, and he had one advantage for, while some settlers probably experienced considerable difficulty in adjusting to pioneer life in the backwoods, his wife was American.

Over seventy years later his son, the Reverend W.S. Blackstock, was to write with all the clarity of remembrance that comes to the old: 'I was but three years old when I arrived on the northern shores of Lake Ontario.' As the boat that was to take them from Queenston to York steamed down the river to Fort George in the fall of 1827, he had stood on the deck holding his father's hand and gazed at the scene below. The fire-room was flooded with water to prevent its catching fire while men, dancing around with pitchforks in their hands, dumped cordwood into the furnace, and all this was reflected in the flame-coloured floor as though it too were on fire. This scene, which surely resembles a biblical hell with attendant devils, was his initiation into Upper Canada.

At York his father engaged a carter to transport them and their effects as far as he could along the Kingston Road, but the carter was delayed and the trio of parents and child walked many long weary miles before the rough conveyance caught up with them to bring them exhausted to Annis' Tavern and eventually to Bond Head Harbour in the Township of Clarke. Here his father decided to spend the winter, for the lateness of the season made it impractical to begin life in the backwoods, and in the spring, with Bond Head behind them father, mother, child, and newborn baby sister set off eastward again as far as Smith's Creek (Port Hope) and then turned northwards. Great-Grandfather says: 'The roads in those days in that part of the country existed chiefly in idea. They had not yet been reduced to an actuality. They were, indeed, euphemistically called the King's Highways, but if His Majesty William IV [but it is in the earlier reign of George IV that this particular journey was made] had seen them, he would probably have looked upon the name as a burlesque.'

The ox-drawn waggon advanced deeper into the forest, the road ever more impassable from the stumps, until one caused the waggon to overturn, throwing out his young mother and baby sister, whom miraculously she saved by jumping clear. On they went until they reached his father's hundred-acre lot, where far-flung neighbours and relations, all of them Scots-Irish, welcomed the new arrivals after their long, cold journey. The novelty of this reception, especially the unfamiliar Scotch utensils that were put before the small boy, greatly impressed him: the wooden dishes with names like noggin, luggie, and cop. A wood sled drawn by oxen pulled up to the door, and stretched out on it lay the body of a huge bear. This was his first impression of Cavan, and here the immediate family were solidly Wesleyan Methodist.

On earlier visits, his father had started to build the log cabin, every detail of which lay embedded in the child's memory; everything inside and out seems to have been made from the wood his father had laboriously hewed. It was a world where wood could be termed both master and servant, where the forest dwarfed every living object and served in every capacity. Many a settler must have flinched at the Herculean task before him, the getting rid of the great trees, in the end only to find himself unfit for pioneer life, and when the child as old man looked back, the task assumed the grandeur of old mythologies, with the settler as protagonist, the great pine forest as magnificent foe. He endowed its destruction with majesty. The underbrushing, chopping, felling, brush burning, logging, and firing become the stuff of epic as though he saw settler and forest playing out the *Iliad*. Everywhere the theme is battle.

The settler is his father; the child sees him waiting for the first streak of dawn, armed with an axe that could split a hair: 'The eight-hour day had not been invented in those times. The working day began with the star-lit morning and it ended with the star-lit evening. I have heard the boom of the big trees falling before it was clear daylight, and I have heard the same music when it had grown too dark to see plainly. But that lonely toiler in the wilderness was cheered in his work and encouraged to persevere by the vision of independence which was before him.' Settlers' independence, however, rested on help received from neighbours, who banded together to help each newcomer. This melding of independence and community was the pioneer spirit that fuelled the century and made this continent and its people distinct from Europe; even today it still marks our society.

The struggle went on; the trees had to fall and lie so that the logs could be rolled into heaps for burning. The felling, chopping, rolling, all the stages of preliminary burning, and hauling took endless months of toil before the story reaches its climax: 'Imagine one hundred huge fires within an area of ten acres, illuminating the whole of the heavens above it, so that the reflection can be seen at a distance of many miles, and surrounded by the dense umbrageous forest blacker than the darkest night.' In the midst of this scene, the settler's neighbours, who must have looked like goblins, ran prodding, pushing, and stirring the fires.

But still the settler's work went on, for he had to drag or cart the burnt logs to form the second fire of branding, endlessly repeating this attack until all was consumed except the timber that had been dragged to the edge of the field for fences. Only the harvest of forty bushels to the acre could reward this toil: 'Of course, this does not end the process of clearing the land. The stumps had to be got rid of. Some of them were left to rot in the ground, some of them blasted with gunpowder, some of them were burned, some of them were dug out with the pick and spade, and some were lifted out by screws, or torn out with other mighty engines after they had cumbered the ground for many years. The hardwood stumps had in about ten years pretty well disappeared, but the great pine stumps measuring often from three to five feet across were good for half a century. These had to be extracted by machinery.' And there were still ninety acres of forest as yet uncleared.

Irony of ironies, the settler who had toiled so long to subjugate the forest had no market for his wood unless he lived beside a river, the one means of transportation; later, with the coming of the railways, it would be a valuable crop, as indeed it was for the Gooderhams in Toronto. Great-Grandfather, the Reverend W.S. Blackstock, paid tribute to these early hewers of wood: 'His work was unique; as he had no predecessor so he can have no successor ...

He laid the foundations upon which we have builded, and are building. If I were either an orator or a poet, it appears to me that I should ask for no better subject than the pioneer settler.' But his romantic view of his father as pioneer is at odds with subsequent silence over the latter, a shadowy figure constantly disappearing and reappearing in the correspondence for many years to come, which suggests some sort of failure or weakness.

His mother was much alone with the children for his father probably continued to work at that everlasting project, the Welland Canal. They saw bears, heard the howling of wolves, and he had seen her suffering from illness and prayed to die with her so that they might never be separated: 'Most boys who are worthy of the name of boys, love their mothers, but though I don't think I was any better than the general run of boys, I doubt whether there ever was one who loved his mother more ardently than I did mine.' The reader senses a lonely child and although there is mention of sugaring-off parties and the gaiety of occasional festivals, the forest can be a silent world where a child is closer to nature than to his fellows.

The child's real friends are the birds and beasts of the forest, and he lay on the ground by the hour to watch the magnificent gyrations of the great hawk: 'I cannot think of his extinction without a pang.' Cavan Township is a Walden before the fact; the constant theme of these early years is self-sufficiency. He saw the forest clearings as an Eden where every kind of wild berry and fruit was to be found; every creature held him entranced, and the forest abounded in game, deer, wild pigeon that came in their thousands, partridge, and quail. His mother's domain included the kitchen garden, which grew at an astonishing rate in the first summer: potatoes, cabbages, turnips, carrots, parsnips, pumpkins, squash. She also cared for the poultry and livestock; hens had accompanied the family in their ox-drawn waggon, and soon piglets and a cow appeared. There is no cloud whatsoever on this happily remembered horizon, no mention of the limitations imposed by the backwoods or the rough manners it probably generated: all is for the best in this best of all possible worlds, or so he would have us believe.

'... God was very near to me in those early days ... I walked and talked with Him as my childhood friend.' This view of life came directly from his hard-working Calvinist Dutch Reformed mother, now a Methodist, a reader of the Bible and books of devotion; through her, he found 'sermons in stones, books in running brooks and God in everything.' Because of the father's long and frequent absences, mother and son remained close indeed. Later he was to show a tendency to introspection and depression, and transfer this emotional dependence on his mother to his wife, our great-grandmother.

His paternal grandfather lent a counterweight to the mother's simple piety: 'My venerable grandfather was a man of extensive reading, possessing many scholarly qualities.' A student of history and the world's great thinkers, he had brought from Ireland his store of books, and pored over them. The child proved an attentive listener, already on the way to the search for knowledge: 'I was a sort of impersonated note of interrogation, with the very spirit of an inquisitor. I seized upon every stray fragment of truth or thought that came my way, put it to the "the question."'

These two strands, religious and intellectual, weave in and out of his life: the first sends him out as a messenger to spread the Good News of the Gospel; later on, the second is his secret vice, the hours spent in reading, marking, and inwardly digesting whatever print had to offer, not necessarily to the advancement of his profession but to the infinite enlargement of his mind. And in his obsessive wish to provide the best education for his sons, that they might have what he had not, he was willing to jeopardize himself and his calling within the Wesleyan Methodist Church in Canada, but this lies many years in the future.

The township's first settler had given land for a school in 1816, but these common schools were most imperfect institutions and his grandfather's learning would have far exceeded the teacher's. Later, both distance and expense were deciding factors in school attendance, of which he says nothing at all, and circumstances were rudely to interrupt whatever formal instruction he had received. Events within and beyond the township heralded the approach of the Rebellion, the causes of which were manifold: a general dissatisfaction with the political power of the ruling clique, the privileges awarded to the Church of England, and, of more immediate concern, recent instances of poor crops, a shortage of money resulting from the tightening of credit, and resentment against agricultural imports from the United States. The inhabitants of Cavan may well have sympathized with some at least of Mackenzie's aims, but his excesses no doubt alarmed them as it did so many others; moreover, loyalty to the Crown ran deep.

On the whole, the County of Durham (the new terminology) and in it the Township of Cavan remained quiet in contrast with the disaffection so noticeable in the West. At the time of the march on Toronto by the rebels, volunteers (including Gooderhams) rushed to its defence, and it has been estimated that about two thousand came from the Newcastle District, which embraced Cavan. Too young to join in this excitement, our Great-Grandfather Blackstock played his minor part in the government's attempt to restore and maintain order afterwards: 'It was in the autumn of 1838,' he tells us, 'that I turned my back for the first time upon my house with the expectation of not returning for several months. There had been a rebellion in Canada, the year previous, and though the back of the insurrection had been broken, peace could scarcely be said to be completely restored. It was still thought to be necessary to keep a considerable force of militia, so to speak, under canvas. An uncle of mine was drafted for this service, and his circumstances, and the circumstances of his family being such that it was quite out of the question for him to leave home, though I was but fourteen years of age I volunteered to go in his stead. Being an uncommonly stout boy for my age, though not very tall, I looked older by two or three years than I really was and, in consequence of this I readily passed the examination and was mustered in.'

This event marked the beginning of the end of his connection with Cavan, which perhaps after so much hard labour proved unproductive. In any case, his father and many of the relations moved to older settlements, and nearly all the next generation reached out well beyond the confines of the original grants of land. When I asked Old Cousin Marion what occupation the father followed when he emerged from the backwoods, she said: 'Not much, a wheelwright I think.' Her tone of voice quite discomposed me, I remember. 'Pioneer' had always had an aura of heroism, now so singularly lacking.

The backward glances by our great-grandfather suddenly cease, but in the mid-seventies when his two sons as fully fledged lawyers acknowledged their debt to his self-denial and struggle on their behalf, he spoke of the missing years following the Rebellion: 'He was a very, very poor boy once far from home and it may be to the kindness shown to him by good people in a higher position in society than himself you owe the position you occupy today.'

'He is a bold man,' he said on another occasion, 'who attempts to write his autobiography. There is so much in the life of everyone of us that we would like to have blotted out, and this being impossible we would like to have forgotten, that to be one's own biographer, and to do the work conscientiously, must appear to anyone who has ever thought profoundly and seriously upon it, to be an undertaking little less than appalling.' If ever he toyed with the idea, no autobiography resulted, and as his life unfolds one can see why.

At eighteen he experienced conversion in the Methodist sense, and in his own words he was accepted and saved, the moment of truth in Methodist lives. He declared himself publicly at twenty. This took place in New York, a week's journey by horse, where he spent the winter of 1844 with his father's brother, a grocer, who is listed in the uncompromising ways of directories as a huckster. Back home again and licensed to exhort, he began his training in Pickering, was soon licensed as a local preacher, and in the last quarter of the year was recommended for the ministry. During the next four years on probation in circuit work, he performed regular pastoral duties under an ordained minister, whose function it was to test him as to his moral and religious character, soundness in the faith, observance and enforcement of the church's discipline, and punctuality in keeping appointments and in the discharge of his pastoral duties, in short, his competency.

He was young and strong, prerequisites to his vocation, or so he tells us, and single: 'There was a great scarcity of ministers in this country when I entered the work. This may account for the fact that I was accepted so soon. I had barely reached my majority and my education was far from being finished. I had however some of the secondary qualifications for the work, which in those days were regarded as of considerable importance. I had good health and a sound constitution; I took no snuff, tobacco or drams. I was not in debt neither was I engaged to marry ...'

He preached the Gospel, visited from house to house, cared for the poor, ministered to the sick and dying, catechized the children, learned much about human nature, and followed the Wesleyan Methodist Church's precise and practical rules of conduct: to be diligent, never unemployed, to be serious, to converse sparingly, to conduct himself prudently with women, to take no step towards marriage without first consulting the brethren, to believe evil of no one, to speak evil of no one, to avoid all affectation, to sing no hymns of his own composing, and to remember that he had nothing to do but to save souls.

The organization of circuit work had not changed since his Uncle Moses' day, indeed since Wesley's. An orderly framework contained Methodist missionary zeal: in every circuit there were several churches and a number of other places of worship, usually schoolhouses, and each circuit was divided into classes, over which class leaders held sway, while the itinerant reigned over class leaders, local preachers, exhorters, and stewards. Once in every quarter, the minister exacted an account of each member's spiritual progress, and every circuit held Quarterly Meetings when those who passed muster received their tickets of membership. Then came the Love-feast and Sacrament, ending with a sermon and scenes of penitence lasting well into the night.

The Wesleyan Methodist Church did not claim to have highly educated men; indeed, few had much claim to learning, but they had a rigorous training. They were examined every year in the discharge of their duties and courses of study; they were expected to read in the faith by borrowing or buying books, and above all they committed large sections of the Bible to heart so that they might quote easily and readily. They were examined on prescribed texts that covered theology, grammar and rhetoric, church history and geography, history, logic, and philosophy. Among authors cited were Wesley, Paley, Plutarch, even Hume, and when it came to Gibbon's *Decline and Fall*, the young preachers were reminded: 'Infidel sentiments in this work are numerous. The student therefore should be on his guard while perusing it.' Preaching depended on the strength of the speaker's own faith for its efficacy; there was no thought here of jumping on the bandwagon of the latest fashionable cause. Only eternal truths. For the ultimate goal of preaching was not wisdom, education, or entertainment but the salvation of the listener, and so the minister learned to expound, persuade, and convert.

The horse was his chief possession, and he had to look after it well. The saddle-bag, made of leather, small, and square, held Bible, hymn book, a few personal articles, and the great woven scarf that, wrapped round the rider at night, served as a blanket while he slept. His accommodation was often a shed, set aside specially for such uses, without any adornment or comforts, for the people were poor, but still they put the very best of their fare before him. One more item lay on the horse's back, the surveyor's chain; as new districts opened up, Great-Grandfather acted as agent of government in the mapping and measuring of the land.

Methodists were shifting ground; the Rebellion, with its bitter divisions, would be a thing of the past; the Clergy Reserves would soon be laid to rest; the church would wear a more sober face, its exuberant forest spontaneity replaced by organized camp-sites. A few years earlier, it had been in danger of losing ground to rival groups and sects, while now Methodism itself was on the way towards substantial union. William Schenck Blackstock entered the church just as it was adjusting to the change from a sparsely populated mission field to towns and cities in a more complex society where economic development was taking place; better roads and, within a decade, the advent of the railways were to end the isolation of some at least of the settlers.

He entered the church just as the sermon began to replace the earlier exhortations, and how many hours of his life were to be devoted to that pursuit. But in some respects he remained an old-fashioned preacher, heir to the early evangelical tradition, and as one of his brethren said of him at the end of his life: 'To the very last he preached and taught the two tremendous facts of sin and salvation.' If he held that only by human effort could the evils of society be corrected, he stood in opposition to any belief in the infinite perfectibility of man, or, for that matter, to the eighteenth-century's maxim of the natural goodness of man. He had only to dwell upon his own motives and actions to see the fallacy of these arguments. He would have held the view, too, that the border between civilization and anarchy is treacherously thin. He was a conservative in politics, but champion of the common man; proud of his British heritage and loyal to the Crown, but admiring of much that was American and of what Mackenzie had hoped to achieve. He had, however, weaknesses and failings that as time was to show proved almost his undoing.

His Uncle Moses, far more politically motivated and aligning himself first with one group and then another, had encouraged his flock to make a stand on issues that appealed to him. For twenty years and more, his great-nephew ventured rarely beyond pastoral concerns, a common reaction to the hostility of the Rebellion, but he had plenty to say, especially in later years, on social problems and politics. Still, his sermons were never a call to arms in the name of a party or platform; he saw no panacea to the world's ills, except the Gospel itself in changing the hearts of men.

In 1846 the Wesleyan Methodist Church in Canada received him on trial, as the training period was called, placing him under the aegis of an itinerant in the hills of Mono, in the forests of Nottawasaga, and beyond the small settlement of Barrie in a vacuum of territory that had begun to attract settlers. But the mission stations that served this hinterland referred to incoming settlers in unfailingly unflattering terms: a singularly discouraging field of labour, where the missionary had better be hardy, courageous, and persevering; where the flock were grossly ignorant of Christianity, poor, and those who were not poor, close-fisted; where journeys were long and the roads bad. One missionary summed up the struggle in this wise: 'He has to contend with drunkards, Sabbath breakers, liars, swearers, and hosts of unbelievers on every hand, and the great evil is, that the nominal professor often disgraces the Gospel which he professes. Indeed it is hard to manage such persons.'

After this introduction to his calling, Great-Grandfather's circuits drew him closer to what constituted civilization, the Humber, the Bradford, and the Oshawa, at which last he made the acquaintance of Mary Hodge Gibbs, and at the New Year of 1850, he sent her a formal proposal of marriage in words suited to the solemnity of the occasion and written on pale blue paper. It began: 'My dear Miss Gibbs, I take the liberty to address you upon a most important subject and one which has weighed heavily upon my mind for some time. [And here he laid before her reasons that led him, after mature consideration, to offer his hand.] ... I have taken the matter to the Throne of Grace and sought direction from above and still my convictions remain. I trust you will do the same; and then answer me with the same simplicity and sincerity with which I have unfolded the feelings of my heart to you.' Mary accepted.

Two years earlier, the Oshawa circuit had received James Gooderham, whom we have already met, old William Gooderham's son, who turned Methodist and ended his life under a locomotive. James was just beginning his abortive attempt at life in the itineracy. On July 23rd, 1850, he married Mary's sister, Sarah Gibbs. At the same church and hour, Mary wed the Reverend W.S. Blackstock, for which the latter was to say over forty years later that he had never ceased to give thanks: 'In her I have found an unfailing source of inspiration and help.' He had also found a firm-minded wife who never failed to remind him that standards must be kept up in parsonages. On the ninth day of the previous month, the Wesleyan Methodist Church in Canada had ordained him minister of the Gospel, and the *Christian Guardian* noted: 'This was one of the finest classes of young men ever presented to the Conference for reception.'

After this account of our great-grandfather, our great-grandmother's family was full of surprises. To sit down and read their correspondence was to set sail, not into entirely unknown seas, for some of their origins we knew, but into a past peopled by many unknown men and women, to be swept along and away into their lives of long ago.

CHAPTER THREE

As IF A DAM HAD BURST, the end of the Napoleonic Wars released a pent-up flood of westward-bound emigrants, and the Wars themselves had greatly aided Great-Great-Grandfather Gooderham. He had served abroad in the Army until invalided home, and a subsequent stint as recruiting officer had enabled him both to emigrate in style and on arrival to deposit the sum that apparently astounded the cashiers of the Bank of Upper Canada. In Ireland events during the Wars had sufficiently disenchanted our Blackstock forbears so as to make emigration eminently preferable, and they brought only themselves, their books, and very little else. A sudden lowering of their standard of living in a disrupted economy persuaded yet another branch of our family tree to transplant itself here. But nothing is clear-cut in the plans of Thomas Gibbs and his wife, Caroline, when they make their appearance in the correspondence, except the decision to leave their native land.

From childhood we were acquainted with two early-nineteenth-century Gibbs silhouettes, which were discreetly set in small black oval frames without any of the flamboyance of the other ancestral portraits in the house, resting on the mantelpiece in the sun-room (it was a living-room, in fact, as distinct from the drawing-room) at 79 Prince Arthur Avenue in Toronto. But we did not know to which generation they belonged: to Philip and Mary Gibbs, our great-great-great-grandparents, or to another Philip and Mary Gibbs, their son and daughter. Different branches of our connection opt for different attributions. Until family letters came my way, I did not know that we could ascribe to this particular stem some of our eccentricities, for old Philip Gibbs and his wife, Mary, had a large family, of whom one daughter was certifiably mad, one son utterly incompetent, and one more might be termed exceedingly disputatious.

I thought, if I thought at all, the name extinct, for like a limb lopped off we had severed connections with this Gibbs tree after our grandfather's death in 1906, as I have already described, but the name was once a household word in Canada, signifying like 'Gooderham' both milling and wheat; not, however, alcohol, since the Gibbs family were not Church of England. Later it came as a surprise to me that here our Canadian roots through Caroline Gibbs, wife of Thomas Gibbs, reached back in Quebec to the eighteenth century, if only in a tentative, unbinding way that precluded us from any equality with descendants of the Loyalists, a distinction that would have raised me in my own eyes. The discovery made me ask Old

Cousin Marion why our great-great-great-grandfather, Caroline Gibbs's father, with the name Monkhouse Tate – so redolent of historical romances – had spent a year or more in Quebec in 1789. She said: 'He was sent out by the British Government to restore the mills of Quebec that had fallen into disrepair.'

The previous year, 1788, had seen such poor harvests that there was a serious shortage in Quebec of wheat, flour, and bread, which seems to have raised the spectre of near famine, galvanized the authorities to action, and sent Monkhouse on his way. His year in Canada put him in touch with the owners of a number of seigniories, often in the hands of newcomers connected with the fur trade in the days when fur was still king, and this in turn benefited his daughter Caroline, who had married Thomas Gibbs, when they set sail for the colony thirty years later. Their western approaches bear none of the hallmarks of Cavan Township; there was no forest.

In their determination to leave England, but long uncertain as to destination, these two had had several changes of plan; chopping down trees, however, was not one of them. They were not pioneers, and while many settlers pushed into forest hinterlands, Thomas and Caroline chose an easier transition, which had its own pitfalls. The road proved often hard, but time in the end fulfilled earlier dreams, and almost fifty years later Caroline could say: 'I think there is not a mother on the face of the earth that has more cause for thankfulness than myself. My last days are turning out to be my best in every sense of the word.' With Thomas she had lived through the

Rebellion of 1837, seen the advent of Confederation, travelled the uncertain road of the century's economic crises, and had had her fill of private troubles.

She walks purposefully through life, unremarkable in herself, noting the changes of half a century by the very trivia of her domestic horizon, but endowed with a steadfastness that lifts her to a kind of minor heroism. Not for years did I realize how independent she had once shown herself to be, nor even what resolute defiance she was capable of showing her stepmother, for I had not yet read the appropriate letters. Secrets lurk in every heart and seldom did Caroline unlock the door to her hidden self; brisk and practical, rarely indulging in introspection or repining, she passes by as a recorder of other people's lives, not of her own. But once in a while there is a cry from the heart as when in old age she said: 'Nothing kills me so much as the recollection of the past, but of what avail is this now? We cannot alter what is done. But how many things in the course of my life could I have wished otherwise, had I seen the end from the beginning.'

An aura of sadness hangs about her childhood, and when I asked Old Cousin Marion the reason for Caroline's failure to keep in touch with her many half-brothers and sisters who pour out of the early letters written in the first quarter of the last century, she merely said: 'Oh, it was all so long ago.' Caroline was born in the City of London in the year 1795; her mother died when she was three months old, and in the same year her father, Monkhouse Tate, bought St Mary's House and St Mary's Mill at Chalford in the Cotswold Hills of Gloucestershire, where he is listed as clothier, a manufacturer of woollen cloth for which the district was famous.

John Tate, the father of Monkhouse, had crossed over from the town of Lochmaben in Dumfriesshire, which incidentally was noted as a centre of Jacobites, and then like so many Scots taken the high road to London, established himself first in Walbrook in the City and subsequently, for more than thirty years, conducted his business at 26 Bucklersbury next to the Exchange. He had been admitted in 1766 to the Freedom of the Worshipful Company of Musicians of the City of London, which offered a speedy passage to respectability, and on the same day was raised to the livery. His business as toyman indicates that he made fine objects or jewellery, and directories listed him also as owner of a warehouse.

In the Cotswolds, St Mary's House dates from the late Middle Ages and is incorrectly reputed to have been the home of Roger Bacon in the thirteenth century. Here Monkhouse's daughter Caroline grew up; sixty years passed before she looked upon the home of her childhood again, by which time it had already lost its medieval charm, a jumble now of styles much added to and altered since her father's time. She said: 'I remarked how very much everything was altered, the front part of the house and grounds particularly, the large iron gates and gravel walks at the entrance all gone, and half the garden turned into pasture land, no wide walks there used to be planted each side with apple trees trained on trellises, not the pretty place it was sixty years ago.' Then she added: 'I shed a few tears at the recollection of gone-by days, which even then were not all of them joyous to me.' This remark, at first seeming inconsequential, unfolded its meaning later on.

In the early 1820s, after she had already been settled for some years in Lower Canada, she enlarged on this theme to her Uncle John Tate, for he replied: 'My dear Caroline, I read with much interest what you said about the days of your childhood and cannot but regret that you should ever have been treated so harshly. It is not likely that the recollection will ever be effaced or that you will be able to contemplate it without a feeling of sympathy towards a poor defenceless girl & of animosity towards those by whom her life was made miserable.' Always the peacemaker, he told his niece: 'The best thing that you can do now is to make as many excuses for her [referring to her stepmother] in your own mind as you can and to be thankful that what appeared most adverse was overruled for your benefit.' This advice went unheeded; the scars of bitterness had cut too deep.

Her father moved his large family of Caroline's stepbrothers and sisters from Chalford to London after the bankruptcy of his cloth business, brought about during the War of 1812 by the defaulting of a large exporting company in London; many of its clients had traded in the United States and suddenly lost their markets. Contributing causes may also have been the overproduction of cloth in Cotswold mills and the inability of clothiers there to compete with the more modern mills in the North of England. His legal difficulties dragged on interminably: 'My counting house,' he told his daughter, 'is now in Bucklersbury [in the City of London] but letters go to Batson's Coffee House.' This establishment was a centre for traders and brokers engaged in trade with Russia, and on November 27th, 1818, he gained admission to the Freedom of the Russia Company, from which country in the previous spring he had sent her an amber necklace inscribed with the words 'forget me not,' signing all his letters 'Your affectionate Father and friend.' Oblivious to their mutual antipathy or anxious to ignore it, he added messages of goodwill from her stepmother: 'She sends her love to you.'

Immediately on his return from Russia, he learned of his daughter's engagement to Thomas Gibbs, the son of Philip and Mary Gibbs of Shindles Mill, Kingsbridge, Devon, whose family consisted of five sons and three daughters. Thomas acted as his father's assistant in the business of the mill. Philip Gibbs had a house in Kingsbridge and a short distance away on the estuary this substantial mill, which had been in the family for generations and which appears on Benjamin Donn's eighteenth-century atlas. Next to the mill as part of the property stood a small Georgian house where several of Philip's sons lived like a hive of fractious bees buzzing round the mill and all about to complain of their father's slowly hatching plans for their future. The mill had produced a sufficient income all during the previous century and in the long war years when the Army needed flour, but a postwar depression put an end to any security and simultaneously disturbed Philip's domestic tranquillity. Hardly had news of the engagement been digested before problems arose.

Suddenly and unexpectedly he refused to countenance Thomas's engagement, which only made his son the more determined so that the marriage took place and added further fuel to the fire of Philip's seemingly irascible temper. 'It is the conduct of the son contrasted with this of the father which speaks so much to his praise & honor as far as his engagement to you was concerned and although I can enter into his feelings when anything disrespectful or insulting is said of his wife, yet there is still a respect due to his own father ...,' said Monkhouse Tate in a communication to his daughter that refers somewhat obliquely to words and angry scenes between Philip Gibbs and his son Thomas.

Almost ten years after his departure from England, Thomas's mother, Mary Gibbs, offered him by way of excuse this unsatisfactory explanation: 'My good husband desires I w^d tell Caroline he never felt unkindly toward her but the circumstances of the times combined with his affliction *etc* gave rise to conflicting interests & trying feelings, but is all passed away...' Monkhouse attributed Philip Gibbs's attitude to the news of his own bankruptcy proceedings as they followed labyrinthine paths in the London courts and the subsequent loss therefore of any financial expectations. He added: 'I was in hopes that when Mr G. sen^r found that his son was married and that he could not in any way change his determination, he would do as others in the same circumstances by making a virtue of necessity and reconciling himself to what he could not change ... But I will say no more on this unpleasant subject than wishing that peace and harmony may reign among you all.' Peace and harmony did not reign, and the young couple's defiance of parental authority hung temporarily like a dark cloud over the first months of married life.

The Gibbs family were to be caught up in the agricultural depression affecting the whole countryside, where many a son saw his inheritance slip from him, his income vanish, and himself uprooted from his ancestral soil. All over England, sons and daughters were to be forced off the land to some other life, for which they were untrained and unsuited, many drifting into shopkeeping and schoolteaching, both of which required little preparation. A desire to emigrate swept over England like a plague, and Thomas foresaw a better life abroad and so too, it seems, did Caroline.

Twenty years of war, coupled with the accelerating pace of the Industrial Revolution, had brought social upheaval and economic distress, in which countrymen were to face as bleak a future as industrialized townsfolk. The flow of villagers to cities and towns had long begun; enclosures had deprived them of land, and their security had vanished. The small trades and crafts gravitated to the larger centres; and agricultural labourers were to become destitute, while even those families who had enjoyed a good standard of living from their land, farms, and enterprises found themselves pressed out of their old life and unable to adjust to the new. Philip Gibbs's sons, hitherto in the comfortable and quite prosperous yeomen class, felt the impact of this ill wind blowing across Devon, where farming constituted the primary occupation. Unlike most other counties, it consisted not of a few great landowners but of minor gentry and freeholders; this last included Philip Gibbs, whose family began to fear for the future.

At first, his son Thomas considered the possibilities of Demerara but soon changed his mind, about which his mother was to write in the following year: 'Taking up the *Edinburgh Review* this morn I observ'd a sentiment which so perfectly coincided with my own that I transcribe it ...' She abhorred slavery and gave heartfelt thanks that her son had not gone to a slave-owning economy: 'No virtuous man ought to trust his own character or the character of his children to the demoralizing effects produc'd by commanding slaves.' Dissenters have been called the conscience of England, a trait that Mary Gibbs frequently exemplified.

Both of Thomas's parents, Philip and Mary, descended from a tradition of dissent in a county that had long been a stronghold of nonconformity, renowned in the sixteenth century as one of the great Protestant counties of England, while nonconformist Kingsbridge, the town in which the Gibbs family had lived for generations, had a Puritan inheritance with a leaven of Baptists, Quakers, and Independents. The Gibbs side had produced a Baptist pastor active in Plymouth for fifty years, and Mary Gibbs's father had been, and her four nephews were at that moment, Baptist ministers.

Her ancestors, hailing from Skye, which they had left two centuries earlier, had a long history of involvement in dissenting religious and political movements, for which some were ruinously fined for harbouring Quakers in James II's reign, others imprisoned, and one hanged, drawn, and quartered for his part in the Monmouth Rebellion. Her grandfather was out in the 'Fifteen under the Earl of Derwentwater and had narrowly escaped capture at Newcastle-upon-Tyne by hiding in the hold of a ship. All this must be part of our inheritance, filtered down through generations and tempered by the fact that we were all swept into the Church of England.

When later on Philip and Mary left the mill and settled in the village of Broadway in Somerset, Mary rejoiced that it had an Independent meeting-house, a term that might lead one at first to suppose a change of allegiance to the Congregational Church, which had recently scooped up many Baptists in Devon when their numbers declined there. But with an army of relatives as Baptist clergy, such a change is unlikely. In any case, from whatever vantage point, she aimed anti-hierarchical shafts at the Church of England, although an eighteenth-century piety instilled in her a gentleness that made amends for the gruff contrariness of her ailing husband. 'Were you to ask me,' she told her son, 'how & by what means I have borne up my fortitude through life's ills, I would answer by retiring, reading my Bible, musing on its meaning, praying for grace to understand it & the influences of the spirit of all Grace to enable me to live consistent to the rules there given; short, very short have I fallen below them yet my soul has gain'd all her strength from this source.' As for her son Thomas's innermost religious convictions, they hide behind a lifelong veil of reticence; he remained a Baptist and staunchly refused to be swept away in the enthusiasms of rival denominations when later on all around him succumbed.

Thomas's second choice of destination rested on the United States – twice as many ships sailed there as to Canada at that time – and in January of 1818 Caroline's Uncle John Tate enquired into the possibility of their joining George Flower's settlement in Illinois. Flower and his friend, Morris Birkbeck, were arranging for two hundred English settlers to accompany them to Albion on what then constituted the frontier of America. Birkbeck was an agriculturalist of some repute, and the community was to have a high proportion of educated people. Her Uncle John wrote to Caroline: '... I have got Mr Flower to give me a statement in writing of the nature of his situation and the probability of success in order that you might be able to make up your mind on the subject.'

Three hundred pounds was the sum named as the necessary preliminary to joining the settlement, and although Thomas had some money of his own, the remainder would have to come from his father or from Monkhouse Tate, who could ill afford it. Uncle John offered a hundred pounds and arranged an interview between Thomas and Mr Flower: 'in order that Mr F. may be able to judge from his appearance and sentiments whether he is a man whom it might be right to encourage and also that he himself might have a more perfect understanding of the concern.'

At first, Caroline's father, Monkhouse Tate, opposed the very idea of emigration, Mr Flower's scheme in particular, and the United States in general: 'In speaking with your Uncle John the other day about the American plan,' he wrote to Caroline in June of 1818, 'I told him I should not wish you to undertake such a scheme without some more engagement on the part of the projector than they seem inclined to give. The truth appears to be this, they are dissatisfied with their own country because there is not scope enough for their ambition, and therefore they will go with their property to one where they can be greater people than they are here, and the greater number of persons they can persuade to go with them or to follow them, so much more will be their importance in the place where they may settle, but the mere representation that *they think a man might do well* who understood the business of a miller or a mealman without a promised engagement to give him assistance or to find him a mill, I should think a very shallow foundation and a very poor inducement to any man who has the means of supporting himself in England.

'It is a well-known fact that a very great proportion I believe three fourths of the English and Scotch who have emigrated last year to the United States have been nearly starved there and have been passed by the British Consul in different States to our own settlements in Canada.' It would, however, be more exact to say that the Consul, James Buchanan, who resented the preference of British emigrants for the United States, actively endeavoured to intercept new arrivals at New York and direct them to Upper Canada instead, especially to Cavan and Monaghan, so that he may have had a hand in pointing our Uncle Moses and his brothers this way.

'If therefore,' Monkhouse continued, 'after a fair trial of what you can do in England and finding the spirit of emigration still with you, I should much, very much prefer your going to British settlements to your going to the United States on any account. In British America the communication by letter is much more frequent and better regulated, the prospects of success in my opinion much greater. I could be of much more use to you by friends and connexions, although I think it probable that there is scarcely a person existing now whom I knew there thirty years ago, but notwithstanding I am sure I could be useful to you in a much higher degree there than in the United States.

'However, I wish you to give your present situation a fair trial and see what further advantage the old gentleman will allow his son for this continuance of his services in the way of partnership and with the prospect of having it entirely to himself in case of the old gentleman's death or inability to carry it on longer.'

November found Monkhouse more convinced than ever of the inadvisability of emigration, which he said might produce misery for life, while for the moment Philip Gibbs's Shindles Mill appeared to hold its own in spite of hard times or family squabbles. Five months later the would-be settlers, caught in the dilemma of uncertainty at home and doubts as to the wisdom of emigrating, had reached no decision. John Tate had read highly unfavourable comments from emigrants to the United States, so that his opinion of Flower and Birkbeck had undergone a change. Recently published confutations were devastating. The Illinois scheme was called 'the el-dorado of that cunning fox, Morris Birkbeck'; travellers returned with stories of corruption and dishonesty in both the Eastern and Western States, and one writer, sent to compare the United States with Canada, wrote: 'The delusions of such visionaries as Mr Morris Birkbeck cannot be too severely reprobated next to the crime of downright falsehood, Mr Birkbeck ... has stifled many important truths in the most shameful and culpable manner.'

John Tate said: 'I should make greater efforts to do something in this country now that the hazard of leaving it appears greater.' Yet, the Illinois venture abandoned, Thomas and Caroline were more anxious than ever to leave England after the arrival of their daughter, another Caroline, in 1819. This time they favoured Quebec, and once more the spectre of financial backing was raised. John Tate allowed them to retain his loan of a hundred pounds, while Monkhouse promised to furnish them with a letter of credit at Montreal for another hundred.

Preparation for the journey meant finding a ship and making a private arrangement with the captain or the ship's broker for stateroom accommodation, a luxury enjoyed by only a minority but the way in which Caroline and Thomas were to travel. Most emigrants sailed on ships which on eastbound voyages carried timber and on the westward journey had temporary decks installed with row upon row of wooden berths and hatches that functioned as portholes. While the Passenger Vessel Acts limited the number of persons per ship, evasions were frequent and officials to enforce the provisions were few. False decks could be quickly fitted up with subsequent overcrowding, squalor, and inadequate food; not until mid-century, with the coming of the clippers and steamships, did conditions really improve. But in 1819, as cabin passengers, Thomas and his wife fared incomparably better for, however long and uncomfortable their voyage proved to be, it never approximated these evils.

After numerous enquiries, Monkhouse reported in February: 'I have an answer from Mr. Pope at Bristol about the ship, the *Charlotte*, which is represented as a very fine vessel with good accommodations, to sail about the second week in April.' The *Charlotte*, however, had already yielded to the *Speculator*, sailing from Plymouth, taken from the French during the late War and condemned as a prize in 1794, a small ship by any standards, only a two-masted schooner of a hundred and two tons, which in winter plied the coastal trade of England and in the summer sailed to Canada going out in ballast for timber for the Navy. Moreover, five years later in 1824 it was lost at sea.

'I hope,' Monkhouse cautioned his daughter, 'the vessel you are going in is not going to take a cargo of live-stock on this sail as I fear you would then have a very uncomfortable voyage.' Her captain instructed Thomas to lay in supplies for ten weeks, which seemed to Monkhouse an unnecessary length of time, although in the event it proved an underestimate.

He advised his daughter to make an agreement with the captain for ship's provisions in such staples as bread, beef, potatoes, and flour and wrote: 'I trust Mr Gibbs has reserved what is called a state room for you, some of these rooms have four or more beds or rather bed places.' He proposed to meet her in Kingsbridge or Plymouth to say farewell: 'As soon as you can fix the day of your departure from Kingsbridge, let me know and I will endeavour to come the one place or the other.'

With these arrangements in place, Monkhouse wrote off to acquaintances in Quebec, some of the colony's leading citizens, whom he had known there thirty years before: 'Col. Mackay [William McKay, fur trader and officer of the Indian Department] left London this morning on his return to Canada by way of New York. He is to embark at Liverpool on Monday and I wrote by him to Mr Monk [(later Sir) James Monk, Administrator for Lower Canada] respecting the mill at Mascouche and also to Sir John Johnson [Loyalist, Superintendent-General of Indian Affairs in British North America; Member of the Legislative Council of Quebec, etc.] for one of his mills in case the other should be occupied and I requested Col. Mackay to speak to the parties which I trust he will do to inform them of Mr Gibbs' going out in the spring, and I undertook to answer for his understanding his business, for his integrity, activity and industry, indeed for his being worthy of confidence in every respect.'

He added one more name to the list: 'Perhaps Mr Forsyth [probably John Forsyth, fur trader of Forsyth,

Richardson & Co.] may also have forgotten me but he will remember my name I dare say.' And quite reconciled to the idea of emigration Monkhouse now encouraged Thomas to think he had chosen wisely: 'Tell Mr Gibbs however not to be discouraged or cast down about these things as I have a very strong persuasion that he will do well and will one day be a rich man, if his life be spared. I think the field is wide open and the moment favorable, therefore do not let him be discouraged by any apparently untoward circumstances.'

Thomas's father, old Philip Gibbs, who is not quite the curmudgeon his eldest son Philip, Jr, would have the world believe, promised two years rent of a mill; a small dividend from the estate of Caroline's grandfather fell due, which her father suggested she lay out in tea and other commodities for a quick sale in Montreal, but his own troubled business affairs kept him constantly on the move and may have stood between himself and Caroline on the eve of her departure. The date of sailing had unexpectedly been advanced: 'I am truly grieved to think that after having made preparations which I had for visiting you next week intending to set off on next Wednesday, I should now be under the necessity of abandoning the idea of seeing you at all, as from what you say it is doubtful if this letter reach you ... Sincerely wishing you health, a good voyage, and every blessing that can attend you, I remain my dear girl, Your affectionate Father, M. Tate. Give my kind regards to Mr Gibbs & to the little one, perhaps I may yet see you.' And perhaps he did.

Thomas's mother, Mary Gibbs, bade farewell to her son with this advice: 'Oh my children bear patiently the trials of life together, never use unkind or reproachful language to each other but patiently bear each other's imperfections, determine to sett out in life in humble appearance & manner, determine to be saving in every department that you may be honest. Think no expence trivial, "tis many littles make much." Be thoroughly industrious both of you each laboring to help the other through your mutual duties. Think nothing so mean as living above your income. Attention to these things in a Tradesman's outsett is of vast importance. I stood aghast when I was first told that a woman could throw out more with a spoon than a man can throw in with a shovel but when I became a housekeeper my wonder ceased. Keep a strict acc't of all your expences or you never know what you are doing, & now my dear Son once more adieu, beware of impatience; as you grow in manhood, grow in calm patient conduct ... Y^r affect^e friend & mother, Mary Gibbs. N.B. When on the seas read the 107th Psalm, it is styled the Mariners' Psalm.' In it are the memorable words: '... they that go down to the sea in ships, that do business in great waters.'

The voyagers spent the last night at Plymouth, where friends gathered to say farewell, which Thomas's cousin recalled many years later: 'How many sad hearts there were that day.' The young couple stood on the deck waving the last good-byes, the baby lay in Caroline's arms, and the breeze that swirled about them filling the ship's sails sent them now into the uncharted waters of a new life. But only after eleven storm-tossed weeks did the *Speculator* reach the further shores, which news in a letter dated 6th of June and arriving in mid-October called forth from Thomas's mother heartfelt thanks to the Almighty for their safe passage and Thomas's speedy employment. If he failed in his original plan to lease a mill, the letters of introduction had born fruit as *maître meunier* to the Seigniory of Terrebonne, a stroke of great good fortune when most settlers probably arrived penniless. His mother observed: 'It affords us pleasure that you both appear quite decided as to the propriety of the step you have taken. Indeed I know of nothing at present to induce you to alter that opinion as things in England do not wear a better aspect since you left us.'

On August 8th in the following year, John Tate wrote to his niece: 'I only received your favor dated 17 Dec. last year about a fortnight ago & set about enquiring immediately after vessels for your part but finding there will be no opportunity of that kind before the spring & fearing that by so long a delay you might suspect me of inattention have determined to avail myself of the American Packet which has not yet sailed.' He too was cheered to hear that she was comfortably situated and contented: 'With regard to the privations to which you are subjected you have to reflect that they are more than compensated by the consciousness of independence & a fair prospect of success ...'

Miller and wife had settled happily into their new home, a stone house set in a maze of outbuildings, grist and saw mills, sheds, stables, kitchen and huge bakery, docks and wharves. The seigniory fronted the St John River by Île Jésus north of Montreal; its land had long been noted for the amount of wheat it produced, and its mills, the largest in New France by 1731, had achieved fame for the quality of the flour which had been exported from an early date to the Antilles and Newfoundland. Robert Gourlay was to describe the Terrebonne mills as the most complete and best in the country, when he wrote his *Statistical Account* in 1822. In 1819 it was still obligatory for every farmer to bring his grain to the seigniorial mill to be ground, an important source of the seigniory's income, and in spite of the dislocations of the war years and the Corn Laws, which limited imports to Britain after 1815, the latter gave Canadian wheat advantages over foreign imports; the Terrebonne mills still exported to Britain, Newfoundland, and the West Indies.

Roderick Mackenzie, always styled in our correspondence as the 'seigneur' but never actually holding that title, had been active in the fur trade; another fur trader, Simon McTavish, had been owner of the seigniory from 1802 to 1804. The latter had built the enormous bakery next to the Terrebonne mills, and each had had a share in the construction of the great docks on the river. The connection with the fur trade had required large quantities of flour and hardtack to be sent up to the Northwest by the brigades. In Monkhouse Tate's time in Quebec in the late eighties of the previous century, fur had ranked as the colony's most important export; fur traders, having amassed fortunes, made the village of Terrebonne, where they built fine houses, a centre for products from the Northwest and for supplies going up in exchange. In his day, English and Scotch merchants were beginning to dominate Montreal and buy up seigniories, the Loyalists and other settlers only beginning to affect the balance of population. Thirty years later in 1819, this stream had swelled to a flood in full spate of English-speaking immigrants, and the economic situation in Quebec had altered, with the fur trade in steady decline and wheat crops deteriorating.

Into this society with its incipient problems came Thomas and Caroline, unaware of cross-currents of conflict or portents of trouble. They began to learn French and to furnish their house, taking some pride in their Canadian purchases. 'I assure you we are greatly entertain'd by your accounts about Canada,' said Thomas's sister, '& our friends consider it a treat to hear particulars of a country so far abroad from persons whose testimony we can believe.' The price of wood astounded them: 'Perhaps Thos may purchase a winter stock cheaper now he knows the country better.' Alas, before the year was out, a fire damaged part of the mill, several buildings, and most of the house and new contents: 'It is a great mercy you were not all burnt in your beds when the fire took place ... It will operate as a caution in future,' said Caroline's father, with no mention of where any blame might be laid; nevertheless an unwelcome beginning.

Without exception, all their English correspondents considered Thomas's situation an improvement on the fate of friends at home, many of whom were sliding inexorably into poverty. His mother said that mass unemployment, low wages, and taxation that squeezed the poor had directly caused recent riots and bloodshed, a reference to the Peterloo Massacre: 'All the manufacturing poor are suffering dreadfully, the woollen as well as cotton & the manufacturers failing in large numbers.' She told enquirers that her son's decision to emigrate had come from the badness of trade, not from a roving disposition, and she reassured him: 'All your Kingsbridge friends think it likely you may ultimately feel no disadvantage by being in the employ of another, before you embark in trade for yourself. Indeed my dear Tho[s] it is my opinion your present situation & circumstances are more free from anxious care than any other you will ever occupy, therefore I hope you will move cautiously & with prudence; by your description of Canada & all I have read of America the middle classes of Society enjoy every mean of earthly happiness.'

Prudence prevailed and at the end of his first year Thomas renewed his agreement with the seigneur, with some improvement in his modest salary, so that Monkhouse Tate wrote to his daughter: 'I was glad to see by what you wrote to me that Mr Gibbs had made another and more advantageous agreement with Mr Mackenzie for a year as from everything that I see and hear from you and others I am confident you will do better in your present mode of life than in launching out on your own account. Mr Gibbs is young, his character, his conduct and his knowledge will in due time be sufficiently appreciated to make it important to his employer to retain him on almost any terms he may choose to require because he must know that it will be more easy for Mr Gibbs to obtain another situation equally advantageous than for him, Mr Mackenzie, to procure another manager equally confidential and trustworthy, for I understand almost all the Americans from the United States who have been employed in the mills in Canada have been found woefully deficient in morals and character.' He was no admirer of things or persons American.

'Think not your past instruction is lost because your hands are employ'd in domestic concerns,' Mary Gibbs told her daughter-in-law, and added for Thomas's benefit: 'It is no small addition to my pleasure that Caroline suits herself so well to her circumstances.' But Caroline's Uncle John Tate had received a more equivocal view from his niece: 'Your present situation does not appear to be such as many would envy,' he said, although he quickly reminded her of what she owed to Thomas: 'If it had not been for the effort which he made you might at this time have been sinking instead of rising in the scale of society.'

At this point, Thomas's family in Devon come to the fore in all their trials, bickerings, and indecisions, envying their brother and sister-in-law in the Promised Land, and yet unable to cross the Red Sea of their present troubles in order to join them. For every emigrant who sailed away from Britain, how many more must have longed to follow, but had not the courage, or found themselves rooted in their native soil by a thousand untoward events that sapped initiative and kept them hostage. The Gibbs family give ample evidence of hope deferred, of disappointments, tremors, hesitations, and plans that are postponed the better part of a lifetime.

Everything seemed to confirm the wisdom of Thomas's decision to leave England. Debilitating illness and onslaught of age had persuaded his father, old Philip Gibbs, to put up Shindles Mill for rent and sell all his other properties, including his house in Kingsbridge, before retiring to the village of Broadway in Somerset. This had precipitated a bitter quarrel with his eldest son, Philip, Jr, who accused him of breaking the entail: '... your father [and his own],' he told Thomas, 'intends to give that to strangers which Providence and policy designed for his family. In temper he is certainly amended but in obstinacy and perverseness of action more abounding than ever ...'

Mary Gibbs turned a blind eye to this latest family squabble and said: 'Our house is a very neat and comfortable one at a low rent.' But the journey to Somerset in a carriage that jolted all the way had severely shaken her ailing husband, who suffered agonies now in failing health, and even she admitted: 'I have felt a depression of spirits on the occasion but do not encourage it ...' Their daughter Cathrine was a chronic invalid in body and mind, unable to care for herself, frequently unmanageable, at times forcibly restrained in the manner of the day. The doctors said she should be locked in her room: 'Her affliction,' wrote Mary Gibbs, 'is a heavy trial to us & my body feels it as well as my spirit.' Thomas's sister Elizabeth was their 'depending hand,' although others murmured: 'What a drudge poor Liz is to them.'

Monkhouse Tate, from a miniature. My great-great-great-grandfather, who was sent out to Quebec by the British government in 1789.

Monkhouse Tate's daughter Caroline, who married Thomas Gibbs.

Thomas Gibbs.

Thomas's brother Philip Gibbs. From a silhouette, c. 1815.

Thomas's sister Mary, who married Silvanus Gillard.
From a silhouette, c. 1815.

Thomas Nicholson Gibbs, the son of Thomas and Caroline,
known to us as Uncle T.N.

Uncle T.N.'s brother, William Henry Gibbs.

Uncle T.N.'s Ellesmere Hall, 1870.

Their sister Sarah Ketland Gibbs, Mrs James Gooderham.
Taken in Japan in 1892.

Mary Hodge Gibbs, my great-grandmother, who married the Reverend W.S. Blackstock. From a daguerreotype, c. 1852.

The Reverend William Schenck Blackstock. From a daguerreotype, c. 1852.

The Reverend W.S. Blackstock and family, 1867(?).
From a daguerreotype. Standing: George, Millie, Thomas.
Seated: W.S. Blackstock, with May, Mary, and Carrie.

From left: George, May, Carrie, and Millie at Milton, 1867.

Thomas Gibbs Blackstock, my grandfather, at about twenty-one, possibly when he set out for the American West in 1872.

Caroline (Carrie) Jane Blackstock at sixteen as
Mrs Donald Downey, Napanee, 1876.

George Tate Blackstock at about twenty-three and a lawyer, c. 1879.

Mary (May) Blackstock at about seventeen, c. 1880.

May a few years later.

Carrie, at about thirty-one, as she begins her career
in New York, c. 1891.

Amelia (Millie) at about forty-three in 1897(?).

Carrie, as Mrs Charles Duer, with her husband, her beloved dog, Jack, and her army of servants in the garden of their house in Rangoon, c. 1910(?).

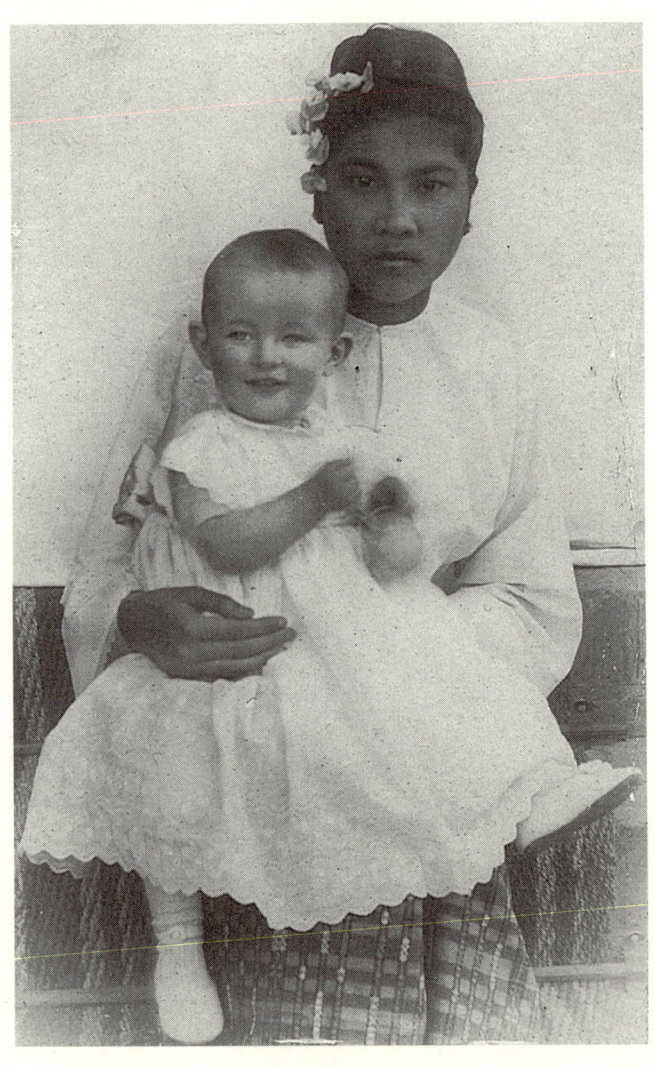

Carrie's adopted child, named Jackie, with his Burmese ayah, 1919.

Frederick Weymouth Gibbs, who had been tutor to
the Prince of Wales, 1890s.

George Tate Blackstock campaigning in England for the Unionist (i.e., Conservative) party in 1910.

The Reverend W.S. Blackstock at about seventy-nine, c. 1903.

My great-grandmother Mary Blackstock, at about seventy-eight, c. 1905.

The mood of the eldest daughter, another Mary, and her husband, Silvanus Gillard, had already sunk into unrelieved gloom, and they constantly complained of their own near poverty compared with Caroline and Thomas's expectations. 'Oh, we long to know if you can still give us such a favorable & encouraging account of y^r situation & prospects as at first. Oh, many stand in need of it & I marvel that so few have courage to quit the land of their birth while they are pressed down with vexation and care,' wrote this Mary. But an unlucky star governed Gillard affairs, for they had intended to follow Thomas and Caroline to Quebec in the autumn of 1819 when at the very moment of embarkation Silvanus's mother fell mortally ill, lingering on for nearly a year and as Silvanus somewhat ambiguously said: 'While life remained it made our removal very unpleasant.' Then his father sickened and he too lingered on, foiling a second attempt to emigrate; only ill-paying shopkeeping kept their heads above water.

'We have lost *much* money,' Mary Gillard informed Caroline; 'we can scarcely tell how & yet have been denying ourselves many things since you left us to endeavor to repair the breach but all in vain. I have kept no servant since you left us.' They moved to the village of Stokenham in Devonshire and tried to make a living out of four fields, a school under Silvanus, and a shop under Mary, who described their house on first seeing it as the very abode of wretchedness and filth: 'Now all my pride of circumstances or situation in life receives the death blow ... Fancy my d^r

Caroline how my heart sank in me when I beheld it.'

Stokenham dispelled whatever optimism they still entertained as history repeated itself; the shop failed, leaving unpaid creditors, and Silvanus's attempts at schoolmastering foundered just as his wife was expecting her first child: 'Poor prospect for my little brat, is it not?' she said. 'I know not what we shall do. This is our only bitterness but a great one it is ... Indeed so adverse have things been to us that it seems as if we were to be crushed almost to the dust here – the fields do not pay at all.' Silvanus added: 'and so here we are in the mire.' Joseph, another of Thomas's four brothers, said: '... they appear to be laboring under difficulties & privations which it has pleased the Great Disposer of all events to visit them with.'

By now every member of the Gibbs family struggled in reduced circumstances, and as not a penny of rent from the mill had come in, the elderly parents, Philip and Mary, in the village of Broadway had less and less to live on. 'What are we come to?' said their daughter Mary Gillard. 'We are really looked down on with pity by some & contempt by others, everyone esteeming us as having thrown away our bread as a family thro' pride, discontent & family differences.' Her husband, Silvanus, went so far as to accuse his parents-in-law, when they were obliged of necessity to reclaim an earlier loan to him, of turning their children penniless out into the world: 'Such revolutions as are taking place,' he complained. 'Some rising in the world whilst they whose expectations have been something comfortable are crushed to the earth; we must not go out of our own families to witness illustrations of this. But we seem to cling to old England as if to an old enfeebled house when one stone after another is falling from under us & are manifesting our determination not to leave it till the whole fabric falls to the ground. Indeed we have already accepted this as we have no means whatever left to us of escaping.'

Silvanus turned to preaching as one way of making a living, writing to Thomas: 'I am now become what you and I once scarcely guessed at, a *Baptist minister*.' He went on to admit that he would never have had confidence enough to assume this role were it not for the ignorance of the flock. His wife said: 'Mr G. has engaged in preaching to the poor villagers at different places since we came here & appears satisfied that it is his duty to do so & anxiously wishes, I trust from pure motive, to be more extensively employed in this work & fancies a more enlarged field.' Always expectant, always disappointed, and forever formulating unrealized plans to emigrate to the United States, which he deemed a more developed country than the Canadas and therefore more worthy of his abilities, Silvanus said: 'I think I shall soon convert myself into a Yankey ... All of our friends and acquaintances that have gone to the States are benefitted & pleased & give a very encouraging account of it.'

To whatever shores they sailed, many Kingsbridge emigrants had judged favourably of their new circumstances. One acquaintance had just sent word from Newfoundland that he was well established and happy, but now at home would-be adventurers suddenly hesitated, increasingly prey to conflicting rumours. Recent newspaper accounts spoke of much disillusionment, and Thomas's sister, Mary Gillard, said: 'No one will persuade you to go to America. Oh no! None but fools for this [venture?]. The Papers are filled, our ears are dinned with the unceasing tale of distress endured there.' However, she told her brother: 'Many seem disposed to listen to y^r accounts that will not hearken to others.' Thomas considered his emigration a success even if in August of 1821 his brother Philip, Jr, was writing: 'I thought your last to Uncle Benjn rather gloomy.' On this occasion, Philip, Jr, ends his letter less plaintively than usual: 'Numerous are the enquiries made for you & the good wishes breathed for your welfare.'

Silvanus Gillard had a friend whose attempt at bettering his lot proved as abortive as his own: 'Poor Smith is another distressed! He too, poor fellow, would feign have gone to the land of deliverance but for untoward circumstances. He took his family & luggage to Plymouth & found to his mortification the capt^n would not take them on board as some of the children were sickening for the measles & they are now at Guernsey; he has day work, 20/ per week.' One Kingsbridge resident left under a pall: 'Pray have you seen anything of Robert Mannin?' enquired Thomas's mother. 'He has left England for Canada, the family wish'd us to write you by him but we thought it best left alone. He brought disgrace on himself by having a base child by Thos Gillard's daughter of Goveton, she who has a hare lip. Mr Mannin permitted him to be taken to Bridewell rather than pay the sum the Parish demanded which was an extravagant one & when he came out of Bridewell he set sail.'

Only Thomas's brother John acted resolutely amidst all the equivocations and hesitations of other members of the family. Making up his mind to emigrate, he had lost no time and sailed for Quebec in the summer of 1821. He was most shrewdly appraised at the time by his sister Mary Gillard, even as he boarded the boat that would carry him away from her forever: 'If I were you,' she advised Thomas, 'I w^d renew nothing old or unpleasant with John, but I hope he will gain a more noble, generous & open spirit by being with you, for he knows nothing of the world & is very narrow-minded, inclined to indolence & exceedingly suspicious, at the same time he is most steady, quiet, orderly & affectionate & has plenty of ability & strength to work.' Time would tell.

Thomas's older brother, Philip, Jr, all the while talking of emigrating but failing to put it into operation, opened a school, which succeeded in spite of his volatile temper, although Silvanus said: 'He is like the rest of us completely tired of keeping school. I know by experience how hateful it is & can sympathize with him.' And Philip, Jr, summed up his view of England in this manner: 'There is no prospect here.' At the same time, he mastered surveying and mapping as useful trades in the United States, his choice of destination also, so that he and Silvanus talked of joining forces. Emigration beguiled even the misfit Benjamin, another of Thomas's brothers, but having already broken one apprenticeship, he was enmeshed in the courts, with all the witnesses siding with his master, and this deferred any plans he entertained of sailing away. His mother said: 'I am sorry to say Benjn is a poor weak-minded young man, stronger in body than he was but as to religious affairs to be given over to fanaticism, carried about with every wind of doctrine, very unsettled, appears to gain no ground in temporals or spirituals.'

From London, Caroline's father wrote encouragingly to her but soon complained of her failure to reply promptly: 'I had indeed thought it long since I heard anything from you after your promise in the preceeding year to be more mindful of your English friends but it has been often said and I am inclined to apprehend with some truth that there is in the climate of North America a sort of oblivious quality which makes its inhabitants unmindful of persons and things across the Atlantic, one cause assigned for this in regard to the inhabitants of the United States was that the letters which they received were chiefly of a dunning nature and therefore it was a convenient thing to be able to attribute the neglect of their correspondents to a natural quality of the air. This however need not in any shape affect you as you receive no letters of this sort.'

The Gillards had received from Terrebonne no replies to their letters for over twelve months: 'Everyone wonders at it. Our anxiety to hear from you knows no bounds. Other people are hearing from their friends but we cannot hear from you.' Thomas's mother wrote: 'Farewell my dear children, do write me. Rest assur'd nothing gladdens my heart more than your letters.'

CHAPTER FOUR

*H*ARDLY HAD THE ASHES of the fire at the Terrebonne mill settled, the repairing of its damaged machinery as swiftly been completed, than family at home heard that Caroline and the children were to live alone on a farm until Thomas joined them, which thoroughly alarmed Tates and Gibbses alike. The spirit of enterprise that had carried him to Terrebonne as miller persuaded him now, with an increase in family in 1821, and the prospect of more to follow five more, as it happened, to turn farmer as well.

Various plans came and went. To the north of Terrebonne the recent opening up of settlement in New Glasgow with English-speaking inhabitants attracted him, but this choice appears to have yielded from the lack of a good road and cleared land to a second purchase of two parcels of cleared land with house and barn fronting on the River Mascouche only a few miles to the north of the Terrebonne mills. (It was in the River Mascouche that three-year-old little John Tate Gibbs was later to drown.)

Thomas's purchase of the first parcel of land, which the seigniory had ceded long ago, involved an outlay of sixteen hundred and fifty Quebec pounds or shillings and a complicated mechanism to pay off a wife's dower rights; the second parcel, within the seigniory, called for minuscule payment but the usual retention of customary seigniorial rights relating to wheat, the milling of wheat, or the cutting down of oak and pine, and so the farm harked back to *ancien régime*. Isolation and hard work awaited its owners. 'Now,' said Silvanus Gillard, 'perhaps since you left the confinement of the Mill you yourself have gone farther in the country & can give the best and earliest account of that kind.'

This bold leap into the future brought immediate problems and on December 5th, 1822, John Tate wrote to his niece: '... from all you say am inclined to suspect that Mr Gibbs has speculated beyond his means. When a man has a family growing up & finds his means insufficient he thinks that he must do something & when there is a good prospect of success it's worthwhile venturing something. Of this he must be the best judge, but as a general principle the only safe way is to reduce the expenditure within the income, whatever it may be & to take no more land than you can manage well.' Thomas, however, would have had one advantage, a knowledge of the more advanced farming practised in England.

Old Philip Gibbs dispatched letters of credit, supplies of seed, and other farm necessities, some of which were for instant resale. Thomas's mother said: 'We sincerely wish you & yours health to enjoy & wisdom to improve it,' but she reacted immediately to the news that Caroline was to go there alone: 'Methinks I would never have you move till you move together for as the family increases in years both Father & Mother are needed to guide their youth but circumstances will direct you better than I can.' In August she wrote again: 'Is your house in a village or alone? If alone you cannot live in it without a man. I do not wish to dictate your plans but hope Thos will weigh one thing over against another before he removes you.'

Removed, however, she apparently was and in December her Uncle John Tate wrote to her: 'I shall now delay no longer to express my wish to know how you succeed in the various plans you mentioned in your last – how you manage with your dairy, pigs & poultry?' Thomas's twin roles of farmer and miller greatly impressed his brother-in-law Silvanus Gillard: 'We cannot conceive how you get thro' so much whilst people at home find it impossible to get on with one concern.' The grinding of wheat and export of flour continued unabated at the Terrebonne mills, where, however, other problems arose.

In 1824 a court case took the seigniory away from Roderick Mackenzie and awarded it to the heirs of Simon McTavish. John Tate wrote to his niece: 'As to Mr Gibbs, what you say about want of rest is very true but let us hope that things will mend and that Mr Henry McKenzie will do all the good you expect & that such an arrangement will be made as will enable you to get forward in the world.' Henry McKenzie, fur trader, exporter of flour, and brother of the 'Seigneur,' maintained his previous function as seigniorial agent, the person to whom Thomas from the beginning had reported, and he came to the rescue. Thomas apparently continued to run the seigniorial mills.

Despite reservations on Calvinist doctrine as too cold and intellectual for her liking and ignorant also of the local Presbyterian minister's shortcomings, Thomas's mother had on their arrival in Terrebonne urged her daughter-in-law to attend his church. But Silvanus Gillard had early noted the minister's failure to please his brother and sister-in-law and now on perusing a newspaper found mention of him: 'Was this the same you used to speak so badly of?' It was indeed. The farm's distance from a church fully exercised minds at home in England, provoking much comment. Caroline's father suggested she invite a few like-minded Protestants to join in prayer: '... though the privation of the means of attending public worship is a misfortune, I do not consider that it is an irremediable one.' Thomas's sister Mary Gillard said: 'Alas, how I lament for you that you cannot enjoy public worship. We hear they are better off in this respect in Upper Canada.' Thomas's mother favoured any missionary as long as, one supposes, he were neither Roman Catholic nor Church of England. 'Surely you Canadians will not suffer yourselves to be kept down by any one religious order?' said she, always suspicious of any established denomination.

She soon wrote on another theme close to her

heart: 'Am sorry you have such impediments in the way of morally educating your children,' for schools as well as churches were weighed in the balance and found wanting. Roderick Mackenzie had sat earlier on a commission to provide free schools, and the village of Terrebonne boasted a schoolmaster, but teachers nearer to the farm proved elusive, unsatisfactory or out of reach. Then, providentially, a Mr and Mrs Hodge entered the neighbourhood to become close friends, Mrs Hodge undertaking to instruct little Caroline Gibbs, and at four years of age she went to live with them during the week. A word of warning came from Uncle John Tate in London: 'A child in her situation ought never to be allowed a voice as to whether she likes to stay at one place or another.' Mary Gibbs said: 'Do my dear instill into her that respect for you & her father which is obtained by kind and sound reasoning accompanied by a firm command without austere rebukes ...'

Throughout these early years, Terrebonne and Lower Canada rise up before the reader only in mirror image as family at home reply to Caroline and Thomas's letters, none of which to England have survived. And on either side of the Atlantic, the postal service, the cost of which was paid by recipients, came in repeatedly for criticism for any letters that went astray as well as the irksome regulations everyone endeavoured to circumvent. Caroline's Uncle John Tate had a friend, Captain Stoddard, who obligingly delivered his letters to Terrebonne unfranked and undetected by the authorities and on the return journey brought letters and first-hand accounts of Montreal and the young couple: 'It would be as well,' John Tate advised his niece with regard to letters the Captain would carry home with him, 'to notice the ship's name on the inside instead of the outside and then the appearance of your letter not being different from an Inland one, there would be no danger in passing it thro' the Twopenny Post Office without further precaution.' When at one point the Captain's ship was seized in England for some minor infraction, it greatly distressed John Tate lest his own attempts to evade postage came to light. Philip, Jr, was to write bitterly that he had received one letter from Thomas 'with a rapidity truly astonishing and it was followed by two others from Brother John to Benjamin the last of which with all my schemes to avoid it saddled me with the postage. My remarks on this mode of transacting family affairs I shall reserve for another part of my letter.'

In the isolation of their farm in Lower Canada, perhaps only the letters from home tied miller and wife still to a world they knew and eased for them the pain of separation, while the assumption that his niece would one day return to England when times improved reconciled her Uncle John Tate to her absence: 'Much as I sometimes regret your being at such a distance yet when I consider all the circumstances cannot upon the whole wish it to be otherwise.' Caroline took to numbering her correspondence, a system he copied without much enthusiasm, and in one letter he remarked: 'At the present time have so little to communicate that I could very easily find an excuse for delay & it has required some little exertion to seat myself for the present purpose.'

'I value your affection,' he told her in another letter, '& feel a lively interest in everything which concerns your welfare.' He, rather than her preoccupied father, related the news, and from the great metropolis of London he provided a door to the outside world by regularly posting books, newspapers, and pamphlets: 'On Sunday last a new paper came out & as they gave with it a print of the King it was an inducement for me to buy it in order to send it to you.' He sent new coinage as presents for the children and obligingly complied with a request for a cookbook: 'Though what great occasion you can have for one I really do not know. However there's no hurt in it & any fancy of that kind which you may take into your head shall be very happy to accommodate you with.'

John Tate commented on every current topic. Despite conditions in the countryside, so he told her in 1824, in town interest rates had dropped, taxes were coming down, and jobs were plentiful: 'It is astonishing to see the great number of buildings about London in every direction & there is continually some new scheme coming forward for either bridges, docks, gas companies, insurance offices etc., besides loans without number & they all get subscribers – the consequence is that some acquire fortunes and others are ruined.' Mr Peek of Kingsbridge, and neighbour of the Gibbs family, was said to be making a fortune in confectionery in London, and a year later John Tate returned to the theme, saying that very large fortunes were being made and many a fortune lost.

The royal row between George IV and his consort had spilled forth in 1820: 'Nothing scarcely has been talked of for these nine months or more but the Queen. Parties are very violent on both sides ...' Caroline's half-brothers Monk, established at the Pelican Fire Office in London, and William, newly articled to a law firm, sided violently with the Queen. 'I have a leaning to the same side,' John Tate admitted, 'but think there is so much to be said on both sides that it is difficult to determine & that very often those who are most positive know the least.' The two young men may have clashed with their father's conservative views; Monkhouse Tate stood on the side of order.

In the matter of the Catholic Emancipation Bill, which rent the kingdom in 1825, John Tate gave as his opinion: '... nothing is so injurious to the cause of truth as coercion of any kind. It is said that last Monday the Duke of York in presenting a petition against Catholic emancipation took occasion to deliver a violent speech, it was of course admired by some few but by myself & many more consider'd a very silly exhibition.' Mary Gibbs spoke of 'the abominable Test Act,' which affected both Roman Catholics and Dissenters like herself.

Her bachelor uncle, so often the voice of reason, assisted Caroline in a very practical way; he kept the children shod, sending his niece an accurate method of judging the size of shoes required. Moreover, he advised her that, much as she disliked it, letting the children go barefoot was preferable to pinching up their little toes in tight shoes, and Monkhouse's sister, her

Aunt Sarah Tate, who was married to Mr Ketland, of Mousley, Cumberland (this conjures up scenes of Mrs Tabitha Twitchit), sent gifts of clothing. The outfitting of all Caroline's growing family in Lower Canada must have required her hard work, and she too, like the local *habitants*, may well have depended on the carding machine and fulling mill introduced into Terrebonne village by Roderick Mackenzie. The journey into Montreal made shopping expeditions there a rarity, although from time to time Thomas had business in the town.

From London, Caroline's father lacked the means to smooth her path even when the courts at last absolved him of his bankruptcy, in which he had been in no way to blame, for he soon found the Russia Company to be a losing concern to everyone engaged in it, which prompted a move to the Island of Jersey; he too became an emigrant of a sort. 'The utmost of my expectations is that he may be able to support his family,' said his brother John, but Monkhouse founded and edited there the first English-language newspaper, *The British Press*, which began publication on March 5th, 1822.

At the same time, he designed and built a ship on a new principle without ribs, tried to settle his older sons in professions, and in the morning instructed his younger children at home. He wrote to Quebec that Caroline's stepmother was apprehensive: 'Our little Charlotte you know is eight years old, but some fausses couches have taken place since.' Mrs Tate's fears were well founded; Lucius Octavius appeared, and Caroline commented rather acidly to her Uncle John that this baby was rather out of season, twenty-three years younger than her half-brother Monk.

'Henry is here for want of being able to do better for him,' Monkhouse informed his daughter. 'He is now 17 & is five feet nine or ten inches high. I wish much to get him fully employed either at home or abroad. Would he do any good in Canada do you think?' But Henry went to work for Mrs Tate's family in the wool trade, and after a year with an uncle in Paris and another under an experienced traveller in Britain, he was entrusted with the firm's business in New Orleans. 'I hope,' said his Uncle John Tate, 'he will acquit himself of his commission in such a manner as to do himself credit.' This Henry did with one exception: 'He is now returned, but he took rather too great a liberty by going up the Ohio crossing the Alleganny [sic] Mountains & visiting Philadelphia & New York.' The excursion did not include Montreal and Terrebonne, which may appear a little strange.

In 1827 John Tate died, bequeathing his niece two hundred pounds, his Bible, and his books: 'Indeed,' wrote Mary Gibbs on hearing this news, 'my dear Caroline, you have lost a good friend.' This she knew and from now on only sporadic Tate news reaches Lower Canada, but this much can be gleaned: later in life, her brother Monk, whom she often mentioned, developed a fever and went insane; John, who had already joined the East India Company, sailed back and forth to China as also did little Charles until, still only a boy, he was swept off the mast in a gale and lost at sea. George, after training at Guys Hospital, became surgeon to the Gloucester Regiment, publishing a treatise on hysteria that ran into several editions. Maria and Charlotte, who never married, were to live together in Camden Town, but of Henry, William, Pitt, Emily, and Lucius Octavius there is no further word.

By contrast, in Devon and Somerset, with pens ever in hand, a more faithful set of scribes, the Gibbs family, kept the miller of Terrebonne and his wife in touch with home, where several talked still of emigration, inspired by Thomas's example. The pipedream of escape continued to dance before Silvanus Gillard, whatever obstacles lay in the way: 'I still lean towards the United States,' he informed Thomas, but if any large town on the Great Lakes wanted a schoolmaster and preacher, he would come to Canada immediately on being apprised of it. Instead, he flitted irresolute from place to place in Devonshire without the fixed determination that every emigrant must have, and he soon found it necessary to supplement his inadequate income as evangelist by turning again to teaching: 'On Monday next it is my intention to open a school in this place, much as I dislike it,' he said, 'and I shall see what the inhabitants of Modbury will do for me in this way. We must do something besides preaching and we have no means for any other thing.'

He enquired after Thomas's family: 'You would laugh to hear the folks in England groaning at the expected approach of increased families. Pray, are visitors so excessively unwelcome in Canada? Cousin J^{no} Nicholson has six daughters and another in embryo unless indeed they should be happily disappoint'd and it turn out to be a boy. But I believe that even a boy would not atone for the horrors of increase.' And even as his wife in uncontrollable fits of coughing edged closer to the grave, which quite escaped his notice, Silvanus congratulated himself on avoiding doctors: 'I hope you don't employ these rats too much. We are the wonder of all the places where we live because we do without them & yet I find we get on as well or better than our neighbors.'

Mary Gillard died leaving two little girls, and although Silvanus truly sorrowed, he sought a replacement in the following year. From nearby Salcombe in Devon, his present address, his former mother-in-law, Mary Gibbs, received a letter comparing past and future wives to the detriment of the latter: 'In which,' she wrote to Thomas and Caroline, 'he introduces the subject of his acquaintance just such as he could wish & adds "I did not again expect an idol nor an object of admiration & delight – the source of my pride in every circle to which it might be my happiness to be introduc'd – but the Mother before the Wife."'

Private trials were multiplied in public woes, and Thomas's mother continued to lament the onrush of progress in industry and agriculture that brought poverty and distress in its wake in Devonshire, where landlords and tenants alike had appealed to the government for help as early as 1823. Her view of the countryside is neither idyllic nor picturesque, a prerogative surely of the rich who dwelt in carefully cultivated parklands. Philip, Jr, too harped upon the upheavals taking place in society and especially in the town of Kingsbridge, where an uncle on their mother's side, though a preacher, was reduced with his wife to poverty: 'Were I to tell you all that I could you would not believe, notwithstanding you know so much of the world as you do.'

Thomas's brother Joseph informed him of changing scenes in Devon and Somerset, writing in 1823 that '... coaches are upsetting every week, being such competition among coach proprietors that they cut & drive every way both in time and expenses.' The Industrial Revolution was speeding rapidly onwards, as Joseph said in the same letter: 'Steam engines are become so general that they are used in most parts of the English coast but there are often accidents arising from them ...' Trevithick's steam locomotive had appeared in 1803; the first railway engine, Stephenson's *Rocket*, would follow in 1829; and seven years later in 1836 the first railway in Canada would run between the St Lawrence and the Richelieu Rivers.

Everyone thought Joseph satisfactorily employed in a village shop, though even this was a sad comedown. He now inadvisedly launched out on his own into ironmongery, at which Mary Gibbs said: 'There never was such times for parents to settle their children – so hopeless!' Joseph's brief and only good luck came in marriage, which had prompted this remark from Silvanus: ''Tis a secret but perhaps your mother has told you that cupid has thrust his dart at Joseph Gibbs. A lady of Abergavenny [in Monmouthshire], very plain in person, a fortune £1500. Hitherto he has been unsuccessful.' But two years later, Joseph was bankrupt, caught a cold while selling off his stock, and died. Philip, Jr, wrote to Thomas: 'Poor Joseph, his widow has married again and has exchanged a dead Gibbs for a living Gould in less than nine months.'

Thomas's parents voiced alarm at the engagement of his sister Elizabeth, the present stay of their old age: 'The young man being I believe a God-fearing man,' wrote Mary Gibbs, 'we do not consider it right to oppose it but still tremble as to their getting into business lest a race of paupers be the consequence, in fact paupers & pauperism are terms in common use in England.' She sent ever more discouraging news of Thomas's brother Benjamin: 'If pride were my governing principle it would be sufficiently mortified at his low estate, but I am thankful he is so far restored as he is & able to act at all.' He too still talked of emigration, talked and did not act: '... a rolling stone gathering no moss but an expense to the family & a grief of mind to us all. When his wanderings will be staid God only knows.' But she told Thomas that Silvanus Gillard was Benjamin's steady and forbearing friend.

The country poor lived more wretchedly than ever; the population burgeoned and the blame for much agricultural misery was directed at the introduction of machinery, especially the new threshing machines. In 1827 Mary Gibbs wrote to Terrebonne, 'It is expected the population cannot continue to pay what they now do for victuals.' This is the constant theme of her letters: '... I cannot but think prosperity in this land will be constantly varying much until the laboring classes have surer incomes. Machinery can do everything here.' She had no doubts at all as to the wisdom of Thomas's and his brother John's emigration: '... Tradesmen cannot or do not keep on their legs but by compounding with their creditors.'

In 1829, when a severe winter had followed a bad harvest, the poor rose in protest in England; there was a demand for reform, and the government's complacency towards the poor incensed her: 'I say in the thousands & tens of thousands of hearts wring with agony not knowing how to obtain employ sufficient & pay equal to support their families & yet the Prime Minister [the Duke of Wellington] remarking on the appearance of prosperity in the very quarters where inability to provide things sufficient to meet creditors is well known to exist.

'Many have lately emigrated to New Holland [Australia], great temptations being held out to form a settlement call'd Swan River [in Western Australia], which some wisely name Goose Island ... It is by no means likely that society can hold together in this manner, but the wisest, the most judicious see not how it can be altered without such a general renovation among all classes as human nature is too selfish to attempt.' Fortunes continued to fall in England.

Seven years earlier, family in England had learned with some surprise that Lower Canada had not contained for long Thomas's brother John, who alone had followed him to Quebec and had found occupation as miller, but at a distance that precluded much companionship. Without warning, in 1822, he joined the flood of settlers into Upper Canada and put down roots at Napanee, where he was employed at its mill, the first west of the Cataraqui River, which had been constructed by the government in 1786 in preparation for the Loyalists. From Devon, Philip, Jr, with a constant eye to improving his own finances and for all his erudition not entirely master of economics, was to make this proposal to Thomas: 'Fur, particularly beaver, bears a heavy profit and we conceive John must be well situated for such a business and wish you might easily get into it.'

Unfortunately, the village of Napanee, on what was called the front line of settlement, lay on swampy ground beside the Napanee River six miles north of Lake Ontario, and its banks were particularly conducive to the ague, from which poor John greatly suffered. Silvanus Gillard sent an enquiry: 'Is he married or trothed? We hope you know something of him for his English friends know just nothing. We think you American folks all very sparing in your communications.'

In 1829 John popped up again like a jack-in-the-box, as he was always to do, and wrote to his brother Thomas in Lower Canada. The ague of Napanee had sent him off westward through the Midland, Newcastle, and Home Districts, where he paused to consider a site for a mill in Haldimand Township, then pressed on to the County of York and the village of Newmarket, where he came to a halt. Here he married, momentarily settled down once more as miller, and made the acquaintance of Eli Gorham, an American settler and owner of one of the first cloth mills in Upper Canada. Eli's son, Nelson, was one day to be an ally of Mackenzie, and there seems to have been some connection by marriage between the Gorhams and the Lounts; the Rebellion is coming ever closer.

Eli's brother Joseph had a fulling and carding mill in the Township of Whitby, still in the County of York, on the north shore of Lake Ontario, and it was through Eli that John heard of the Cleveland and Dearborn Mill in that township at what was known as The Hollow, not far from Skae's Corners, which later became Oshawa. In October of 1830 John dispatched a long enthusiastic description to his brother Thomas with special emphasis on Joseph Gorham's encouragement to buy the mill, which had long been idle for want of repairs: 'all the farmers in Whitby Township would be rejoiced if some capable person or persons would come immediately & carry on the business in a proper manner as many of the farmers have to go upwards of 20 miles to get their grinding done as it should.' He urged Thomas to come up and see for himself with a view to forming a partnership: how could the enterprise fail?

John tumbled breathlessly over himself in extolling the advantages of the mill: only one mile from the stage road between York and Kingston, four miles from a good harbour, the back settlement of fertile land quickly filling up, three hundred settlers having arrived in the previous year alone, all of whom would clear the land, sow wheat, take it to the nearest miller to be ground, and sell him the surplus. He wrote as settlers surged into the Upper Province, the second stage of whose history had now begun; this was a society in which a good miller was of some importance since the fastest crop was still wheat and the day of extensive mixed farming had not yet begun. Various changes in the British Corn Laws continued to favour Canada wheat, although it was subject still to import duties; exports from Upper Canada via the St Lawrence flourished, and by the 1830s these exports were rapidly increasing; no one saw any obstacles in the way.

A regular steamboat service had been established on Lake Ontario at the end of the War of 1812, and by the time of John's arrival a stagecoach ran between York and Kingston. Many small settlements grew up at the junction of this Kingston Road and the streams that emptied into Lake Ontario; such were the origins of Whitby, Oshawa, Bowmanville, and Port Hope, when the streams were far larger before the forests disappeared and were reliable sources of water power for the mills and industries of the new villages. Gristmills, sawmills, carding and fulling mills, asheries, distilleries, and tanneries sprang up wherever there was water power; its importance could not be overestimated, so that emigrant handbooks noted the suitability of certain places for mill sites, at the same time warning the would-be settler against so-called neverfailing creeks and extensive water privileges, which in reality might prove to be but trickling streams. The Oshawa Creek was already attracting the manufacturing that presaged the town's industrial future, convincing John of excellent business prospects.

Only the indecision of its owner delayed this mill's purchase: 'Sometimes he wishes to sell very much & at others he will not sell at all & has sometimes sworn that no man shall have the situation short of 36 hundred dollars.' However, Mr Cleveland reduced the sum to three thousand dollars and a bargain was eventually struck: five hundred dollars down with yearly instalments of seventy-five pounds with interest, and he agreed to wait three years for a decision. 'Dear Brother,' wrote John to Thomas, 'I think I have made a fair statement of the place to you & have mentioned every particular necessary that I can think of but I think if you were to see it yourself you would be satisfied.'

Old Philip Gibbs said that John would have to work a good deal harder than he had in order to pay off the sum required. This was a discouraging start, and Mary Gibbs told Thomas: 'You are not devoid of knowledge that it will take money to stock the estate, alter mills, etc. We are quite anxious that you may maturely judge before you act, you know your own resources, we do not nor do we know if John has saved anything to go on upon. You say it has a smart saw mill, we scarcely understand the term.'

Their father promised to help both his sons, and even Philip, Jr, talked airily of contributing several hundred pounds himself to his brothers' venture in Upper Canada. He had hoped to import timber, wheat, or 'anything yielding a profit' from Terrebonne and in his patronizing way had written in the previous year: 'Mr Balkwell & myself much wonder how it is that you who appeared to possess such spirit and enterprise for himself should on your getting into America have dropped everything of the kind.' Mary Gibbs warned Thomas: 'Your brother P. is a scientific man, calculate on him as no other, a mathematician.

Somehow these men never appear to feel like others & altho' he was train'd to business yet he does not act like a man of business.' Meanwhile Philip, Jr, spoke most disrespectfully of his ageing parents: 'those who now receive all the attentions of the growing second childhood.' Yet Mary Gibbs lent a hundred pounds from her marriage settlement, and only the violence of winter storms delayed their father from venturing out of doors to transact the business of forwarding funds.

The Cleveland and Dearborn Mills were to be known in time as the South Oshawa Mills, and if the partnership between John and Thomas lasted only four years, it launched a commercial enterprise by which Thomas's sons became the leading citizens of the town and ranked amongst the largest millers and produce merchants in the country, gaining and losing fortunes, their successes and failures reflecting the periods of expansion and depression in mid-nineteenth-century Ontario.

From a miller's standpoint, the Upper Province offered several advantages over Lower Canada, where the seigniorial system limited the amount of land available for purchase, and where by 1830 Upper Canada wheat had to be imported. The Upper Province abounded in good mill streams and sites; the English language and English law prevailed; and there were fewer restrictions, it seemed, and greater opportunity. Not that the years in Terrebonne were considered a failure, quite the reverse; the miller had received a salary supplemented by his farm, and in 1828 he had acquired a tannery. His mother had observed:

'It is a mercy my dear children that with so numerous a family you have food & raiment for all without fear – a most mortifying one to an honorable man – that you shall injure others to provide for your own decently.' But the prospect of owning a mill and the future advantages to the father of a large and ever-growing family persuaded Thomas to consider this second migration.

In Montreal the cholera epidemic raged in 1832, striking down great numbers of the population, and although Thomas and his family seem to have escaped, he had recently suffered a lengthy and serious illness; only after his recovery could he marshal his family for the journey into Upper Canada. The death of his benefactor, Henry McKenzie, in June of 1832 probably hastened his decision to join his brother John; by the 22nd of the following December, he had already left the seigniory, a new miller took his place, and on the 31st the seigniory was sold at auction to the Honorable Joseph Masson.

There is no word as to how the little expedition consisting of Thomas, Caroline, and their children travelled from Terrebonne to The Hollow, or South Oshawa as it eventually became. Mary, our great-grandmother (who was to marry the Reverend W.S. Blackstock), was five years old when she made the journey with her brother William, and her sisters Caroline, Sarah, and Amelia. Their brother, Thomas Nicholson Gibbs, known to us as Uncle T.N., already attended his Uncle Philip, Jr's, school in England in spite of that gentleman's eccentricities and temper.

The uncle had written encouragingly to Lower Canada: 'He will have advantages which it is impossible he should avail himself of in your neighborhood. I propose mathematics and geography and one of the best writing masters in England will superintend that department of his education ... Mind the boy, let nothing prevent you from sending your boy to England.' Accordingly, in 1829 at the age of eight he had sailed from Montreal. Within two months of his arrival, Philip, Jr, assessed his abilities: 'At his young age, they are by no means contemptible.' He showed a marked aptitude for mathematics. 'But his temper too soon flags & in this single exception he is not a Gibbs, but this we will endeavor to rectify.'

Philip, Jr's, catholic and singular learning embraced a smattering of Greek, Latin, Hebrew, and Arabic. He wrote now to his brother Thomas: 'No man knows where he is to be placed in society, where in the world he may be call'd on business & a knowledge of Latin and Hebrew in dead languages with a knowledge of English & Arabic in living languages will take a man with very little additional trouble and time through every market of the living world and all the valuable books of the dead.' In the autumn of 1833, young Thomas told his grandmother, Mary Gibbs: 'I can assure you I have but little time to spare as I am always to work at reading, writing, or mathematics & astronomy.'

A few years later, young Thomas apprised his unsuspecting grandparents of an untoward event at the school: 'This is a subject on which I cannot trust myself to comment,' Mary Gibbs wrote to the elder

Thomas in Upper Canada, '& will merely add the moral evil, the bad example has wounded your father & myself sorely.' Her schoolmaster son, Philip, Jr, had married his servant girl a month after she had borne him an illegitimate child, and he understandably kept his distance, nor had he answered any communications: '... but having since heard of the event your child alluded to we cannot wonder he does not write us.'

Philip, Jr, remained indifferent to all his mother's pleas, even though she warned him she might die of a stroke and '... that I could not but say my head, hand & heart might soon & suddenly cease to act.' With a sick and often grouchy husband, mad daughter Cathrine, son Benjamin the cause of much trouble, the deaths of her son Joseph and her daughter Mary Gillard from tuberculosis, and now Philip, Jr's, unwelcome behaviour (and some of all this oddity will have seeped into our genes), her sweet temper never flagged.

Young Thomas remained at the school for several more years until his future came up again for discussion. He sent his grandmother a wistful letter: 'Tell Father I have a great desire to come home & see them again ... Ask Father whether he will let me come home or not, tell him I should like to see my brother & sisters again.' But at this point there arrived sudden and surprising news of discord and disappointment at his father's mill for the mid-thirties saw some depression in business, a drop in the price of wheat, and instances of poor crops. The brave new venture in Upper Canada foundered on the rocks of human frailty and hard times, to which Philip, Jr, reacted with his usual bite, scarcely able to credit his brother Thomas's letter. It had struck him as one of the gloomiest and most fanciful descriptions ever penned by a Canadian settler, and it persuaded young Thomas that he might return home only to be starved, that his father was almost penniless, barely able to support his large family.

'Some of the remarks which you make about the largeness of your family make me smile,' Philip, Jr, told his brother. 'Why a short time since, I passed an evening with a Canadian who declared that the maintenance of one child in England incurred an expense which would maintain half a dozen in Canada.' But the needs of Thomas's brood probably competed with the payments of interest on the mill purchase or the cost of its extensive repairs, and brotherly squabbles had dealt the *coup de grâce* to an already deteriorating partnership. It soon dissolved, and Thomas spared no delicacy of feelings in the calumnies he heaped with some justification upon his brother John. 'Sorry, very sorry we are for the trial his temper must have been to you,' said their mother, while even Thomas's brother Philip, Jr, sympathized, but added: 'I fancy clumsiness, want of politeness rather than want of brotherly feeling caused John to give that milk to his pigs which would have been acceptable to your family. We have made up our minds to believe it this way.'

John's roundabout path took several turns – milling, farming, then shopkeeping – for he seemed incapable of sticking to any place or task, and with that ruthless candour so evident in the relationships of this family, his brother Philip, Jr, said: 'Even when an infant in arms, he was marked for the tenacity with which he held fast all that was imparted to him ... a natural disposition joined to mediocrity of talents, a mind fond of ease, unfitted for great enterprise & uncultivated by great study & education, ever pointed him out to me as one on whom no one dared lean very heavily.' But Thomas had directed malapropos remarks at Gibbs foibles in general and delivered some anti-English jibes or praise of things French, a telling indication perhaps of views nurtured in Lower Canada. Philip, Jr, quickly retaliated: 'To the remark that the French are more open or love truth better than the English or that their language is half so honest, I can not, can not for one moment entertain. It may be so in Transatlantica but 'tis not so in Cisatlantica.'

In Upper Canada, Reformers charged that both taxes and laws favoured millers at the expense of farmers, but millers had their own problems. Then came the Rebellion, which threw the countryside into turmoil and brought depression in its wake. Some have called it an agrarian revolt, and this appears to have been particularly marked in the countryside known later as Ontario County, where the farmers had strong Reform sympathies. It harboured such famous rebels as Peter Mathews of Pickering, and just outside its boundaries Nelson Gorham of Newmarket, son and nephew of John Gibbs's friends.

Thomas Gibbs and his brother John came from a tradition of dissent and belonged to that rising independent merchant class which had little in common with the Family Compact and much to gain from the Reformers, but like most of Upper Canada they remained loyal to the Crown and British institutions even if their friends the Gorhams were inextricably caught up with the rebels. Two local millers, John Borlase Warren and Abraham Farewell, men of moderate Reform views, broke with Mackenzie; the majority of the inhabitants seem to have longed for an end to the unrest and all the while, along the Kingston Road, not far from the mill, there would have travelled great numbers of troops – regiments, volunteers, and militia – called up for the defence of Toronto.

Faint echoes of these events come from England, where Philip, Jr, summarily dismissed them: 'We have received Canadian papers two several times for which we are obliged, but we are sorry to learn from them that the Lower Province is so discontented and unhappy without the slightest cause for it.' And when it was all over, Monkhouse Tate wrote: 'I have sometimes had apprehensions that Mr. Gibbs might have taken a view of public affairs totally differing from mine, and which must prove so ruinous to his interest and to the comfort of his family. So shall rejoice to hear that this was not the case and that you have all maintained your loyalty in the strictest sense of the word and have remained undisturbed in your dwelling and personal comforts.'

In the Rebellion's aftermath, many Upper Canadians besides rebel sympathizers left for the United States in hopes of escaping the poor crops of the thirties, the discord, and depression. Many left in search of land, as that commodity grew dearer at home, in an exodus that reversed the trend of the first part of the century, when American settlers flowed into Upper Canada. Joining the exodus sometime during the forties, John chose Ohio, now a well-settled and rich agricultural state on the frontiers of the American West. His wife had died. With a new wife, Charlotte, he began life again.

Young Thomas Nicholson Gibbs had returned from Uncle Philip's school in Kingsbridge in the autumn of 1835, at which point his younger brother William was packed off to school in Montreal for the following six years, presumably in the care of friends. Young Thomas Nicholson made his way by boat from Montreal to the village of Darlington and walked the twelve miles or more to the home at The Hollow, which he had never seen, to find himself acting at fourteen as assistant to his father. His schoolmaster uncle poured out advice from afar to keep up his Latin, practise French in the bosom of his family (he and William were later reputed to speak the language with ease as members of Parliament, so much so that they were said to be bilingual), and concentrate on history since the Canadas were becoming every day more important geographically and politically: '... it will be desirable,' said Philip, Jr, 'that her members should be furnished with the best weapon of assault and defence.'

He showed himself uncharacteristically sentimental: 'When my nephew left me, I felt that my friend, my companion, my little counselor [sic], the human being who of all others was allied to me by ties which bound no other mortal to me on earth was gone and

I felt listless for a long time afterwards.' His own two little boys determined to buy a horse and ride away to America to see their cousin, and Mary Gibbs said: 'He is a youth of peaceful spirit.'

'I hope,' said Philip, Jr, to his brother Thomas, 'every means will be used to prevent his mental and bodily powers from being depraved by that intoxicating curse upon the trading part of men called grog & as he travels I cannot be too urgent with you as a father to caution against that which more speedily shuts up the mental powers than any other beverage or food, compared with this all the stimulants which are in use are very slow poisons indeed.' Now, however, a skeleton emerges from the family cupboard as disaster after disaster befell the South Oshawa Mills and broke Thomas's spirit.

Fire destroyed both grist and oat mills in 1840, two days after the insurance expired; a new and larger mill rose upon these ashes, but it too was razed in a second fire two years later, again without insurance, this time because the friend who had been entrusted with the premium forgot to deliver it. Worse still, the second mill was built on borrowed money, and for Thomas it was the final straw. He had struggled in Lower Canada only to lose everything now, and he took with a vengeance to drink, which appears to have been the national tranquillizer.

A crushing load fell on young Thomas Nicholson Gibbs's shoulders, and many years later our great-grandmother, his sister Mary, said: '... What would have become of us is difficult to say, if the boy of fourteen [when he became his father's assistant], educated, had not been there to keep us together, for the one that should have done so was most of the time utterly incapable of understanding the terrible state of affairs in which we were placed.' He began the long haul of paying off his father's debts, and our great-grandmother remembered all her life the depths to which her father sank, her mother's courage in the face of adversity, and what they all owed to young T.N.

CHAPTER FIVE

SCARLET FEVER RAVAGED the village of The Hollow, carrying off first one and then another of the miller's youngest children; diphtheria struck with such ferocity that little Victoria died almost immediately. Sickness laid low half the family, and in England the death of all the older generation had already cut Thomas and Caroline adrift from their old moorings. To make matters worse, Caroline and her father had quarrelled in a breach never properly healed. Thomas had written him such an offensive letter, its contents never divulged, that Monkhouse Tate had committed it immediately and angrily to the flames, while Caroline had angered him too by her continued antipathy to Mrs Tate, which she showed by never mentioning her name or reciprocating her messages: 'one to whom you owe,' said her father, 'and have frequently acknowledged yourself to be under the greatest obligations.'

Although Monkhouse sent his forgiveness as far as any injury done to himself (but not for transgressions to his wife), he instructed her to address all future correspondence, not to himself, but to her half-brother William, the lawyer in London, for forwarding (presumably under separate cover) to Jersey. This injunction merely adds to earlier straws in the wind, taken in the agregate now but signifying little at the time, and they point to the conclusion that Caroline may have been Monkhouse's natural daughter, hence the reason for subterfuge and the earlier references to her childhood misery.

There is even an unsubstantiated tale of how at four years of age she attended a boarding-school, from which veritable Lowood Mrs Tate was apparently willing to rescue her and permit her to join her baby half-brother Monk in Chalford. This is surely the obligation to Mrs Tate, to which her father now refers. In old age, Caroline was to speak sadly of the intolerable regrets of life, and this quarrel with her father and even perhaps with her stepmother must have been one of them. He died in 1841, the first of our family to arrive in Canada over two hundred years ago, when he carried out the British government's commission in the late 1780s to restore mills in the colony.

Old Philip Gibbs, successful miller as were his forbears, had given his son Thomas a useful trade to bring to North America and some financial help. He died in the year that his grandson, young Thomas Nicholson Gibbs, returned home from his uncle's school in Kingsbridge. A few years later, during the winter in which the Rebellion festered in the Canadas, Thomas's mother, Mary Gibbs, fell ill. Philip, Jr, wrote: 'She has been confin'd a considerable part of the winter to her room and bed, has been also visited with an epidemic which has run through the greater part of Europe, a violent cold which the medical men call an influenza.' Then a letter from Thomas's sister Elizabeth told how on August 26th, 1838, at five o'clock on a Sabbath morning, their mother turned her face to the wall and murmured: 'I am dying, I am happy, my Saviour has made my passage easy.' Her last words to Thomas were: 'Only remember to serve your heavenly Father to whom I commend you & yours.'

Her son wandered far from the straight and narrow path, as was abundantly clear at The Hollow, and this particular thread of Thomas and Caroline's story is only picked up in 1843 after a visit to Newmarket, where their daughter Caroline, who has leapt from childhood to matrimony, is now Mrs Joseph Collins. Caroline Gibbs wrote to her: 'Having so favorable an opportunity I willingly embrace it to let you know how we are getting along in this miserable world – a fine anniversary of my wedding day, your Father as drunk as he can be and has been so all this week so far ... Your Father took his old road the Monday morning after we got home and has continued it pretty well ever since.' Even his neighbours would have been glad to see the last of him.

A year later, Caroline Gibbs wrote again in the same vein to the younger Caroline, but she ended this letter as follows: 'I have hitherto been supported through all my trials, and shall endeavour from henceforth to cast all my care upon Him, who knows better what is good for us than we do ourselves. I am better off than thousands, and if I had not this trial, I might possibly have it elsewhere. When I look on every side I see more cause for thankfulness than repining. I will not give your father up as lost yet, but rather pray, and hope that he may soon be brought to see his danger.'

In short, faith carried her through the vicissitudes of life as a member now of the Presbyterian church, a building conveniently vacated by the Anabaptists and possessing in local terms an unrivalled orator as minister. Her husband and his brother John stuck loyally to the diminishing Baptists. But the whirlpools and eddies of multiple denominations easily swept the faithful of one church into the arms of another, and all Thomas and Caroline's children joined the Wesleyan Methodist Church in Canada. Religion has become the staple diet, affording comfort to some, endless cause for argument to others, and a subject of interest to nearly everyone. The role of religion both privately and publicly is not to be underestimated in nineteenth-century Canada and especially as it relates to our connection.

In Newmarket the younger Caroline's husband, Joseph Collins, belonged to the Disciples of Christ or 'Christians,' an American church formed by dissident Presbyterians and Baptists, with a large following in this Quaker town, and here the second daughter, Mary, our great-grandmother, found a sanctuary away from unedifying scenes at home: 'I often spent months there when I was between twelve and twenty years of age. That was in the long, long ago,' she said, and if Joseph, descendant of an early Pennsylvania settler, hard-working and highly esteemed by his neighbours (for thirty years he was to be clerk of the township), had his idiosyncracies which came in for family comment, Mary never alluded to them; she owed too much to her sister and brother-in-law.

Like Job, Joseph Collins suffered many undeserved afflictions, including carbuncles and erysipelas, nor did his hard work and spirit of enterprise always succeed, as hints and directives from Thomas Gibbs later on make clear. From his vantage point as a Disciple of Christ, Joseph held strong views on religion, and in 1842 when John Gibbs, now resident in the United States and equally firm in his Baptist convictions, visited Newmarket, he told Joseph why he would no longer be drawn into argument: 'I do not, as I am well aware by experience how the common and subtle enemy of mankind takes the advantage on such occasions ... It is generally the case I believe that when men argue even in religious matters they too often contend for victory more than truth.'

A recent writer noted that Ohio Baptists had feeble if numerous churches, and although John much admired the way in which the United States – 'this giant country' – thrived, he could only lament the Baptist decline in the state he now inhabited: 'Religion is at a low ebb.' If he saw satisfactory outpourings of grace in the local church, the thoughtless sinners outside remained annoyingly untouched. But he owned a third share in a grist-mill and, full of schemes for a mill in nearby Elyria, he sang the praises of wheat fields between his home in Twinsburg and the metropolis of Cleveland to the south, all of which prompted him in 1848 to send an invitation, couched in his usual curious blend of religion and trade, to his erring brother Thomas in Canada: 'I have a good little business at present and hope by the blessing of God to do better than when in Canada. I know not a more pleasant and suitable situation for business and society either for Baptist Methodist or Presbyterian and water power and if you think anything of it waterpower is gaining so fast in value that it would not justify delay.'

Thomas must have been wished Godspeed by everyone, nor would the mill have suffered in his absence for the reins of management had already shifted to his son Thomas Nicholson Gibbs, or T.N., who ran the South Oshawa Mills. In nearby Columbus, the second son, William, had already taken over a mill and store, the usual adjunct of every mill, which had once belonged to John Gibbs. William had taken up this enterprise upon his return from school in Montreal, and he did so well in 1845 that he showered muffs and boas on all his female relations. 'There are five stores in Columbus now,' said Caroline, 'but he says he is not afraid of one of them.' With stock amounting to fifteen hundred pounds worth, he went into business, and as miller he shipped out eight hundred and fifty barrels of flour, only to crash several years later in unwise speculations in grain.

A marked improvement in wheat crops fed the local mills, attracting customers from all the back townships, so that in winter great consignments of wheat on sleighs poured into the village, while Simcoe Street, running north from Oshawa to Prince Albert and right through Columbus, where William had his mill, crossed one of the greatest grain markets in the province. His store developed into a singularly prosperous business when a few years later he moved to Oshawa, formerly Skae's Corners, now an important centre for trade with several more industries and stores.

Wheat production increased dramatically; and it had already been possible to import wheat from the United States and export it again as flour to Britain. The canal system had improved, and shipments to Britain could be moved more quickly. This was the great impetus that founded so many milling industries, even if the introduction of Free Trade in Britain and repeal of the Corn Laws in 1846 ended the entry of Canadian wheat and flour on a preferential basis and adversely affected Canadian millers.

William and T.N. formed a partnership, Gibbs & Bro., grain dealers, their mills and store serving as stepping-stones to banks, insurance companies, and other financial concerns; the days of grist-milling long past, they were merchant millers. They entered local politics as reeves and first warden of the county, and sat on various committees, which prepared them for the maelstrom of faction in national politics. T.N. superintended the Wesleyan Methodist Church's Sunday school and saw to the building of one church; William joined the Missionary Society.

On receiving John's invitation in 1848, their father had no intention of jumping into the quagmire of partnership with him again, but Caroline delivered an ultimatum on reform; and so he crossed over to the United States in the autumn of that year by an overcrowded steamboat, the stench of which he described as overpowering. He soon found that John had been building castles in the air. A long, cold winter followed and in the spring cholera rampaged through the neighbourhood, making farmers afraid to take their produce to market. 'As to the nature of the epidemic,' said John, 'I do not know but is past finding out as it baffles the most experienced of the medical faculty. Our doctor in Sandusky if I mistake not thought he had discovered a never failing remedy and said he was ready to make it known and stake his life to the community for a fair compensation but he was soon cut down with the rest and his remedy fail'd.'

The California gold rush of '49 swept up the young men of Twinsburg, Ohio, and Thomas heard a rumour that at home even T.N. and William thought of going: 'I should think if they feel desirous of being rid of wives & children, it is a first rate chance,' for by this time both his sons were married men. T.N. had married Almira, daughter of Joseph Ash of Cobourg, which raises an odd confusion for there were in the area several by that name and one was ignominiously involved in the unsavoury Cobourg Conspiracy, an aftermath of the Rebellion involving a murder. Perhaps there was some connection, but Almira was well educated, a pillar of rectitude and church alike. William married Frances Colton of nearby Whitby.

Thomas Gibbs returned to Oshawa from Ohio in better shape, leaving his brother John to think pious thoughts and continue indecisive in his many plans, complaining that Charlotte, his wife, was as firmly attached to her farm of chickens, cows, pigs, and a horse as ever. 'I expect,' Thomas said, 'he would not grieve much if they were all dead & she attending to something (in his opinion) of more importance.' John dreamed of ever larger schemes, bought shares in a plank road, and talked of importing oats and barley from Canada, but above all he was devoted to his ferrets, Ezra and Fouchee, imported from Oshawa, whom he taught to dance on the kitchen table to his accordion and doctored with homeopathic medicines. When Fouchee jumped on the stove and was burned to death, both he and Charlotte were desolate; the ferrets were their friends.

'The older I grow,' he told Caroline, 'the more I think I esteem friendship particularly when I think it comes from a benevolent heart.' Here he was thinking not so much of his ferrets as mankind, who had in general let him down. As he surveyed his life, it also occurred to him that in tossing about the world he had seen much of human nature, its selfishness, coldness, and man's inhumanity to man, which had made him both despondent and at times misanthropic. On the other hand, when he looked into his own heart he too was laid in the balance and found wanting: '... upon reflection I find I have come to the conclusion that we must look beyond this world for a more perfect state, it will be a great transition indeed even among Christians.'

'I wish,' John informed his sister-in-law, 'my brother Thomas could once be resolved with God's help to give up all for God and unreservedly give himself and all he has into His hands.' But Thomas kept his religious views to himself, returning to home and mill restored, forgiven but not quite cured – 'I must have a little at times,' he said. Delighting all with his wit (which, sadly, has vanished without trace), he was called henceforth by Caroline 'dear Father,' valued for his sound advice by his sons, and achieved moderate success at the South Oshawa Mills, which he shared with T.N., all the while slipping into great deafness.

If a fortune eluded his grasp, in time he regained his respectability, and the mill brought in a sufficient income to enable himself and Caroline in the summer of 1855 to sail home on a visit to England. The vessel dawdled across the ocean, and its passengers fished for their meal on a calm day off the Banks in a crossing that took more than a month when already packet-boats achieved astonishing speeds. At times rain poured into their cabin, and the noise of the caulking nearly stunned them. Caroline said: 'We long to get on shore to get a good cleaning up & a piece of good bread & butter. I have often wished I had a crust of bread that I had given to the dog at home.'

The ship ran out of potatoes and several other commodities: 'Our accommodations are better, than what we had on the *Speculation* [i.e., *Speculator*] coming out, but the *Delia* is something like myself the worse for wear and tear ...' 'Father,' she was pleased to say, had behaved like a gentleman. They hurried off to Thomas's sister Elizabeth, now Mrs Blake, thence to Kingsbridge, where Thomas persuaded his brothers Philip and Benjamin, both well past life's prime, to turn emigrant at last and join the family in Oshawa.

Whatever challenges faced farmers in Upper Canada, now Canada West, in England upheaval and poverty had left farm labourers crushed, to which state, in Devon, Thomas's erring brother, poor Benjamin Gibbs, had long ago descended. By 1830 their plight had reached desperation; uprisings throughout the countryside had set farmers' ricks ablaze, as Mary Gibbs had duly noted, and in Devon their standard of living had plunged to such depths that the member for Parliament, Lord Ebrington, appalled by their low wages, had raised them on his own estates, for which it was said his party made him apologize.

Improvements in agricultural machinery had made Benjamin write feelingly to his brother Thomas of an England where men and horses were made useless, their labour worth nothing, and of the horrors to come upon labourers 'when old age, poverty, misery and sickness chain their powers and fetter them to that which is the dread of human nature.' He had turned to peddling wares throughout the Devon countryside, a mode of selling that had greatly increased during the Industrial Revolution before shops existed in the remoter areas, welcomed by factory owners but anathema to shopkeepers, who, ever on the lookout for evasions, saw to the enforcement of the licensing laws. Benjamin was soon put out of business by these laws and by the taxes exacted on himself, his donkey, and his cart 'besides innumerable turnpikes that I am constantly in the fire of outgoing & as my income is limited the wisdom of the serpent is necessary to prevent it into too small a sum as I may live to want it when I am done for labour.'

Over the years he had made several plans to join Thomas, picturing himself in a Canadian cottage where every flower and vegetable grew in his garden and where he would be self-supporting and happy. He had asked Thomas to use his influence with master bakers, pastry cooks, and gingerbread bakers, his earlier troubled apprenticeships: 'All I want is your approbation, help and instruction until I get on my legs.' But these plans were aborted by his short-lived marriage, entered into against all advice according to his brother Philip, whose bark was so much worse than his bite and who remained Benjamin's true friend. She was a strumpet wife, said Philip, and her extravagance threw all that Benjamin owned, which was little enough, into pawnshops.

Soon everyone viewed him as incapable of earning his living: 'I thought this some time ago,' said Philip 'although many of the family declared it nothing but a will that was wanted.' Thus, later on and to no one's surprise, Benjamin's career in the New World pursued these well-worn paths. His journey, so long in the making, took him in 1857 from Devon to Oshawa and on to pastures new in Twinsburg, Ohio, as helpmate to his brother John, a plan that was bound to fail for, as Caroline remarked, their horses did not pull well together. He returned to Oshawa. Two more years passed before he found employment again, this time as a baker at two dollars a week in the nearby village of Brooklin: 'This is better,' said Caroline, 'than earning nothing.' But this venture also failed. Once more in Oshawa, he settled down in a small rented cottage chopping wood for his nephew T.N.: 'He is going to keep bachelor's hall,' said Caroline, and this arrangement lasted to the end of his days.

Sixty-five and a widower, Thomas's brother Philip, the schoolmaster, whose son had preceded him, landed with his daughter at Port Darlington near Oshawa on May 25th, 1859, transporting with him his books, those repositories of information on the many subjects that had captured his interest or the languages he had endeavoured to master. Years ago he had requested young T.N. to send him all possible information on, and specimens of, fossils, fauna, shells, minerals, Indian artifacts, and any other items that might enlighten the citizens of Kingsbridge. It was the great age of cataloguing and classification. With him came treatises on homeopathic medicine, an art he practised on his daughter: 'she has great confidence in him as a physician,' said Caroline.

A few years earlier, Philip's son, known as P.H. Gibbs, bird fancier, bank clerk, bibliophile, and the father of a number of children, had settled in Guelph. All over the province, from exhibition to exhibition, he transported his collection of prize birds until, as Caroline reported, he gave them all up in order to concentrate entirely on business and religion. His medical history weaves in and out of the correspondence, and by the end of the sixties, Caroline said: 'He has had another operation. Two hours and five minutes under chloroform, the effects of which were so severe that he fairly rolled on his bed in agony, sick, nausea, vomiting, headache and frightful pain of the kidneys, he had no rest whatsoever.'

More Kingsbridge names reached Oshawa, amongst them yet another Carrie, the daughter of Thomas Gibbs's long-dead sister Mary Gillard and the now deceased Silvanus, who made her home with her aunt and uncle in Oshawa, calling them 'Ma' and 'Pa.' Past thirty and heading for the cruel category of old maid, she received a proposal of marriage from a Mr Dixon: 'I think her prospects very encouraging,' said her aunt, 'but I tell her she must expect some dark days like the rest of us. I am glad she is going to be comfortably settled.' But Carrie's future was never settled and dark days filled her life.

These latest additions might have completed the family circle had the tide not ebbed early in the marriage of the daughters, carrying them away from Oshawa, and Caroline Gibbs began her network of letters, spinning a web that bound all together, for family was still the basis of society, the fracturing late twentieth century not yet dreamed of. The first to leave was Caroline Collins as the young bride at twenty of the upright, high-principled Joseph, who soon succeeded in exasperating his brothers-in-law. In the mid-fifties, a botched operation by the village quack, in whom Joseph had untold confidence, nearly killed her: 'The proper place for his friend,' said Oshawa's doctor, arriving post-haste with her brother T.N., 'is the Provincial Penitentiary.' And he added, without further elaboration, that he found Joseph an extraordinary man.

It was in 1850, the year after Thomas Gibbs's return from Twinsburg, that Mary, our great-grandmother, and her sister Sarah took on the tasks of the Wesleyan Methodist Church in Canada by marrying respectively the Reverend William Schenck Blackstock and the Reverend James Gooderham. Sarah was spared the births and miscarriages that so imprisoned her sisters, and because her husband's physique failed to stand up to the strain of preaching, she had no acquaintance with parsonages, but she bloomed in the Church in the last twenty years of the century. Mary moved house every two years or so as the Wesleyan Methodist Conference dictated, and her migratory life occupied more and more of her mother's correspondence, so that the parsonages in myriad circuits come to vie with Oshawa. For the moment, the two younger sisters Amelia and Emily are still at home. Amelia's husband will be a diligent Baptist layman, and Emily's, an active Methodist.

Mary, whose tale has now begun and whose childhood and youth are a blank, had grown up in a town that stultified, that lacked cultural or intellectual advantages, and offered little to free its inhabitants from the tedium of life. In short, 'culture' was a word scarcely to be associated with Oshawa. Caroline Gibbs had constantly complained of the lack of a good school and had sent her daughters to one or other of the small local private establishments with no claim to distinction whatever, one of which Thomas Gibbs described as being run by a go-ahead grass widow, scarcely a compliment, and it rankled with Mary that she had not had the same opportunies as her two brothers.

For one year, in 1847, she attended Mrs Hurlburt's

Female Academy in nearby Cobourg, a town of infinitely superior culture to Oshawa's. This establishment had opened its doors in 1843 when the Methodists' Upper Canada Academy in Cobourg, after several years of admitting girls, lapsed abruptly into a male bastion in the previous year. It constituted for Mary a sort of finishing school, and the odour of the Female Academy still permeates one of her compositions, which begins: 'There is no trait in the human character that shines with so much lustre and loveliness as piety and particularly when it is exemplified in the female.' A smattering of music, French, and drawing may or may not have rounded off the Academy's polish.

Mary escaped the boredom of home and town by the visits to Newmarket, and occasionally she and her brothers journeyed down to Terrebonne; while, in Oshawa, the Wesleyan Methodist Church must have offered her society, occupation (Sunday-school teachers being in constant demand), and stimulus of a sort; it may have fitted her for her destiny. 'I was born old,' she said later in life. 'As soon as I began to think, life seemed to wear a serious aspect, a dark shadow rested upon it and questions kept coming up for solution that made existence and the government of this world a great mystery.' This outlook suited her to join the ranks of Methodist ministers' wives, that call to high office as helpmate to her husband, perfect wife and mother, keeper of high standards, and, as has always been the fate of ministers' wives, under the constant scrutiny of congregations: community property.

She did not have to wait long before the full meaning of her husband's calling dawned in all its uncertainty. At the Streetsville parsonage on the Brampton circuit, where her husband was a junior minister, as he would be until the Newcastle circuit in 1854, their first child, Thomas Gibbs Blackstock (our grandfather), was born on November 11th, 1851, and in June of 1853 the situation at the parsonage was described as one of special affliction. The circuit had defaulted, unable to provide the means for its two ministers' support, a common occurrence in the Wesleyan Methodist Church; it would be months before the Contingent Fund made good these deficits. Salaries, paid quarterly, frequently in kind with additional sums for rent, fuel, moving expenses, and allowances for each child and the indispensable horse, often fell short, and even with the aid of the Contingent Fund, ministers' families experienced difficulties: it was a life of some hardship and uncertainty.

All circuit wives contended with the frequent absence of their husbands. In every circuit the minister travelled constantly, and there were always the sick and dying to be visited, often at night. He preached three times or more on Sunday at his own churches or meeting-houses, which were many miles apart, as well as preaching several times during the week, visited his flock in town or countryside, organized Sabbath schools, Bible classes, revivals, prayer meetings, and occasional camp meetings, at which several thousand worshippers had to be accommodated in tents, and devoted many hours to prayer, study, and the composition of sermons.

In 1852, on the Brampton circuit, the Reverend W.S.B. preached in October before several thousand worshippers congregated in twenty large tents (each tent 36 feet wide, 148 feet long, and warmed by stoves) at a camp meeting that lasted from Saturday to Wednesday. Luckily the tents were watertight, since it rained all Sunday. In 1849, when he was stationed in Oshawa, the *Christian Guardian* had reported him as the speaker at a soirée (this is the exact word) of the Oshawa Methodist Sabbath School, where tea was served to seven hundred boys and girls: 'It was stated that the pupils had committed to memory at least between 30,000 and 40,000 verses of the Holy Scriptures during the past year.' The minister had to be a master of logistics and statistics.

Every minister led his troops into battle, often with an assistant minister, and always with his battery of lay or local preachers, exhorters, class leaders, and stewards, until once a year in May the District Meeting reviewed the circuit's work, its finances, and statistics on everything from the number of sermons to volumes in libraries. It also reviewed the minister's performance, asking of each, 'Does he pass?' The highest and strictest standards prevailed: no tobacco and no drams whatever. In June, Conference sat in judgment on all the circuits, reviewed the work, ordained men for the ministry, and dealt with matters of doctrine, discipline, and the behaviour of its clergy.

'I hope you do not think of remaining alone if you continue to be poorly and Mr. Blackstock so much from home,' Caroline wrote to her daughter in March of 1854 with the first intimation that poor health is to be a factor in her life. 'I hope your dear husband keeps well amidst all his toil and labours of love,' she added. Three months later, when attending Conference in Belleville, he sent word to his wife: 'Though absent I have not forgotten you. My heart is with you.' Twelve days after this, their second child, Amelia Eliza, was born at the York Mills parsonage on the Yonge Street circuit, and in another ten days, while her husband was already at work on the Newcastle circuit in the Cobourg District, she packed up children, some furniture, and all their belongings to join him, as she was to do with every change of parsonage.

Her husband found the Newcastle circuit weak and divided; a year before his arrival it had lost a hundred of its members to the Primitive Methodists, an inauspicious beginning, and the previous minister's illness had left it without a pastor for three months: 'I need say nothing about the state of things which I found when I came here,' he said, and on New Year's Day he began a diary. Mid-nineteenth-century Methodism was still a religion of the heart; the journal served both as an examination of his feelings and as a spiritual exercise. Pouring into it his innermost thoughts and fears, he gave way to morbid introspection, an ever-present tendency amongst Methodists if our family is anything to judge by, constantly viewing and analysing his own and his flock's imperfections: 'The work of decomposition is everywhere in progress,' he said.

He admonished the faithful for their indecision, procrastination, and despair, all the sins of which he himself was guilty, saw evil in many guises, as when young Miss Turley insisted on attending dances and stoutly maintained that she enjoyed them: 'May God in mercy lay trouble on her conscience,' he entered in the diary. Depressed and anxious, he blamed himself for not having spent enough time in prayer or in the preparation of his sermons, and if he swung briefly to happier moods and congratulated himself on backsliders reclaimed, sinners converted, new penitents gleaned, the narrowness of the Methodist outlook suspected danger and pitfalls everywhere: 'I feel very weak; nothing but the power of omnipotent grace can keep me from falling.' He wondered that God did not cast him out; two weeks later, their third child, George Tate, was born on April 1st, 1856.

The Brighton circuit in 1856 had five churches, seven other places of worship, and an estimated Sunday attendance of two thousand five hundred; minister and assistant prepared twenty sermons a week. In the following year the Church divided the circuit in two, and on his own again, he had two churches and ten places of worship. In a burst of optimism, he reported to the *Christian Guardian* on a highly successful camp meeting, but in a second communication he had to admit that the missionary anniversary celebrations in December attracted few, that some of the speakers had failed to show up, and that the circuit was in arrears in its financial obligations, which must have included his salary. The economic depression of 1857 was to have all of North America in its grasp.

Mary feared her husband had reached the point of exhaustion, and of herself she told a friend: 'The past few months have been a season of much mental disquietude and I fear of spiritual loss. A weak and enervated body has not tended to fit me for meeting the constantly recurring and increasing anxieties of life.' A fourth child was born, which sickened and died; she fell ill, and after months of silence the Reverend W.S.B. took up his diary again on New Year's Day, 1858: 'I humbly hope a few have been brought to God through my exertion, but alas how few.'

On this ciruit, however, old Pieter Van der Heyden's conversion was remembered by the congregation half a century later at the time of the minister's death and, in its small way, deemed a triumph by the faithful. The farmer had never been to church, except to a funeral, for more than thirty years, a fact of which he continually boasted and a challenge the minister immediately took up, setting out to catch this recalcitrant member of his community by guile if necessary. The opportunity soon arrived as he trudged along the road one day on his parochial rounds, and begging a lift on old Pieter's waggon, the minister began to praise the horses' good points, knowing that their owner took great pride in them, and he himself as saddle-bag preacher was no mean judge. 'Vell, if diz kennen die Pferden I will go & hear him preach,' said the farmer, who turned into a regular church-goer and later donated a hundred dollars to put up windows in the church as a thank offering for this particular pastor.

His was a most personal ministry; it was not only by sermons and services that souls were to be won. Mary thought he wore himself out in the performance of his ministry, and now fate recoiled to spring upon them with a crash. Her husband was now thirty-three years of age, and if in the previous years he was one of the ministers appointed to attend Conference and in 1857 had represented the district on the committee for the training of probationers, events soon dispelled this confidence in him.

On May 18th, 1859, at the town of Dundas, the Hamilton District Meeting reviewed as usual the moral and religious character of all its clergy, and it examined the case of the Reverend W.S.B., who had placed his whole pastoral future in jeopardy and been suspended from office for three months. Ten days before the District Meeting, he had returned to his diary, oscillating between despondency and hope: 'Oh my God,' he wrote, 'what wouldst thou have me to do, Thou seest my perilous condition.' But the next day, he added: 'Have faith in God.' And, because he acknowledged his fault and exhibited a truly penitent spirit, the District Meeting resolved that his character now passed and prepared to reinstate him not, however, without the misgivings of two of the brethren.

Minutes of meetings show that suspension or dismissal was a common enough occurrence but rarely if ever give details of the cases before them, and his transgression can only be surmised; it seems to have been a brainstorm brought on by exhaustion and overwork. Every minister at ordination forswore the taking of tobacco, snuff, and drams; caught once in such delinquency, he would be suspended and warned; caught twice, he would be instantly dismissed without redress; anything worse would also have brought instant dismissal; even disagreement over matters of policy could bring expulsion.

The reinstatement in May permitted him to attend Conference in June, but there a dispute arose over his pardon on the part of the two clergy who had earlier objected to his reinstatement. They moved that he be deposed from the ministry and expelled from the Church: 'Bro. Blackstock being absent he was sent for and in the meantime the case was laid over.' It was decided that he had been sufficiently punished and that neither his name nor the case should be included in the printed minutes. Instead of a year's suspension as one of the two objectors (and more about him anon) wanted, he was to be employed in 'some distant part of the work,' in effect to be banished to the least popular district. To this he had descended after thirteen years of labour, he who at the outset of his ministry had been described as 'compact and healthy, studious and possessed of a great deal more than the average measure of mind.'

During the three months suspension at Hamilton, he had received no salary, and when the Church put him to work in Toronto for six months at what must have been a poorly paid post, clothing, fruit, vegetables, butter, and other sundries arrived from Oshawa to help out his family in all their difficulties; the children paid long visits to their Aunt Sarah Gooderham at Meadowvale, their Aunt Caroline Collins at Newmarket, and the uncles in Oshawa. Throughout, and without any words of reproach or blame, Caroline Gibbs remembered him always in her letters, sending him her kindest love, writing in

September to Mary: 'I am pleased to hear you have been and still are so wonderfully supported under present trying circumstances, and sincerely do I hope the event will turn out for your future good both for time and eternity,' which certainly covered the ground.

Conference, the arbiter of justice and fate, sent them to Three Rivers, one of the most remote of all the circuits, other than the mission fields, with a membership of twenty-five and an average Sunday attendance of sixty-five. But the minister weathered the storm of his temporal and spiritual chastisement with surprising cheerfulness: 'On the morning of the 27th of January,' he entered into a brief and much happier journal in 1860, 'at about half past two o'clock I reached here with my little family; found the Mission house warm, Bro. Clarke waiting for us, and provision made for our comfort until we should have an opportunity of providing for ourselves; and though every cent of my money was spent I have been ever since provided for and have had need of nothing.'

He set to work visiting the members of his little church, but ever mindful of his own shortcoming he viewed with alarm the magnitude of the task to evangelize and convert as it gaped before him: 'If my life had always been what it should be,' the diary continues, 'if my course had not been marred by crooked steps, I could have done this with a good heart, but it is hard for one who has been so defective as I have been in his own life to lift the Gospel standard so high or to present the claims of God so strongly.' Mary looked on the bright side, for part of her husband's salary came from the Missionary Society, which, as she told her mother, was more certain than depending on the people.

At one time, Three Rivers had a numerous English-speaking population largely in control of its industry and commerce, an enclave now in decline and, or so it seems, a gossip-ridden little community struggling to survive. Moreover, the very person the Reverend W.S.B. replaced as minister was the one who had wanted him dismissed from the ministry and who on hearing he was to be his successor, lost no time in spreading the news of his fall. Caroline Gibbs answered Mary's letter promptly: 'I am sorry to hear of such impudence and unprincipled conduct on the part of Mr M.' These machinations effected the withdrawal from the church, or as it was termed the Society, of its most influential member: 'We were repeatedly told,' Mary reported to her mother, 'that she never would enter our church in Three Rivers and, as she expressed it, Methodism had received its deathblow here.' But the lady soon reconsidered her position and returned as friend, supporter, and benefactor (she gave the children five whole dollars), and was even heard to say that she had never met a minister's wife so well suited to her position, which Mary passed on to her mother: 'I would not repeat this under ordinary circumstances even to you, but as I said before, I know you are to a certain extent anxious about us.'

In the previous fifteen years, Three Rivers had not seen one conversion, and Mr M. had taken the congregation to task for the smallness of the collection, telling them he had preached a first-rate sermon but got only one and tenpence-ha'penny in return. It now averaged ten and sometimes thirteen shillings: 'and this,' Mary wrote to Oshawa with some satisfaction, 'from a comparatively poor people.' Attendance almost doubled in a year. She could not forbear to exult in these minor triumphs which so thoroughly undermined the reputation of Mr M. Only a few irritations surfaced: 'Lent is over and whether the poor Catholics are glad or not I am sure the Protestants are for it would seem as if they would neither eat meat themselves nor allow anyone else to.'

The circuit of Three Rivers had turned out to be a pleasant surprise even if winter brought isolation – the railway had not yet come through – and the St Lawrence was a constant source of delight as were the bright days and clear skies. Mary reported with pride that little Millie, that is, Amelia, at six took French lessons and spoke the language well: 'She is very observing for her age and a fine sweet child. I often say, if Grandma saw her she would say that she was the smartest of the lot.' (This was the great-aunt who wore a green cloche hat and used to converse with us from a third-floor window on Homewood Avenue when I was a child.) On June 3rd, 1860, Caroline Jane was born.

One incident ruffled Mary. The Prince of Wales made his visit to Canada in 1860: 'I see by the papers the Prince has not given as much satisfaction in western Canada [i.e., Canada West] as he did before. I think the old Duke has done no good by his advice,' Mary wrote to her mother. The Fifth Duke of Newcastle, accompanying the Prince, had refused to let him become the pawn of any one faction and when, at Kingston and Brockville, Orangemen wanted him to pass under their arches, the Duke forbade it. The real cause of Mary's pique, however, lay in the presentation earlier to the Prince of twenty Roman Catholic priests and the Church of England rector before herself and the Reverend W.S.B.: 'It looked as if the intention was that we should be the last.'

The parting from Three Rivers saddened both pastor and people, and on the occasion of his leave-taking, they printed a poem in his honour; its last verse ran:

> Farewell dear Pastor go,
> We part with thee in love:
> And if we meet no more below
> O may we meet above.

Conference sent men where they would be most effective; all salaries were more or less equal, but L'Orignal on the Ottawa River in 1861, where they spent several lean troubled years, had little to recommend it. Beautiful scenery masked its reputation for sickness, and already a passing Presbyterian had noted: 'Evangelical religion in this part of the country is at a very low ebb.' A large circuit deficit from the year previous to his arrival greeted the Reverend W.S.B. Caroline wrote her daughter: 'I sympathize with you in your trying position, but hope you will have your wants supplied so far that bread shall not be wanting.' The spectre of want, however, was dangerously close, and here each succeeding winter brought mass sickness in the countryside; little Millie coughed incessantly. Caroline said: 'I shall certainly rejoice when I hear you have left that miserable part of the country,' a sentiment vigorously repeated in the following year.

On March 29th, 1863, the third daughter was born, Mary Elizabeth, known throughout her life as Mary, Mollie, and May. In June from Conference in Quebec City, the minister wrote to his wife: 'I never know how dear to me you are until I am separated from you for a time.' Again, in the lottery of life, he drew L'Orignal, where once more winter produced mass sickness in the countryside, which added to the clergy's daily round until overwork and the prevailing epidemic brought the minister so low in March that he could not rise from his bed for over a month and Caroline came down to nurse them all. He could scarcely descend the stairs to receive a delegation to the parsonage which bore the princely sum of one hundred dollars for himself and thirty-four for his assistant, these 'donation visits' being a circuit's way of apologizing for arrears in salary; they spoke of him as their highly respected and esteemed minister.

CHAPTER SIX

THE FIFTIES had ushered in a period of general prosperity, and Oshawa, with eleven hundred inhabitants, enjoyed an increase in trade. Gibbs & Bro. expanded, and both T.N. and his brother William accumulated wealth; Caroline said: 'They dine now at six o'clock,' an indication of upward mobility, while their sisters, with the exception of Sarah, who had married a Gooderham, were tied to tedium, housekeeping, and motherhood's joys. The brothers travelled on business, cautiously at first, to the United States and England, and the horse-drawn coaches that had plied between Montreal and Toronto since the War of 1812 yielded in 1856 to the Grand Trunk Railway when everyone went out to view the first passenger train as it sped through the countryside, taking fourteen hours to make the journey. In that year, William opened his large department store, W.H. Gibbs & Co., in the centre of town, where the new premises of Gibbs & Bro. drew attention to that firm's importance also.

Small towns attracted industry, and mid-century Oshawa swelled with new factories, foundries, an ironworks, and a new type of venture, a joint stock company of farm machinery, which T.N. helped to found (but which failed in the depression of 1857 and was promptly taken over). Everything appeared to favour milling: the Reciprocity Treaty, the Crimean War, which prevented Russian wheat from entering Britain, thus opening its market to more from Canada, modern machinery, which increased the amount of flour ground from wheat, improved communications, which coincided with a larger than usual wheat crop, and the impact of the railways, which revolutionized trade.

T.N. entered the portals of high finance, at least as interpreted in small towns. The expansion of industry and commerce in the province required improved methods of financing, and the Bank Act of 1850 enabled local banks to spring up in these towns. Both brothers were large shareholders in the new Ontario Bank, founded in 1857, based in nearby Bowmanville and owned largely by Montrealers. T.N. became a director, then vice-president, and everywhere banks played an increasingly important role in the grain trade.

Mammon, however, was not always dependable, and the bubble burst as the very factors that had assured prosperity reversed themselves: the end of the Crimean War, the loss of such favourable terms of entry into the British market, poor wheat crops, and the great depression that hit first Western Europe in 1857 and then North America, making the winter of 1858 a wretched one for the country and multiplying the difficulties that faced the Reverend W.S.B. on the Brighton circuit. A year later, T.N. was writing to his sister: 'Everybody groaning with liabilities more than they can well stagger under.' Such was the background to an event beyond the realms of trade and industry that marked the year 1860 in the town.

A minor domestic upheaval had almost prevented T.N. and Almira from joining the throngs sailing down the St Lawrence to welcome the Prince of Wales to Canada, for the opening of a straw-hat factory in Oshawa absorbed all the local female labour and this had had immediate repercussions; Almira found herself entirely without help for six weeks. 'Part of the time had to go into the washtub even & do that. No one to be had,' said T.N. At the same time, as far removed from the washtub as possible, in England Thomas Gibbs's second cousin received a pension of £800 a year from the Queen, for Frederick Weymouth Gibbs had been the Prince's tutor: 'Handsome remuneration for his services, is it not?' said Caroline. He will reappear. The town of Oshawa's great event took place in December, a spectacularly successful revival.

'I must confess I never enjoyed a series of meetings as I have these,' Caroline informed her daughter Mary in Three Rivers when the revival, a means to conversion of the already converted, was in full sway. The Reverend Mr Dickson of the recently combined circuits of Oshawa and Whitby had organized services with several of the Protestant denominations as his target, for revivals were thoroughly ecumenical in this respect. How often the Reverend W.S.B. had returned home, and was to do so in the future, tired out, despondent or exhilerated, from similar services that he himself had initiated, all entailing a great deal of work and organization but offering glorious opportunities, if successful.

The churches shaped Canada, tamed the backwoods, guided the men and women who founded nearly all our institutions social and political, underpinned the state, and the nineteenth-century Methodist Church ranks second to none. Yet this said, when we peer into the lives of its members, much evangelical piety goes against the grain: the cocky self-congratulation of the saved and the gloomy soul-searching of the penitent, two extremes often within the same person, at least in our family; the exuberant display of their innermost selves, holding listeners to ransom in the telling; and, not least, the probing into their neighbours' spiritual business.

An awareness as Christians of the inherently fallen nature of man, all too evident in the world around them, and belief in the biblical threats of eternal damnation drove Methodists on to affirm their faith dramatically and visibly, to stand together as a pilgrim band in a hostile world. Services that effected such conversions gave rise understandably to scenes of joy, fostering that very cult of emotion which Wesley had warned against. The public face of mid-nineteenth-century Methodism, with its emphasis on strict Sabbath observance, hard work, honesty and integrity in private and public life, sobriety, and self-discipline, coexisted with emotional outpourings of religious enthusiasm.

The Church now marched hand in hand with men in politics and business, better educated and more sophisticated than earlier generations. Such were T.N. and William, but to be a member of the Church, even as regular in their attendance as either of them, was not the same as a man's emotional response to the Lord's bidding. Both brothers had long served the Methodist Church as laymen. But Thomas Gibbs said he did not believe his son T.N. had ever been converted: 'he does not believe it possible for anyone who has tasted of the goodness of God, to go back as he has,' Caroline told Mary. The word was 'backslider.'

His backsliding was distressingly evident at times in his flippancy, which could not be tolerated and which was in marked contrast with the serious tone adopted by others whenever church came under discussion. From the parsonage, his sister Mary had recently taken him to task on his birthday, delivering a lecture on his need for salvation, to which he had replied that it was like so much water on a duck's back. Of the anniversary celebrations of the Presbyterian church, which his mother attended, he said: 'The Methodist choir was there, admitted at half-price, an instance of Scotch liberality. The edibles were spoiled by the cook ... I was much pleased with the whole affair, appearing to me in such striking contrast to the miserable affair at the missionary meeting here ...' William was very active in missionary work.

William had recently returned from a business trip

to England, where he made the acquaintance of James Lobb's sister (James had married their sister Amelia and was William's deputy at the department store), who loudly expressed her dismay on hearing that, notwithstanding his many business duties in the mill and his dry-goods store, William did not devote at least one hour a day to prayer, and she sent word to Canada that she had already begun to pray for his conversion. But it would be wrong to attribute this all-consuming occupation with someone else's most private affairs to nothing more than inquisitiveness or mere want of delicacy; an absolute obligation lay on every Methodist, and indeed other evangelicals, to save whomever it might be from the risk of eternal damnation.

At about this time, the Methodist Church was beginning to take the lead amongst Protestant denominations in the already popular Holiness movement, whose search for Christian perfection, a state of grace termed sanctification, required a very visible conversion. Methodism had, as already stated, drawn all Caroline Gibbs's children into its orbit, even if she herself had been enticed away from the declining Baptists of Skae's Corners by Oshawa's outstanding Presbyterian preacher. Having been satisfactorily set at liberty herself on an earlier occasion, she welcomed the great revival of 1860 with enthusiasm and rejoiced at the saving of the backslider. Several weeks had passed with disappointing results until at last it could be reported in the *Guardian*: 'Some of the leading people of the community are among the saved of the Lord.' Amongst them were T.N. and William. This is when Caroline wrote to Mary: 'I think there is not a mother on the face of the earth who has more cause for gratitude and thankfulness than myself.'

A week earlier, T.N.'s wife, Almira, had offered to put up one of the speakers, a Mrs Dr Robinson, although T.N. had particularly requested her not to do so, having an antipathy towards that lady. Even the Reverend Mr Dickson, chief architect of the revival, wondered at her assurances that for twenty years she had lived without sin; once inside T.N.'s house, she effected a miracle. But, in comparison with other participants in the revival, T.N. could not indulge in such claims as fell from their lips, and if at one time he had said, 'Tho' all men deny thee, yet will not I,' he was now rather disposed to say: 'Let him that thinketh he standeth, take heed lest he fall.'

After a few false starts, William underwent a spectacular conversion, which reminded his mother of Saint Paul's on the road to Damascus. It took place on a Monday night just as everyone was leaving the meeting and caused such a stir that a small crowd gathered. First, William's wife, Frances, was set at liberty and her face shone like an angel's, and William's own conversion so excited him that he hoped people would not think him mad; the revival could be termed an almost unqualified success. Only Thomas Gibbs, growing old and deaf, failed to come forward, despite the pleadings of his wife or the regular visits of Mr Dickson. 'If only dear Father,' said Caroline, 'were converted what a happy family we should be!' But he remained firm in his refusal to board this emotional roller-coaster in spite of being a Baptist and steadfastly maintaining he was a Christian.

The good work did not stop here; T.N.'s seventeen-year-old son, Charlie, wrote off to his brothers at boarding-school in Toronto: 'I have been convinced of sin for nearly six weeks, but Satan kept me back from coming out ...' He too was set at liberty: 'When you come home,' he continued, 'you will find a difference in this village. The house that was once a house of business is now turned into a house of prayer.' He asked his brothers to shun the devil and all his works. William's only son, Willie, also responded favourably to the mission, as did his daughter Helena, although she tended to waver. The conversion of James Lobb, Baptist, started him off as a lay preacher: 'He spoke very well last Monday night,' said Caroline, his mother-in-law, and she quoted T.N.: 'For a man who talked calicoes and everything for a week previous, he did exceedingly well.'

T.N. and William celebrated these events with a large dinner party, to which they invited all their relations Methodist and non-Methodist alike, 'besides the young men at the store, our own boys and some others, in all nearly fifty.' Only Mary and her husband in Three Rivers could not attend, as also their sister Emily with her husband Erastus B. Holt far away in the West, but John and Charlotte Gibbs made the journey from Rochester, New York, their present humble home. At four o'clock the company sat down to dinner; at seven they adjourned to the parlour and hall, where T.N. and William explained their object in gathering friends together, inviting them to join in songs of praise. T.N. began with a prayer, when all of a sudden their Uncle Philip Gibbs, the schoolmaster, so bitter of speech and so frequently sour in temper, who had arrived in Canada a year earlier, amazed everyone by jumping to his feet and delivering an impromptu exhortation, which ended with the words: 'God is indeed and of a truth in our midst.' Earlier a debate had taken place as to whether Uncle Philip should even be invited, and William had said no false delicacy should persuade them to ask him, but T.N.'s wife, Almira, thought otherwise. Philip declared it to be the happiest evening of his life, and he led them all in prayer.

The scene and mood so affected Joseph Collins of Newmarket, that staunch member of a strict sect, holder also of many strange views, husband of Mary's sister, that he wanted to know what conditions were attached to becoming a Methodist when no one had ever expected to hear him express disenchantment with his own church. This celebration is the high watermark of religious enthusiasm, which now becomes increasingly more private and restrained, manifest in good works on a large scale and, by the end of the century, in far-flung missionary projects. Methodism had entered into its prosperous age, and nine years after the revival of 1860 T.N. and William were the principal and munificent donors to Oshawa's new Methodist church, which once more offered its people scenes of jubilation. At its consecration, a thousand worshippers attended the morning service, twelve hundred in the afternoon, and two thousand in the evening, and all by ticket only. At one of the services, the Reverend W.S.B. preached the sermon; he informed his wife: 'I can give you no idea of how they were packed together.' The *Guardian* reported that hats, bonnets, and clothing suffered terribly in the crush.

But the sun does not necessarily shine on the just, and in May of 1861, five months after the successful revival, on every side the firm of Gibbs & Bro. was owed large sums. T.N. wrote to his sister Mary at Three Rivers: 'I never saw money melt away (not even by fire) as it has done this spring. Upon the whole it is the most eventful period in my history, hard as has been a portion of it. No human wisdom, foresight, judgement or experience seemed of any avail whatever.' The entire milling industry in Canada suffered in the early sixties from a multiplicity of causes: hot summers, poor crops, the expense of importing from the United States the spring wheat that was then much in demand, inadequacies in the transportation system, and the early souring of Canadian flour.

So bad was the situation that at least one large shipment of imported wheat, which Gibbs & Bro. had sent off to another mill to be ground, was not properly returned, which made T.N. talk gloomily of dishonesty and unfaithfulness to trust in the trade, and he wrote from a hotel in Boston: '... there sits a man at my left to whom I gave 3000 barrels of flour to grind & he appropriated 1800 bls of our wheat to his own purposes & leaves us minus so much in the operation & so it goes.' Far worse news followed when shipments of Gibbs flour to Britain reached Liverpool and Glasgow heated and out of condition with an estimated loss of over forty thousand dollars; before the days of proper insurance, a damaged cargo abroad could mean total ruin.

William rushed to Quebec and sailed on the following night in a ship that narrowly missed a fog-bound iceberg; it had loomed up in the darkness of night directly ahead of the frightened passengers, and only the captain's earlier refusal to increase his speed beyond four knots per hour and his subsequent 'hard port, hard down' had saved them. Recently three Oshawa men had gone down in a vessel that had rammed one. The hazards of Atlantic crossings were real indeed. William arrived in Liverpool to find their worst suspicions about the flour confirmed, and on his return voyage on the *Great Eastern*, the ship that was years ahead of its time and which on a previous trip to London he and many thousand sightseers had viewed as one of the great achievements of modern engineering, she encountered the storm that nearly sank her. The steering failed and the ship gyrated on the sea, the interior a shambles, all the furniture smashed, the staterooms battered, the passengers left without food or water.

Caroline reported every detail to her daughter Mary: 'He says the scene for two or three days beggars all description, he never wishes to pass through such again ... It is supposed but for the strength of the vessel she must have gone to pieces as she was quite unmanageable.' William suffered a stroke, loosely termed apoplexy, and on his return the doctors of Oshawa tended the patient without success. His mother wrote to Mary: 'I think he was going through a course of medicine when you were here, bleeding, leeching, salivating and blistering.' It was two years before he felt himself again.

In the summer of 1862, T.N. sailed to England with such urgency that he drew up a new will, signed it, and boarded the train for New York within the space of a few hours. But he soon wrote cheerfully from London to Mary in insalubrious L'Orignal: 'I like it, yea I may say more, the filthy dirty old place I love it better than any city or town I ever saw.' London and Paris, however, unfitted him on his return for the small-town claustrophobia of Oshawa: 'At times,' he told her, 'I feel a lingering desire that the Providence of God w^d open up a way to leave it. I have a strong desire to go to Montreal if my path was clear. Unless there is a change in business matters for the better before long, one thing is certain, there must be an exodus & I see none that can swarm so easily as myself.' A hot summer had resulted in a poor crop, flour was now five dollars and rising in price, crop failures were reported everywhere, and news of the fearful war affecting their friends in the United States made him wonder what the end would be.

Caroline wrote in the same vein: 'He told me he felt like a man used up, had not a bit of energy or ambition for anything, losing money all the time.' But in part with a loan from the Ontario Bank – in those days, conflicts of interest do not appear to have been as serious as they are now – the firm made good much of the loss of 1861, and T.N., more deeply rooted in Oshawa than ever by the purchase of the other half of his father's mill, said: '... here I must remain & after all my history is so thoroughly identified with the place that I c^d not expect to find another which would seem more to me like home.'

Two years later, a visit to the western United States left him as dissatisfied with Oshawa as when he had come back from England, until a by-election reanimated him. An admirer of John A. Macdonald, as he was to be for the rest of his life, he hoisted this flag and joined battle. An earlier foray into the minefield of politics had occurred in 1854; the old parties were in the process of breaking up and realigning and his views had coincided with the Reformers, especially on the question of the Clergy Reserves. This had prompted the *Globe* to describe him then as a clever man of excellent business habits who was once a Tory but now held sentiments entirely in union with those of the Reformers. However, the defeated Tory candidate, supported by Orangemen, accused him of splitting the vote, and of duplicity and worse in soliciting the candidates of either party to withdraw in his favour; T.N. had maintained that he held a middle position.

The same hesitancy and indecision characterized his second attempt when his name appeared as Conservative candidate in December of 1857, and he withdrew. On the much debated issue of government support for Roman Catholic schools and possibly on other issues, he had sided once more with the Reform party. But in 1864 the *Globe*, now his enemy, said: 'It is notorious in Ontario County that Mr Gibbs has always been quite devoid of fixed political principles. Sometimes he has been quasi-Tory and sometimes quasi-Liberal, sometimes indeed, he has been on both sides of the same election.'

As he stomped the riding in December of 1864, he

fired off salvos at annexationists, against whom the most effective defence at the time lay in the strength of Canadian attachment to the British Crown and British institutions, so that earlier laudatory remarks about the United States were thrown back at him and equivocation in the election of 1854 exhumed. As Conservative candidate, he accepted the basis of Confederation that had been agreed upon by the representatives of the provinces; he extolled the economic advantages of Confederation and added the time-old electoral promises to reduce taxes and eschew local visionary schemes. Few expected him to be the victor with a majority of 194 votes, and his election was taken to signal the country's approval of the terms of Confederation, but throughout the campaign the strength of the annexationist sentiment in the countryside had quite shocked him.

T.N. and William reigned as undisputed masters of Oshawa, the rise of their fortunes coinciding with the eclipse of their closest rival, J. Borlase Warren, known as the Squire of Oshawa, whose mill, house, and tannery came up for sale in 1865, when Gibbs & Bro. bought the lot. William took over the squire's Prospect House, added a belvedere to it, and spent lavishly on the embellishment of the grounds, but the house, like others of the period, was quite inadequately heated, so that in the winter all the pipes froze, the furnace had to be stoked night and day, and a tinsmith kept busy putting up stoves in all the rooms to thaw them out. The winter's supply of vegetables in the root cellar was ruined. A few years later, T.N. put in motion his plans to build just as splendid an establishment.

In May of the previous year, his sister Mary had reported to her husband: 'Wheat up – not much in the country except what they hold,' and in 1865 Gibbs & Bro. cleared twenty-five thousand dollars in the wheat and flour trade alone between January and September. By September of 1866, their profits since the beginning of the previous year had reached a hundred and thirty-five thousand dollars. The Reverend W.S.B. sent his warmest congratulations: 'May their prosperity continue.' But although Caroline said she was glad to hear they were doing good with all this money, she wrote to Mary at Drummondville in September: 'Provisions of all kinds seem to be going up, which makes me think of your little family; they have put flour up to $7. here.' It was on the Drummondville circuit that Mary had great difficulty in making ends meet.

The circuit, which bordered Lundy's Lane Battlefield at Niagara Falls, had extended a friendly welcome on the Reverend W.S.B.'s first Sunday in June of 1864. The first sermon to each new flock was a straw in the wind with which to judge every new minister and a subject for much discussion by the listeners afterwards: 'Though I did not succeed as well as I sometimes do,' he told his wife, 'I think the impression made upon the congregation was of the right kind.' He expressed his customary cautious optimism in reference to the parsonage, which although only a modest cottage was superior to the one at L'Orignal: 'What I am sure will please you everything is pretty clean ... It is not the kind of house that promises or I could desire for such a family as ours but still it has something homelike in its appearance and I rather think that on the whole you will like it.' Painting had begun, some furniture acquired, and the circuit talked of building a kitchen.

Everyone soon agreed that the parsonage had reached such a deplorable state of disrepair and dilapidation that a committee of inspection, jolted into action, promised immediate repairs and renovations; it planned a round of teas to raise sufficient money. At times, parsonages had the barest amenities or were wanting in essentials; at others, they were even a danger to children, and Mary, a stickler for standards, quite possibly a thorn in many a circuit's flesh, prompted her husband on several occasions to remind circuits of their duty towards him. This time she had as usual to await events in Oshawa with the children, while her husband either lodged at a boarding-house or moved from house to house, the guest of his new flock: 'Everything goes on smoothly,' he told her, 'and I am full of hope as to the future, if we only can manage to live very near to God. My only fear is in regard to myself.'

Mary wrote: 'These short separations give me some idea of the unutterable loneliness I must feel should God in his providence ever take you from me.' He replied: 'I have always valued your letters but somehow I do not remember any one that ever affected my heart so deeply as this one.' Time passed but the parsonage remained as before. 'My silver is about exhausted,' she said. The long-promised repairs made slow progress, and then only after many sociables, which he had to attend, with tea and ice-cream at twenty-five cents per person: 'The whole thing went off very quietly, orderly and pleasantly,' he told his wife, when, after all, one would not expect such events to be disorderly. It was early autumn before the family was reunited.

'Never did I enter upon the labour of a circuit with a deeper sense of my responsibility, with more self-distrust or a deeper sense of dependence upon God,' the Reverend W.S.B. confided to his wife when the cost of parsonage repairs produced a deficit. Even a second round of teas in November failed to raise the required amount, and the circuit could not pay his full salary, which many a minister experienced until the Contingent Fund stepped in. Families lived meanwhile on credit, anathema to Mary, and as in pioneer days when little money changed hands, some at least of what the circuit owed still came in kind; potatoes, fruit, vegetables, hay, wood, and other commodities arrived in lieu of salary at every parsonage; at times it was uncertain, even perilous.

The Reverend W.S.B. heard from a fellow minister on another circuit who had not received in any form since the beginning of the year the hundred and fifty dollars owing to him: 'I fancy he is considerably discouraged, I confess I felt a considerable degree of pity for him.' Shortly afterwards, in June of 1865, Caroline wrote to Mary's sister in Newmarket: 'I fancy it is pretty hard times with them. Provisions are very dear, butter 22 cts, meat l2/, flour 6.75. She thinks it is as much as she can do to furnish bread, butter and potatoes. She has not had a bit of meat for three weeks.' This was the year that her brothers in Oshawa made twenty-five thousand dollars on flour alone between January and September.

Mary's anxieties had grown as the Drummondville circuit's debt forced it to launch a subscription fund, and this coincided with the onslaught of repeated illnesses that weakened her and were to disrupt parsonage life for several years. Others observed that incessant toil had brought her to this state, which sent her hurriedly to Oshawa again. 'Dismiss all care and go in for enjoyment,' said her husband cheerfully, but the price of flour was constantly rising, now nearly ten dollars: how were the poor to live? And she counted the parsonage in this category: 'I often check myself when enjoying a hearty laugh for being so forgetful of the many discomforts that you and the little ones have,' she said and added: 'I suppose we must only look to God.'

Here a chance remark by her brother William, who had so generously contributed towards the children's clothes and had just given his sister a substantial cheque, who had sent a piano to young Millie when he found that she loved music, who had in every way tried to help his sister and who had not even had the Reverend W.S.B. in mind, crushed Mary and caused a sudden and uncharacteristic explosion of anger to erupt at the parsonage. Before William had time to apologize or explain, she had written off to Drummondville. Never again was the Reverend W.S.B. to write in such a bitter vein: 'Tell your brother W.H. for me that he is grandly mistaken if he imagines that fidelity in the discharge of ministerial duty and the cheerful payment of ministerial salaries have a necessary and invariable connection with each other ... Never have I been in my life so faithful a minister as I have during the time I have spent on this circuit and I have not found fidelity on my part and liberality on the part of my people in exact ratio.' But he ended his diatribe on a softer and sadder note: 'Who cares for a faithful, plodding minister ...?'

Mary thought of the unrewarding path he had tried to follow, of his years of self-denying pastoral work that her letters bear witness to; for such is the portrait she has painted of him over the years when he sat night after night by the bedside of the sick and dying, took upon himself the troubles and cares of his flock, visited them in terrible winter weather, wore himself out in the conscientious performance of his duties so that every member of his churches had a friend and guide.

'Have faith in God, all is there,' he comforted Mary, reminding her that this is the panacea that cures all the ills of life, but, faith or not, the inability of the circuit to support them delayed her recovery; visits to Oshawa and her sisters at Newmarket and Streetsville failed to restore her, and only increased her aversion to Drummondville: '... I care little to see it if it were not for my own loved ones that are in it and a few kind friends.' The congregation made more and more pressing enquiries as to her return: 'All appear to be anxious to see you again,' her husband wrote, 'I need scarcely say this feeling is pretty strong at home,' and little Mary at two and a half said without prompting: 'I'd like to see me Ma.'

'I humbly trust your gloomy anticipations regarding home will not be realized,' the minister soon replied to his wife's assessment of their present situation, but the bleakness of Drummondville forced upon them even more stringent economies. At last this prompted Mary to remonstrate more strongly than ever, and her husband said: 'Poverty does not come with such a grinding weight upon me as it does upon you.' But he knew that it was she who had to feed and clothe them all, and he had so often seen her sorely tried. 'The Saviour would have us live in the present, leaving both the past and the future to God to whom of right it belongs. This appears to me to be properly a life of faith,' he tried to encourage her. But consoling as this might be, it was precisely the present that worried his wife.

A pattern unfolded of Mary's recurring illness and her husband's inability to organize himself and his work as he felt he should, so that in Drummondville the old depression and introspection returned to plague him, bringing in their train frequent and disabling headaches as he brooded sadly over his want of self-command and perseverance. Ever ready to blame himself for their predicament, he wrote to his wife: 'I have drifted without rule so long that to whip myself into the traces of anything approaching a systematic life seems almost, if not altogether, impossible.' Reading and studying in the late hours of the night, when all was quiet and he could surround himself with books and papers, made rising late a certainty and thus began a disordered day.

The mistress of the house resumed her duties in mid-October of 1865 without, it seems, any perceptible improvement in her husband's mode of living, and Caroline informed her eldest daughter in Newmarket at the end of November: 'I heard from Mary last week. They are all well except Mr B. who was complaining of his head a great deal. I am sure it is not good for him to study so late and then get up so late in the morning.' So bad were these attacks that by the following June of 1866, on his way to Conference, he sent word: 'My poor head is very bad. I am extremely nervous and my hand so unsteady that I write with difficulty.'

The life demanded strength, health, which in his case now fluctuated, and organization. 'To retire promptly at ten o'clock every night and rise at five in the morning seems a very simple thing,' he admitted to his wife, 'and to many persons the self-denial involved in it would appear so trifling as to scarcely deserve the name, but I have my doubts as to whether any amount of pressure could induce me to persevere in it. I am persuaded it would be conducive to my physical and mental health, it would enable me to do far more than I otherwise can ever do, it would save me from many forms of temptation, would greatly lighten your burdens, would be a great advantage to our family and would in all probability add years to my life, and yet with these tremendous considerations staring me in the face, I am writing these lines at the noon of night and will be in bed at seven or eight o'clock tomorrow, and in all probability (I scarcely dare write it in the presence of my Maker & yet I am afraid to do otherwise) I will continue to live as I have done to the end of the chapter.'

In this month, the inhabitants of Drummondville had a rude awakening that dispelled any tendency to similar self-examinations, at least in their correspondence; the Fenian Raid burst upon the town. The end of the Civil War in the United States, strong anti-British sentiment there, and the failure of the American government to control the Fenian rabble prepared the way for attack on British territory; excitement gripped even Oshawa: 'T.N.'s boys are all three gone,' Caroline wrote to Mary; they had gone to defend Queen and country. The government had hastily created a large volunteer force; rumour had it that thousands of Fenians prepared to invade on St Patrick's Day, which also marked the end of the Reciprocity Treaty. As minister of militia, John A. Macdonald had mobilized the volunteers on March 7th, 1866, mustering ten thousand within twenty-four hours, every little town and village answering in a great wave of patriotism as evident in Oshawa as anywhere else.

The order went out to the Oshawa volunteers; the Oshawa Infantry Company marched down to the station with bands playing, boarded the evening train for Toronto, where they were billeted in hotels, began a rigorous drilling, and on the first fine day marched smartly out on parade. But with no immediate danger apparent, the Grand Trunk Railway brought them home again in cattle trucks, this time with their uniforms besmeared in thick black grease. One month later, T.N.'s sons were training at the Military School in Toronto.

The Fenians crossed the Niagara River at Fort Erie on Friday, May 31st; the Province of Canada mobilized twenty-thousand volunteers, and the three boys rushed back to their units in an Oshawa at fever pitch with marching troops, brass bands, and flags; no one could remember anything quite like it before. But the volunteers from Oshawa arrived either at Fort Erie to find that the enemy had fled or too late for the Battle of Ridgeway. At home, confusion and anxiety reigned: 'What a state of affairs have these reckless Fenians put the country in again, it is really fearful to think of,' Caroline said. 'Sunday was more like a day of mourning than the Sabbath, many sorrowful hearts here as elsewhere – at the telegraph office all day to know what was going on.' The mother of one young man, known to all, fainted when she heard the news that he had been killed. Business came to a standstill and there was talk of mounting a guard at the bank.

'Mr B. will surely not leave you just now,' Caroline wrote to Mary so close to Ridgeway, the scene of action, unaware that four days earlier Tom, at this time fourteen and a half, had jumped down at night from his bedroom window in the Drummondville parsonage, followed the troops, and next day observed the battle from the sidelines, while the Reverend W.S.B., already on his way to Conference, found himself stranded because most of the rolling stock had been commandeered for the troops. The battle, so insignificant in the history of military feats and tragicomic in its errors, stirred up national pride as nothing else had done, and the provincial parliament had much to occupy its attention as it came to grips with the Fenian threat. Caroline quoted T.N. in July: 'He said it was hard work in dog days to be shut up in that ill ventilated room with so many in it for so many hours ...'

After this excitement, the circuit extricated itself from debt, but, as the tide of its minister's affairs continued to ebb, in the spring of the following year Tom, fifteen and a half, placed the note which began this tale on his mother's pincushion: 'Dear Mama, 'Ere you find this in all probability I shall be far from here. I leave because I think you are not able to support me.' And his father had wept bitterly. When a letter arrived from the rail-head at Marion, Ohio, where Tom was working on a farm, it only worried his mother the more; he had arrived in the rain, caught a cold, and had not wanted to say anything about it. She replied: '... Day after day passed without any tidings as to your whereabouts ...' But she had put her faith in God. Some weeks later, after much persuasion, Tom returned home. The move to the Milton circuit required his aid.

The question of his education came to the fore. The peripatetic nature of their children's schooling troubled Mary and the Reverend W.S.B., and the solving of this problem occupied their attention increasingly. 'I never wish to see any of my children inconvenienced as I have been all my life for the want of a good education,' said Mary on more than one occasion, while her husband hammered home the importance of a trained mind and instilled in his children from an early age a knowledge of the Bible and Shakespeare, which he had made his own by diligent reading. It was often told in our family how Tom's younger brother George (our eccentric but brilliant

Great-Uncle George) at four years of age would stand up in his high-chair and recite long passages of the bard (here was the future orator with a phenomenal memory).

The episode of the farm in Ohio and the news that Tom, having once tasted of independence, was trudging along in the summer holidays (with his parents' unwilling consent) hoping to earn enough to take him to Paris and the Great Exhibition prompted Mary's brothers in Oshawa to pay for his passage. T.N. said: 'I thought the boy gave signs of courage, able and willing to try to overcome the difficulties of his position that were not to be lightly esteemed.' But Mary replied: 'It does not seem right to take so dear a pleasure at another's expense.' Then T.N. and William offered their nephew a choice, Paris or an education, and, said his grandmother, he opted wisely for the latter. The uncles sent him to Oshawa's grammar school and paid for his board with his grandparents; William's store outfitted him in clothes.

Until now the children have scarcely made any appearance, sending messages to their father whose return they always welcomed with joy, or he in turn never failing to tell his wife how good they have been in her absence and she reminding him, as he tended to be forgetful at times, that Millie was counting on him to bring home a parasol for her birthday. Tom is already setting out in the world, and arriving in Oshawa he drew up for himself a plan of action that probably did not last long, to concentrate on his Greek, improve his composition, and send home weekly essays on disparate subjects for his father to correct. His mother remarked that a recent letter, though she was glad to receive it, was not what she thought a letter from him ought to be. He was to work hard and remember that other people were paying for his education. From afar she kept close watch on events that might lead her son astray.

Into this town with its parochial interests, Tom arrived in the summer of 1867 to enrol in its grammar school, only to be caught up in an election of national importance as helper and factotum in a campaign that see-sawed between George Brown of the *Globe* and Uncle T.N. in the riding of South Ontario. Brown was the leader of the Liberals. T.N. burst with self-confidence, looking upon his re-election as a certainty, and said: 'Brown has been named as the only man that can defeat me, but I doubt if even he can do it.' All the same, on July 11th, Macdonald wrote to him: 'I would not at all be surprised if you had a fight with Brown, but if so we must try to strengthen your hands as much as possible.' He did not elaborate on this suggestion. T.N. had the advantage of being a local man and had managed to give the impression of a certain independence, by which, so long as he maintained this line, he had the support of the town.

The campaign had scarcely begun when the highly partisan Oshawa *Vindicator* and Brown's equally partisan *Globe* gave quite different versions of the rowdy meetings that took place. Brown accused T.N. of jobbery, bribery, and corruption, and his *Globe* warned that if Mr Brown were not elected it would be because of Mr Gibbs's money-bags, which were heavy, far heavier it seemed than the principles of the Reformers of the riding of South Ontario.

The *Vindicator* replied in a lengthy poem, which began:

Brown told his party that he knew they could be bought
He feared that they would sell themselves, but didn't think they ought,
He'd like to buy them up himself, but he was rather short in South Ontario.

Both parties seem to have thrown in all their resources. The *Globe* reported their candidate's defeat: 'All through the night, every concession and side-line was traversed by Government, well supplied with new crisp Government notes.' The *Vindicator* said: 'the unscrupulous measures which Mr. Brown uses to win the election is undoubtedly the chief reason why he so seldom turns a second time to the same constituency.'

T.N. and William, busy entertaining with the help of Webb's catering firm from Toronto and the delivery by Grand Trunk of barrels of oysters from Nova Scotia, no longer complained of the dullness of life. On New Year's Day, T.N. had a dinner for thirty guests (the political men of the riding), and three weeks later another for forty more. Aunt Almira requested Tom's help. He related to his mother: 'I think they intended it should be a tip-top thing. There was about ten courses of all the delicacies of the season. Slater was the only minister present. I got to bed about two in the morning, felt sick for a day or two aferwards as you might expect.'

Caroline found her grandson Tom a quiet, well-behaved boy, fond of reading; he got on well with his grandfather and for the moment diligently pursued his studies, but before two years were out his reputation had declined; 'too careless by one half,' she said, in the same breath referring to 'that dear good-natured Georgie.' His mother discovered that Tom had attended a party at the Drill Shed that did not break up until two in the morning: 'Remember you are consuming other people's money as well as ours in getting your education.' She laid before him the straight and narrow path of Sabbath observance, daily prayer, and the shunning of smoking or drinking: 'I have but one ambition as far as you are concerned, that is that you may be wise and good.' Soon parents and grandparents concluded that he required some discipline.

Oshawa's grammar school by 1863 had had the signal distinction of never having sent a single student to university, and the sons of T.N. and William, who attended various schools in Toronto until they entered Upper Canada College, all moved swiftly into trade, although it seems that one of T.N.'s sons diverged to a French-speaking college in Quebec, an unusual move for a Methodist, again with trade in view. William's daughters, after governesses and boarding-school, attended finishing school in Switzerland in 1867: 'to learn French to perfection, other branches of course,' said their grandmother in Oshawa, but a querulous note sounded on their return when she wrote to Mary: 'And what do you suppose all this running about, as W.H. said, schooling, etc. cost by the time they reached home? One thousand pounds, a handsome fortune for someone.'

Oshawa thought that William's Carrie put on airs, and his Helena earned her grandmother's displeasure now by all too frequent visits to Toronto merely to see the fashions, compounding the error by taking her younger sisters with her. She had also engaged herself to the son of a Gibbs & Bro. business associate in Halifax, but an acquaintance of James Lobb, Amelia's husband, described him as F.F.D. – a fop, a fool, and a drunkard – with whom he would not allow his daughters to associate. No one could credit the news until an engagement ring arrived by post, soon to wing its way back again; and Helena engaged herself to someone else. 'Helena is a very nice girl,' said her grandmother this time.

The town of Oshawa remained the one fixed point for Mary as she moved across the provincial map. For her parents, Thomas and Caroline, it had changed beyond recognition since their arrival in 1832, even if by the time Tom entered its grammar school in 1867 the maple-lined streets still lacked gas lamps, cattle and other farm animals still ran at large, and wooden sidewalks and an imperfect drainage system left much to be desired; King and Simcoe had only recently been gravelled. Among the leading citizens were his uncles, T.N. and William, who now controlled much of local banking and industry. They ranked with the province's most successful businessmen, and the cornerstone of their prosperity was milling and the grain that poured into their mills, as Caroline reported to Mary in May: '... they are actually coining it now ... I was told they held 20,000 barrels now, on which they expected to make $3. a barrel. There is $60,000 (slap), enormous profit, is it not? They are not grinding a bushel here now.'

The real boom had begun in 1866 with the shipping of sixty thousand barrels by Grand Trunk alone, the price going up and up: eight dollars, then ten, and by August of 1867 twelve dollars. A year later, Gibbs & Bro. was reported to have made twenty thousand dollars on barley. In such a way fortunes were made; they were just as easily lost. In 1868 they put forty thousand dollars into the Oshawa Cabinet Company and William took over its management. T.N.'s and William's houses echoed with the sounds of music and dancing, for they had thrown over the Methodist embargo on that pastime, and the young people amused themselves with charades, amateur dramatics, and musical evenings, which made up for the town's cultural deficiencies. For them life seemed eternally buoyant. They travelled; they crossed the Atlantic repeatedly; they took the train to Montreal and New York. Their houses welcomed guests by the carriagefull. The boys joined hunting expeditions in Michigan and one summer sailed the Great Lakes with a group of newspaper reporters.

But from time to time, Oshawa appeared to justify T.N.'s wish to escape its clutches. There is nothing in Caroline's letters to suggest that she aspired to intellectual heights, nor is it surprising that her daughters remained fixed in lives of piety and good works. Her daughter Amelia, silent and invisible until the sixties, is materfamilias replete, and Amelia's husband, James

Lobb, active in the great revival, had long been William's right-hand man at the latter's department store, W.H. Gibbs & Co., appearing at first in Caroline's correspondence as a most superior man of business until doubts arose on that score when he overstocked in William's absence. From the start, he and William had indefatigably covered the hinterland for the Missionary Society, no doubt mutually advantageous to both pursuits.

Amelia and her husband, invariably known as Lobb, had a large household of seven children, all accident-prone, where nursemaids came and went and where every epidemic lingered: 'I don't know how Lobb does with so little sleep, then came stocktaking in the midst of it,' said Caroline. On one occasion, he broke free to Montreal, saying he was sick and tired of country life, only to return because he could find no congenial work elsewhere, and William made him a partner in Gibbs, Lobb & Co. as the firm now became, until the business closed in 1869, when the pull to Toronto affected all the outlying smaller towns. 'It is not so easy to begin again with seven children as with one,' said Caroline as Lobb, without employment, journeyed to San Francisco and then England in search of insurance agencies.

He had earlier imported one of his brothers from Devon, but the experiment failed. Herbert Lobb came sight unseen to act as bookkeeper at Gibbs & Bro., arrived brimful of expectation and liked Canada, but the feeling was not mutual. He proved unequal to the job, put his brother to much expense, and was soon sent packing. T.N. said: 'He made three starts. Once he returned from the station, second from Bowmanville and lastly he wanted to return from Kingston but while hesitating the boat carried him on ... Of all the specimens this last importation from England is the poorest. He got to be nothing short of a nuisance. His friends in England were as glad to get rid of him as we were and as sorry to hear of his return as they can well be.' Another Lobb proved just as unsuccessful, tried his hand at teaching, and blamed their mother, old Mrs Lobb in Plymouth, for never making her sons learn a respectable business. Caroline said: 'He lacks energy of character, and has never been taught thorough business habits.'

The chronicler of these events scarcely mentions any of the great controversies that shook mid-Victorian complacency, but then a woman's work was never done at least until the child-bearing years had passed, at which time she had said: 'I am in a measure weary of this world.' Her vision usually rested on South Oshawa, once called The Hollow, and in their births, deaths, misadventures, and good fortune many of its inhabitants pass by, while in the domestic sphere everything depended on 'the girl,' so that 'my girl' and 'your girl' pepper the correspondence. Every family had one. They worked hard at low wages and, seldom staying long in the household, by the end of the year were often off to pastures new. Rising at five, making up the many coal fires, blacking the boots and shoes, doing the laundry, ironing, and other household chores, and, as one of them said, 'all the time on your feet,' they were the indispensable necessity in even modest households, where the mistress herself was seldom idle.

But an increase in the town's manufacturing dried up the source, in outlying farms, of this supply of domestic labour, and Oshawa by 1860 had to pin its hopes on transatlantic schemes of assisted emigration. Caroline informed Mary: 'There are a lot of Scotch servants coming out under a patroness. Thomas spoke to the agent in Quebec ... Almira told me there were a lot of children coming out also from ten to twelve years of age to be disposed of.' Chattels. For five years, Amelia Lobb's Bridget proved a treasure, until James sent her packing because, as Caroline reported, 'James will not have a Catholic any longer.' William's wife had an ideal servant who thought nothing of ironing eighteen shirts, but suspicion entered Frances's mind. She searched the girl's trunk, which met with Caroline's disapproval, and found stolen articles. The culprit maintained they were her own property and immediately informed her two brothers. They worked at the foundry in which William had shares, and with their supporters they marched noisily and en masse to William's house, denounced him, and threatened to take the matter to court, even to organize a strike. Caroline said: 'The story is in everybody's mouth and like all these things loses nothing in the telling.' Two more servants came and went: 'You don't know what injury such peoples' tongues will do.'

CHAPTER SEVEN

*O*THER NEWCOMERS to our shores, besides Lobb's brothers, failed to adapt successfully; such was Mr Dixon, husband of Carrie, the daughter of Silvanus and Mary Gillard of Devon, although she thought him endowed with all the virtues. Long ago the Gillards too had been predisposed to failure. Caroline Gibbs viewed this Carrie as a daughter and grieved to see her story unfold, for Mr Dixon lacked the stamina to conduct business in any form, moving from town to town – London, C.W., Montreal, Oshawa, and nearby Whitby – the society of which latter place he considered preferable to neighbouring Brooklin, where Benjamin Gibbs had failed as a baker. Here Gibbs & Bro. employed him to buy up wheat in the back townships, but this undertaking unfortunately coincided with the firm's heavy losses during the almost unparalleled scarcity of grain in 1861 and it ruined Mr Dixon, whom T.N. and William had to bail out to the tune of five thousand dollars: 'He sees no opening for anything here,' Caroline had said, 'and he is so disgusted with the way they do business in this country.'

Perpetually on the move, he sold on commission, but what he made on butter in Toronto he would invariably lose on potatoes in Montreal. Finally, he took his wife and daughters home to England, where he worked in London for a shoe store on a pitiful salary, and Carrie wrote to her Aunt Caroline in Oshawa that she was trying to live each day as it came, praying to submit to God's will whatever it might be: 'I often wonder if this anxiety for the future will continue to the end of our days.' But we have not heard the last of them, and the course of their lives flows like a river in Caroline's letters to her daughter Mary.

At the many parsonages that were her home, Mary received with regularity week after week accounts of her brothers and especially of her sisters; Caroline Gibbs sat at her desk as soon as a letter arrived from one daughter in order to relate its contents to another. She kept Mary abreast of all that occurred at Newmarket, where the Collins family managed to hold its head above water as Joseph juggled two farms and a cheese factory. Farming had diversified at mid-century, requiring more machinery and capital investment, while larger landowners were buying up small farms, and Caroline Gibbs reported: 'Collins wants to sell his farm to make him independent or more properly speaking to put him out of debt.' Here the sad parents watched as their dear son John died slowly of tuberculosis, so tenderly cared for by his father. The funeral was delayed for a week to take place on Sabbath so as not to disrupt everyone's August harvest, but in Oshawa his grandmother said: 'It is time he was buried,' the weather being so very hot.

John's sister, another Carrie, who planned to go to Normal School if Aunt Sarah Gooderham would pay a little, played the organ ecumenically for the Disciples of Christ on Sunday morning and the Methodists in the evening. Full of spirit and enterprise, announcing too that she had no intention of sitting around waiting for matrimony, she turned down one of her Uncle James Gooderham's younger brothers (with all his money) because he was not manly enough: 'It will be a peculiar sort of man to suit her ideas,' said Caroline Gibbs in Oshawa. But a young Methodist minister swept her off in his gig to a circuit a hundred miles distant, whence she sent word that she was well, happy, and contented. 'What can a mother wish more for a child than this?' said her grandmother this time.

With three of her daughters, Caroline Collins, Sarah Gooderham, and Amelia Lobb, anchored in the triangle of Newmarket, Streetsville, and Oshawa and with Mary's parsonages shifting in an unpredictable arc, only Emily, or 'poor dear Em' as her mother was to call her, repeated her parents' exercise in emigration, and Caroline Gibbs compared this transplanting with her own experiences in Lower Canada forty years earlier in the 1820s. British Columbia, which is Emily's destination, appeared as difficult a country in which to bring up children, the distance as great, the voyage as long and perilous.

If virtue has any reward, the venture at first augured well for the Methodist Church had a faithful layman in Emily's husband, Erastus B. Holt. He observed a strict Sabbath no matter at what cost to himself, led Methodist class meetings, and never put mammon before God, but he had no business sense. The great depression of 1858 that engulfed all North America had wiped him out as a builder in the town of London in Canada West, and in an entanglement of debts he left creditors behind him, and Emily and little James with her sister Sarah, to join the throngs of men surging westward to the shores of the Pacific, and westward he must have hoped that the land was bright.

On September 17th, 1858, he set out on the long circuitous route and arrived as history was in the making at Victoria, capital of the Colony of Vancouver Island and headquarters of the Hudson's Bay Company. Here Mr Holt found thousands of American miners waiting to cross the Straits of Georgia into what would shortly be the new Colony of British Columbia. The interior had hitherto been the preserve of the Company, but as exploration progressed its reign drew to a close; expeditions were mapping and surveying further and further west. In the previous year, the British government had sent out John Palliser across the Prairies, and in 1858 Canada had dispatched Henry Youle Hind as far as the Assiniboine and Saskatchewan Rivers. The gold rush had started with the first finds on the Thompson River in 1857 and on the Fraser River in the spring of 1858, while the discovery of gold on the Upper Fraser suddenly opened up the country. On November 19th, 1858, at Fort Langley at the mouth of the Fraser on its south shore, British Columbia was officially proclaimed a colony.

The hordes in Victoria – some estimates running as high as twenty thousand – and Mr Holt in pursuit as a builder, pressed into the Lower Fraser, arousing fears that the territory would fall to the United States just as the Oregon Territory had, while in Victoria the governor of both colonies attempted to exercise some control by instituting licences and tolls on the canoes and boats going up river. Fort Langley soon gave way to Queensborough on the north shore when Colonel Moody and the Royal Engineers arrived, selected this site in preference, felled trees, and laid out lots, affording Mr Holt opportunities as builder and surveyor. Caroline wrote to Mary: 'If he gets constant employment he will send for Emily. I hope she will not be too premature or hasty in going to a new country like that for I am sure she cannot endure much hardship.'

Disturbing news reached Oshawa of the near starvation of acquaintances working or mining on the Fraser, where several men had been frozen to death, and a friend in Bowmanville, so close to Oshawa, returned home saying he was disgusted with all he had seen there. Such reports could only discourage Emily, who had not heard from Mr Holt, his letters having gone astray in the overland mail via the United States; it had been robbed. Caroline said: 'I think she has kept up wonderfully under all the circumstances. I shall rejoice to see them together in a comfortable home in Canada if it be ever so plain. Emily does not see much now in the prospects to induce her to sacrifice society and dear friends for a wilderness.'

Oshawa heard that clouds of menacing mosquitoes had driven Mr Holt back to Victoria again. Here he constructed a lighthouse for the authorities and a house for the leader of the Black community, a Mr Gibbs, recently arrived from California and grateful for the guarantee of freedom in a British colony. But the uncertainty of Mr Holt's future made Caroline say: 'I am sure Emily is not a fit subject to endure much fatigue and privation. I hope his pride would not keep him from coming back and his creditors would not trouble him if he was to write to them.'

Nevertheless, in December Emily's brother T.N. escorted her and little James to New York and, underwriting all costs, placed them aboard a ship that was far superior to the *Speculator*. At once Emily sat down to write to her mother: 'On board the splendid ship Baltic, I am afraid I shall have to bid you good night. The language of my heart since I have been on shipboard has been: I will praise Him for all that is past, and trust Him for all that's to come.' T.N. declared his sister had 'good grit,' and Caroline wrote to Mary at Three Rivers that surely Emily's expectation of seeing her husband again would keep up her spirits: 'Was it not for that little word "hope," where would half the world be?'

The *Baltic* sailed to Aspinwall in Panama, a passage made doubly congenial by the number of Methodists and Presbyterians aboard, and from there Emily travelled overland by train to the coast, thence by ship to San Francisco, accompanied all the way by twenty women who were joining their husbands in that city – one family with their hives of bees. But on arrival in Victoria, she learned that a fellow traveller, a Methodist who sailed on a different vessel, had lost her young life in a shipwreck off the California coast.

A hazardous expedition of a different kind was just then being undertaken by another Gibbs family acquaintance, John Jessop, schoolteacher in Darlington and Whitby close to Oshawa, who made his way with a few companions overland across the Prairies, fell in with Blackfoot guides, crossed by the South Kootenay Pass, thence to Fort Colville on the Columbia, a journey of eight months. T.N. heard that they reached Fort Colville hatless, bootless, and almost shirtless. Twenty days later, John Jessop was expected in Victoria; he makes several appearances in Emily's early letters, and in the future he will found the educational system of British Columbia.

Every prospect pleased Emily: 'I forgot to say,' Caroline informed her daughter in Newmarket, 'Emily heard of the arrival at San Francisco of her melodion, boxes, *etc*. Is she not fortunate – only one hundred and eight days from New York?' But she had hardly settled in at Victoria when Mr Holt decided to return to Queensborough, now become New Westminster, and Emily had to say goodbye to the superior ambiance of Victoria. Arriving at her new destination on the mainland, which at the time had little to recommend it, she wrote to her mother: '... he thinks it better to be king among hogs than hog among kings. There is an amount of wealth and aristocracy there which this place does not possess. Indeed, I thought as I neared the capital of B.C., surely this is the jumping off place that the boys used to talk about. I have got to the end of the world at last.'

Mr Holt put up a cabin within the space of several days, and the beauty of the lot, rising gently from the river, redeemed this modest shelter in a settlement of shacks amidst stumps. It satisfied Emily: 'Some of our neighbours think us rather aristocratic with our netted windows and knitted bed curtains, melodion, ottomans, and of course they do something towards making a home attractive.' Her husband's integrity won him accolades now and later in the town, but the fine plans for New Westminster as laid out by the Royal Engineers took shape slowly because of the extreme difficulty of clearing the land. Moreover, the little capital in the wilderness failed to attract either the anticipated wealth or number of settlers; trade still gravitated to Victoria, and on the mainland an endless procession of miners moved on, without halting, right past the small community and up the river.

The town's residents, chiefly Canadians engaged in trade and believers in responsible government, saw no reason why it should be denied them in the colony, resented the presence of their governor in Victoria, and established a reform movement, the leader of which was John Robson, a good friend of Mr Holt's from Canada West. In his *British Columbian*, he described Mr Holt as possessed of large property and more than ordinary enterprise, experience, and intelligence, a tribute the latter might not have received either in Victoria or in Canada West; here he was indeed a king among hogs, and to 'Joiner, Contractor, Surveyor' in his advertisements he now added 'Architect.' A larger house had replaced his family's shack.

New Westminster elected him in February of 1861 to the reform movement's first convention, and it, in turn, appointed him to draft a memorial to the governor, who in any case had not authority to act, but this did not deter Mr Holt from standing up at the second convention in September to denounce the governor as having interests so completely at variance with those of the colony that it was not in human nature for him to do them justice. In the following year, he continued his war against authority by attacking Judge Begbie, who almost single-handed prevented the mining country from degenerating into the gun-toting West south of the border, but Mr Holt believed that in one case at least justice had miscarried. After this, one acquaintance wrote home to Oshawa describing Mr Holt as one of the best men, if not the best, he had ever known.

A steady stream of friends arrived from Canada, including James Crimp, previously employed by Gibbs & Bro. and once of Kingsbridge, Devon. As he sailed into Victoria, he wrote home of the beauty of the harbour, the huge encampment of Flathead Indians, and the barnlike appearance of the governor's residence in comparison to T.N.'s old house in Oshawa. 'They were frozen up at New Westminster,' Caroline informed Mary at L'Orignal, 'no communication with Victoria.' In this coldest of winters, mules, cattle, and horses died by the hundreds. A few months later, she said: 'I fancy it must be worse than Lower Canada was in our day to bring up a family.'

As soon as weather permitted, Crimp crossed to New Westminster and delivered the sewing machine that her brother William in Oshawa, suffering still the effects of his terrible voyage on the *Great Eastern*, sent Emily as a gift, Crimp having taken lessons in order to instruct her. In the early spring of this year, 1862, he lured Mr Holt into accompanying him to the mines of the Cariboo, where a discovery at William's Creek in 1860 had begun the gold rush and where in 1862 the finds at Barkerville and Cameronton acted as a magnet, which for Mr Holt proved a disastrous chimera.

On this long and difficult journey, he sent word to Emily from the Forks of Quesnel that he was in good spirits. Four days later, tired and sore, he reached Antler Creek, having packed sixty pounds all the way and having covered twenty miles over deep snow on the first day. Prosaic in so many ways, he had marvelled at the beauty of nature as the sun sparkled on the whiteness around him. At William's Creek, a hive of activity, he began work as builder and surveyor. But, on the trail, men had journeyed up in hope only to meet others returning in despair, and by the summmer reports reached Oshawa of near starvation at the mines so that many, rumour said half, were leaving the Cariboo.

In the early spring, Crimp had already heard far from reassuring rumours, which he communicated to Oshawa. Reality proved far worse and the price of flour reached astronomic levels. The prohibitive cost and scarcity of supplies in the interior, owing to the primitive conditions of the route and the numbers to be fed, clothed, housed, and equipped, rendered proper provisioning impossible, nor could the government exercise any real control at such a distance. The *British Columbian* reported that provisions were at famine prices and doled out only in small quantities.

Caroline wrote to Mary at L'Orignal: 'I feel very anxious to hear from that quarter. I trust if Mr Holt has luck, he will alter his mind about spending his days in that country.' Still, a little over a year later, with transportation improved and communications secure, the country opened up, and its first tourists, Viscount Milton and Dr Cheadle, were hurtling full tilt down the Royal Engineers' Cariboo Road in a coach provided by Mr Holt's friend, Francis Barnard, on the last lap of their transcontinental journey.

In an annual ritual, men went up to the mines in the early spring, down in the late fall. James Crimp spent the winter at Salem, Oregon, where living was cheaper and where he read by day and attended revival meetings by night, while in New Westminster Mr Holt, a builder by day, devoted his evenings to the Wesleyan Missionary Society, the British Columbian Bible Society, and Methodist class meetings, in all of which Emily joined him whenever she could, until the call of the mines lured the class, himself, and James Crimp back to the Cariboo in the spring and the town emptied itself. 'As to his making a fortune this season it is hard to say,' Emily wrote to her mother, and added: 'I dread the time of their departure.' Lonely and homesick, she travelled to friends in Victoria with little James and baby Carrie: 'I just wish I were now on my way home to see the dear, dear ones, but it is useless wishing.'

At the birth of her fourth child, Mr Holt was away at the mines. She named him Alfie, and she was alone again when at two and a half he fell into a pot of boiling water. Day after day the elderly doctor ordered dosing powders and the application of Castile soap and sweet oil, constantly reassuring Emily in spite of the child's rapid and visible deterioration: 'Mrs Holt, he could not be doing better.' A year later, when another baby lay in the cradle, Emily's eyes were sore with weeping: 'and though I do rejoice at his birth, the circumstances and time of year lead my mind back to the loved one that has been taken away. I am constantly calling him, "Alfie dear."' The cradle filled with one child after another, at whose births Mr Holt had already left for the mines.

By now misfortune pursued him relentlessly. With capital acquired in his many building projects, first in Victoria and then New Westminster, he had bought into claims when the new deeper mines required funds to finance their deep shafts and complicated pumping mechanisms. He lost heavily and people said that if only he had sold his shares a few months earlier, he could have paid off his debts in Canada with a gain of six thousand dollars. Caroline wrote to Mary in L'Orignal: 'If this is true, why did he not do so?' The mines became less and less attractive; a depressed economy eventually affected New Westminster, and in March of 1866 four hundred men left the town for recent finds at Big Bend on the Columbia, Mr Holt amongst them. Emily wrote: '... had to pack 50 pounds and walk over ten and twelve miles a day over snow ten feet deep. The day he reached the Columbia he walked sixteen miles in order to rest on the Sabbath, leaving his companions ten miles behind.'

Big Bend proved such a disappointment to miners and a disaster to traders, builders, and suppliers that he returned to the Cariboo in the spring of 1867, and although Emily was delivered of their sixth child on December lst of that year, yet he did not come home. His absences had grown longer and longer, lasting at times eight and nine months. Caroline said: 'I fear she will be in a constant state of anxiety as to the event of things unless she has strong faith and confidence in the Lord.' For by now a web of confusion entangled Mr Holt's mining shares, and according to Emily the whole country from William's Creek to Victoria was in a state of bankruptcy. Perforce, with ever expanding family, she now managed a sawmill, cows, and a small dairy in New Westminster: 'Dear child, she has lost none of her ambition yet,' said her mother, remembering perhaps her own dairy, pigs, and poultry in the loneliness of Thomas's farm on the Terrebonne seigniory in the 1820s.

The *coup de grâce* fell upon New Westminster; it lost in 1869 its status as capital of the two colonies, Vancouver Island and mainland British Columbia, which had been united in 1866 to the tune of a large debt and depression. The holders of lots threatened to sue the home government since the original advertisements had clearly stated New Westminster was to be the seat of government: '... the officers with their families,' said Emily, 'number about eighty. Of course with our present small population we should feel their removal and for a time confidence in the place would be materially lessened.'

In the previous year, the town of Barkerville, the scene of Mr Holt's present activities, had burned to the ground, and friends said that if only he had left mining alone and stuck to building he would have been well off, which offered small comfort to his wife. At last, in her husband's absence and to his annoyance, 'considering,' he said, 'the obligation we are already under to him,' Emily turned to her brother T.N. for help: 'I feel desirous that our future steps should be taken cautiously; we have a comfortable home, but what is it without the head and master? Not worth a cent.' Mr Holt had been away more than a year, nor was there any talk of his return; he held persistently to the belief that tomorrow his affairs would be in order. But Emily had had enough and arrived in Oshawa in the spring of 1869 with her children.

Caroline wrote to Newmarket: 'She must be treated with kindness and tenderness, which I have no doubt she will be ... Poor dear Em has gone through a sea of trouble in the last eight years.' Mr Holt promised to follow, but time passed without word of any such plans and when Emily said at Christmas time, 'Mr Holt will surely be home soon,' her mother replied that she had no encouragement to think so from his letters. The admiration that Mr Holt's two brothers-in-law, T.N. and William, had once expressed for his integrity in difficult surroundings changed to anger at his procrastinations in returning home. They sent him a peremptory note to come back and look after his family, and Caroline said: 'I look upon this as a sad affair from beginning to end.' He arrived in the early summer of 1870 by the new transcontinental railway across the United States, the Central and Union Pacific, which took only a few days. 'If we were not living in a day of wonders, we should not be done talking about it for a long time to come,' Caroline wrote to Mary.

Cap in hand, Mr Holt reached Oshawa to find both T.N.'s Ellesmere Hall at last completed after several years in the building of it and William's Prospect House resplendent proof of success and wealth, the very names more reminiscent of Old World landed gentry than New World trade, Ellesmere being also the name of Gibbs & Bro.'s finest brand of flour. 'It is quite a walk from the top to the bottom of T.N.'s house and it is beautifully and elegantly furnished,' Caroline said. But the Hall like William's House had its drawbacks. There were too many windows: 'They make a house so cold,' said Caroline again. 'Only think of burning 30 tons of coal independent of wood and none too warm, but it is an immense place to heat.'

T.N. and William, however, had other concerns as distant rumblings from the West reached Ontario, which Canada West had become. The Prime Minister, now Sir John A., the architect of Canada, told T.N. he hoped against hope that the insurrection at Red River would die out. By the spring of 1870, public feeling ran high as events led up to the Riel Rebellion, and after Scott's murder meetings convened all over the province urging the government to act; this is when William as deputy reeve of the county seconded a motion condemning 'that infamous upstart Riel.'

As for British Columbia, the gold rush was over and thousands of miners withdrew from the colony, leaving it before farming, lumbering, and later mining ventures brought it prosperity. The exodus signalled an end to a chapter of its history. It seemed a failure in settlement and trade, but one month before Mr Holt's departure, in June of 1870, delegates from British Columbia arrived in Ottawa to negotiate its entry into Canada. He had aligned himself with reformers and had surely lent his weight to the Confederation League since both Barkerville, the scene of his more recent operations, and his close friends John Robson, one day premier of the province, and Francis Barnard gave it their full support. In his own way, Emily's husband, most of whose friends left their mark on the province, contributed to the making of this country, and Emily did too, while her parents, Caroline and Thomas, who had landed in Quebec one year after the ruination of Lord Selkirk's plans for a settlement in the West, saw now the farthest reaches of continent settled and incorporated in Canada.

Emily began her last years as an invalid; her brother T.N. sent young James to Upper Canada College, an experiment that did not last long, and for a time Mr Holt worked at a menial job at Gibbs & Bro.: 'His position,' said Caroline, 'is very humiliating. I think he feels it.' He moved his family to Toronto, where his business methods so exasperated his brothers-in-law that they were heard to say he should have stayed at his carpenter's bench. Emily fell into a long decline; six years later, Mary came down from the Napanee parsonage for three months to look after her sister and the younger children, returning home from the funeral on a winter night in February on the last train before the engineers' strike on the Grand Trunk Railway: 'I found my dear husband at the station waiting in the midst of a terrible storm for my arrival,' she said.

This scene takes place long after the Reverend W.S.B. and his family have left Drummondville, where the reader has last seen them, and it is time to return there briefly in the early summer of 1867, when Mary was writing cheerfully to her mother: 'Where we are to find a new home or rather where we are to make our next stay, is impossible for us to know at present. No doubt it will be the right place in the end.' And to her husband at Conference, she said: 'Your kind and loving letter came to hand a couple of hours ago and quite renewed the dreams of my youth ... Love grows stronger with us as life wears away.'

The circuit of Milton, a town with five different denominations, a grammar school, and several academies, presented immediate problems. The Methodist minister was well supplied with the usual lay cohorts, but Mary summed up the parsonage's defects at a glance; neither dry nor warm, it had quite inadequate heating for the winter, even in the kitchen, and the committee in charge of repairs appeared strangely inactive, for the circuit already had a large debt binding upon it. Promptly, Mary fell ill, and the kindly flock rallied to take in the younger children as she began a round of visits to restore her health. Her husband reassured her: 'The report from the little ones is that they are as good as they can be, and you are not to hurry home on their account.'

As the months passed, the congregation enquired more and more anxiously after her, while weariness and loneliness combined to sound in the Reverend W.S.B. a melancholy note. In November he informed his wife: '... in regard to the house, it remains just as you left it except that the cistern has been plastered.' The circuit's financial problems, a legacy of the year before his arrival, delayed the promised renovations; the parsonage remained untouched and perishingly cold: 'The large debt makes the Trustees cautious.'

A year earlier, the Niagara District camp meeting had taken place on the neighbouring Grimsby circuit, the high point of that summer other than the Fenian Raid, and he had written a laudatory article in the *Guardian*, although a note of caution had crept in with a hint that a decline in values spiritual threatened the body ecclesiastical. He wrote now to his wife: 'I suppose you wonder how I have been spending my time ... I have not been entirely idle but have accomplished very little.' And Mary began to regret that she had ever complained, although the season of the children's colds and coughs had begun: 'I hope Providence may save them from all harm and you too, my dear, dear husband, for I fear you will be exposed too, shifting from bed to bed and perhaps our own house torn up and comfortless.' He replied: 'I have a terrible cold myself.'

'I am not to be depended upon for one hour,' she reminded him, which made him almost desperate: 'I scarcely know what to do,' he told her as, harried by her repeated directives on the subject, he scoured the countryside for a servant. 'I fear my friends will not be very anxious to care for my little folks again. They have been so imposed upon this time,' said Mary, but at last when a new servant appeared Mary instructed her thirteen-year-old daughter, Millie, to supervise the cleaning of the house, the blacking of the stoves, and 'setting things to rights,' and on the day after Christmas the Reverend W.S.B. travelled to Oshawa to fetch her: 'If you come,' she said, 'put on your best bib and tucker and I think you might get a new hat of some kind.'

A second and more serious illness spirited her away again in the spring to her sister Sarah's at Streetsville and the children hither and thither to friends and relations. In Oshawa, Caroline Gibbs said she supposed it was one more miscarriage: 'She will surely be sick unto death before long with such continual illness.' Mary's brothers, thoroughly alarmed, sent her in the summer down the St Lawrence to the Gaspé with detailed advice from T.N.'s wife, Almira, on the correct kind of bathing attire. In a rapturous mood, she wrote home of the majesty of Quebec, where every prospect delighted. The traffic on the river afforded an endless source of interest, but she returned no better than before, and her almost chronic indispositions caused anxiety and talk. Once more it was Christmas before they were reunited.

It was in this setting that their son Tom worked on a plan most advantageous to his own future. Accordingly and with some help from Uncle T.N., he enrolled in September as a day boy at Upper Canada College in Toronto in the hope of winning a scholarship to university. 'Feel lonely and sad,' Mary wrote in her diary after seeing him off on the train to Toronto, 'and no little degree of anxiety as to how the means are to be raised to keep him there, but shall try and lay it all before God who has often helped me in similar emergencies.'

All the Gibbs boys had boarded at Upper Canada College, the principal of which, Mr Cockburn, had a prodigious reputation, but Tom and an Oshawa school friend shared a room in lodgings at two dollars and fifty cents a week: 'Luke tells me washing is extra so I will use paper collars and no cuffs.' He found needles too fine or thread too thick as he began to patch and darn his wardrobe, while far behind and much discouraged he was almost at the bottom of the class. At home his younger brother George tried to cheer him up: 'I shall be pleased if I leave as good a name behind me as you have.' He moved to another lodging and share of a room at a dollar a week, where he and Luke laid in their own supply of coal and lived frugally. Bread went up a penny a loaf and meat a cent a pound; he moved to even cheaper lodgings.

He heard that his mother was ill again: 'I had rather learn a trade than that you should be pinching yourself,' to which she replied: 'Someday I have a hope that God will open up our way.' His father said: 'You feel the inconvenience of being poor. You are going

Great-great-grandfather William Gooderham, 1870s.

Harriet Tovell Herring, William Gooderham's wife, 1870s.

William Gooderham, Jr, c. 1868.

My great-grandparents George Gooderham and his wife,
Harriet Dean, at the time of their wedding, 1851.

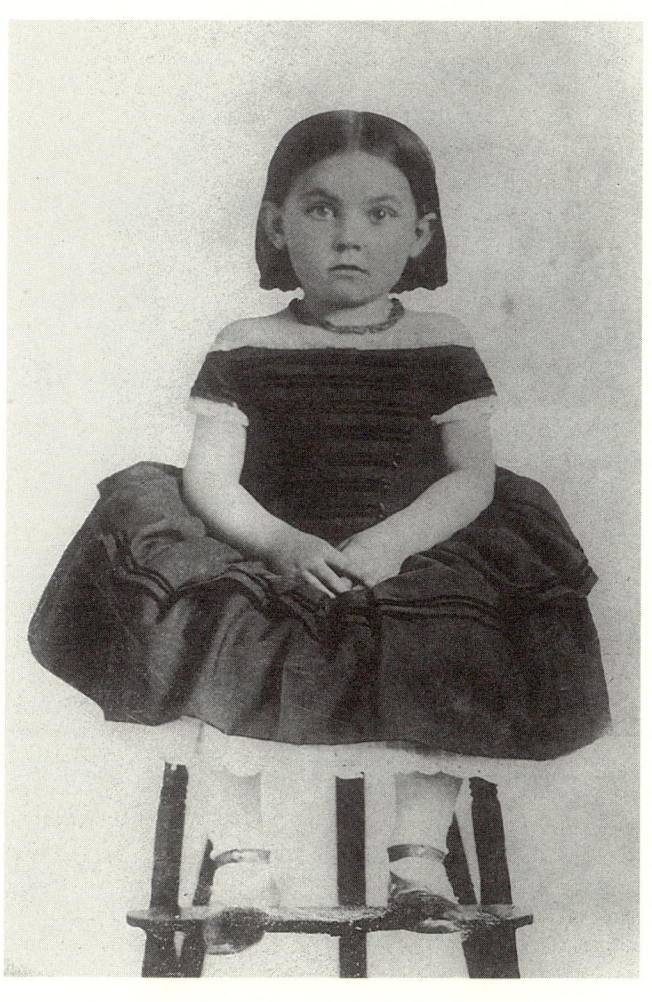

My grandmother Harriet Victoria Gooderham (Hattie),
aged four, 1859.

Hattie, aged seventeen, in 1872, the year of the Grand Tour.

Gooderhams on tour in 1872. Hattie writes: '... how we looked riding through the streets of Belfast.'

Hattie (left), aged about nineteen, and her sister Lizzie, c. 1874.

Grandfather, Thomas Gibbs Blackstock, 1880s.

Tommie, who died of diphtheria at the age of four, 1887.

My father and his older sister, Lizzie, 1888.

My father and his younger brother, George, 1898(?).

79 Prince Arthur Avenue, my grandmother Blackstock's house, showing the back verandah and sunroom, from St George Street, 1906.

Part of the front hall at '79.'

The drawing-room fireplace at '79.'

Grandfather Blackstock's yacht, the *Cleopatra*, 1890s.

Great-grandfather Gooderham's yacht, the *Oriole*, 1890s.

Egypt in 1889. On the right, Great-grandfather Gooderham and, third from the right, Grandfather Blackstock, with two of Grandmother Blackstock's sisters and a host of other tourists.

1914, Christmas leave in Scotland; my father, his brother George and sister Elizabeth.

My grandmother's touring-car being converted into an ambulance in England, 1915.

Father's sister, my Aunt Barbara, as a probationer at the London Hospital, 1915.

Longwood, my grandmother Blackstock's summer
house at Lake Simcoe, 1930.

through what your father has had to go through before you.' Then Mary sent twenty dollars, a sixth of their quarterly income: 'God has provided it just as we needed it.' God did not always act so promptly. In June, Tom passed with honours but without the coveted scholarship: 'A little more attention to details a few years ago would have been to your advantage,' said his father, 'but let that pass.' 'I do not look so fat as I did when home some way or another,' said Tom as he set off to work on a farm.

His father was a tired man: 'He returned home from Guelph last night, quite wearied out,' said Mary as he left home early the next morning to conduct a series of services in another town, preaching every night and visiting from house to house in the day, while ahead lay preparations for Conference and the need to leave Milton in good shape for his successor. But the new circuit of Goderich looked promising from every point of view, a prosperous town in an agricultural area where the railway had arrived in 1858 and in 1866 the discovery of salt mines brought employment. In 1870 attendance at this circuit's eight churches, which averaged between seven hundred and a thousand at Sabbath, exceeded even Milton's.

A sizeable deputation met the Reverend W.S.B. at the station and, forming a procession, led him triumphantly through the town, stopping to introduce him at all the offices and shops that belonged to Methodists: 'I everywhere received a very cordial and hearty reception.' Everything met with his approval. 'I am feeling my way forward as quietly as I can,' he told his wife, and when at last the house was ready to receive her after the cleaning, plastering, painting, and papering, all cheerfully undertaken by the circuit and without any prompting, Mary arrived to be greeted by another deputation and walked to a pleasant afternoon tea party followed by a splendid supper for sixty with enough food left over to start the week well. The house delighted her, and only a few imperfections ruffled its new chatelaine: the maid of all work, the 'girl,' rebelled against a bedroom in the basement, but Mary told her mother that they were going to be more comfortable in Goderich than they had ever been before.

In the autumn of 1870, his parents in these happy circumstances in Goderich, Tom entered University College at the University of Toronto, the pinnacle of his father's earthly ambition. No other members of the connection seem to have aspired to scholarship as did the Reverend W.S.B. and his wife, and an avalanche of advice came down on Tom to study English literature and the Greek and Roman authors, which the Reverend W.S.B. had so assiduously cultivated in quiet vigils in his study late at night and which, in turn, had interfered with early risings. He warned his son: 'Beware of one sidedness; general proficiency is the thing that has real honour attached to it.' Other reminders repeated all that he had been taught before: 'Set God before you by night and by day. Take up every cross, perform every duty promptly and conscientiously. Let the Bible be your constant companion.' Tom joined the Literary Society and took part in debates, a theme on which his mother enlarged: 'Don't be too much afraid of making an exhibition of yourself,' she said. He bought a fourth share in a flute and discovered how easy it was to play.

One advantageous vista opened; through his Aunt Sarah and his Uncle James, the Gooderham clan welcomed him. Old William invited him to play croquet, and on Sundays after church the carriage of Methodist William, Jr, waited for him: 'He took quite a fancy to you as a little boy,' said Mary, who hoped that any invitations to dinner from these quarters would be promptly accepted: 'I sometimes fear that you do not live well enough at your boarding house.' This was only too true, and Tom had also taken on pupils scattered throughout the town, which kept him perpetually on the run.

A cheque from T.N. – 'He is a princely man,' said the Reverend W.S.B. – and another from William – 'My good brothers,' said Mary – sent George, now fifteen, as a boarder to Upper Canada College, where the housemaster, seeing in him a future luminary with great oratorical powers, took him under his wing and steered him towards rhetoric. Tom called him 'the immortal gobbler,' and indeed earlier at Milton, George had almost brought down the roof with applause when invited to speak at the Lodge (the only reference to what was probably the Orange Order): '... speechifying seems to go well with George according to what I hear,' his mother had said. 'I would not wonder, if he minds himself, to see him do something pretty clever in that line, should his life be spared.'

With the uncles' help, Millie too left home to enter the Wesleyan Female College in Hamilton, which gave reductions to ministers' daughters: 'I never knew how much I loved you until now,' said her mother, as she wandered through the parsonage lonely and sad. She entertained the highest opinion of this daughter's intellect and application: 'For though I say it, I don't know the boy or girl that does better at books than she does.' At the end of term, Millie distinguished herself, but Mary declined to join the other parents at the annual display of pupil excellence: 'I suppose they put on a good deal of style at that time and I fancy I should look queer among such fine folk with my ordinary mode of dress.'

With deadening regularity, she reminded her daughter that the only prospects lay in schoolteaching. The very thought made Millie miserable, and Tom, coming to her aid, said: 'I hope she may get out of that as soon as possible for of all things I hate "school marms."' Yet no other career or occupation offered itself. Neither then nor later did she make any attempt to earn her bread, and if some women were beginning to clamour at the gates of higher learning, she was not one of them. She went on perfecting her French and her music at home buried in books, but the subject did not go away. A few years earlier, William's daughter, returning from a visit to Drummondville, had reported that Millie was not much use to her mother: 'Her head is more for books and music than anything else.' In Streetsville, Millie's Aunt Sarah and Uncle James frowned upon this failure to make practical use of the money spent on her: 'They have not much sympathy with our educational views,' said Mary.

Always the indisputable leader of a large group of merry schoolboys, George tasted his first freedom, but a growing tendency towards hypochondria, excitability, and volubility, often excused at home, troubled his parents, whose friends reported to the parsonage that he ran about too much, read newspapers too much, and, from all accounts, spent too much; there was something irrepressibly attractive about him that the censorious wished to curb. Someone saw him smoking and lost no time in delivering the news. His mother confided to Millie: 'I hope he is doing better than I fear he is, if he is not he may have occasion to be sorry for it. There is no certainty about your Papa's health and if he were laid aside we shall all have to look around for something to do.' This ominous note soon rang louder and clearer.

The summer of 1871 had already foreshadowed trouble when the town of Goderich, promising so well, catapulted into a local depression while the rest of the country enjoyed a period of comparative prosperity; its chief industry, the salt mines, closed. Shops shut, men searched vainly for employment, and ministers, dependent on their people, suffered with them. The Reverend W.S.B.'s circuit failed to pay his salary on time or in full, and in the following year history repeated itself with the flock again in financial difficulties: 'I am afraid we shall have to live on credit this summer too, which goes against my inclination,' said Mary (the pincers of uncertain salary and the cost of higher education were equally to blame). Then every kind of epidemic hit the town, so that her husband, weary and quite unwell, talked of leaving Goderich.

'Your Papa has been very poorly,' she wrote to Tom. 'If it was not for the mite we were entitled to when superannuated, he would get a transfer at once to New Jersey, or some place contiguous to the sea.' New Jersey was his mother's birthplace. And Mary added: 'I never heard him talk more decidedly about anything. He says he must have a total change of some kind.'

'I am sorry things have come to such a pass with Pa,' said Tom. 'Your Papa is on the go all the time,' Mary replied. With an eye to his own future, at first Tom abetted his father's new plans for he had heard at the university that its graduates were doing well in the United States, but such reports soon changed with tales that they wished they had never left home, that ministers there did not enjoy the same social position as in Canada, and living costs were higher. In Streetsville his Aunt Sarah, so very comfortably off, gave it as her opinion that Mary as a minister's wife was as free from care as any of her sisters, having a regular income to depend upon without any of the anxieties of business.

Tom practised every economy, gave up meat, and took milk instead, which resulted in two days of hiccoughs: 'I don't know that I ever felt so miserable.' At the end of the summer term, his mother said: 'Thomas came home last night and looks thin.' Next day he set out to canvass the countryside of Goderich for an agent, based in Stratford, of subscription books. 'You need not mention this to anyone,' she told Millie, 'as he does not care to say what he is about until he sees if he succeeds.' Tom informed her: 'Today I commenced business.' But he soon found difficulties in getting farmers to buy: 'It requires some energy to keep the ball moving. The business is, to say the least, precarious.' In nearby Galt, only the working class expressed an interest, but this meant calling upon them in the evening, and shortly afterwards he told his mother: 'The farmers are not so very hospitable here as in Bosanquet.'

Thus began his initiation into the dynamics of commerce and trade as he learned the rigours of a salesman's life, returning footsore to his various lodgings late at night, but on the way he also received kindness and invitations to 'socials.' George plied the same trade in the Bruce Peninsula quite successfully; he had great charm and everyone liked him. In October, Tom delivered the books he had peddled so assiduously, began the collection of payment, and with this last act of entrepreneurship departed from the scene, leaving his mother to deal with any dissatisfied customers.

In the United States the railway opened up the West; the continent unfolded and, as it did so, beckoned young men with any spirit of adventure. The urge to join this throng proved irresistible, and Tom set off in high spirits with a railway pass from William Gooderham, Jr; adventure and the prospect of hard cash beckoned. The tentacles of his summer employer had reached as far as Kansas, or possibly it was vice versa; there Mr Lyon was making a fortune in real estate: 'Why shouldn't I?' said Tom. 'May the Lord bless you and keep you from evil and bring you home again safely,' said his father, but his mother added: 'I do not just like your photo. It has a vacant, frightened look, just like I feel when mine is being taken.' Looks deceived, for he was anxious to be off.

As the train rolled onwards, he sent home reports to his father of a West so ill defined as to be the Mysterious West. As everyone's understanding of it differed, it was a point of no fixed certainty on any map; everyone seemed to have his own view of where it began, and yet it symbolized the hopes and aspirations of so many. Tom looked at it from several points of view, not least as a future home for his parents weighed down at present in Goderich by the inability of the flock to support them, living on credit, and yet in pursuit of their dream to educate their children. 'We must get out of debt,' said Mary.

Tom arrived at Topeka, Kansas, where his cousin Willie Collins had been sent by his parents, Caroline and Joseph Collins of Newmarket, so that he too would not go the way of the brother who had died of tuberculosis. Five months earlier, the Atchison, Topeka and Santa Fe Railway had also reached the town. 'It is pretty,' Tom told his parents, 'the most easternlike of Western cities, certainly the most church going.' He had already paid a good deal of attention to farms and farming as the train rolled through Indiana.

The Kansas Territory had begun its rapid agricultural development at the end of the Civil War and the coming of the railway, which held enormous land grants and offered these for sale to farming settlers in preference to either ranchers or speculators. Settlers flowed in, yet many ebbed homewards again for one reason or another and sold out cheaply. 'Society in the country here is in a pretty primitive condition,' Tom reported from the vantage point of boarding-houses, hostels, and farms. 'You may dress pretty much as you please without losing caste. The only thing they are particular about is their eating that is generally served in great style, abundance & variety. I hear more dishes announced for my dinner every day than I ever saw or heard tell of in Canada. Yet we all wash out of the same basin & are supposed to comb with the same comb.'

His father wanted details of government, free land grants, and opportunities for ministers in the neighbourhood of Topeka, its society, churches, congregations, ministers' salaries, and living expenses, but neither its largest and most influential church nor its congregation impressed Tom: 'All seemed quite ordinary to me.' His mother wanted to know the prices of common household articles and, with an eye to Millie's future, the salaries of music teachers and schoolteachers. She added: 'What styles do the ministers generally live in?'

CHAPTER EIGHT

*I*N THE AMERICAN WEST, a bitter winter set in while unemployment made the times thoroughly unpropitious for any young man seeking work in real estate or book selling, on which Tom had set his hopes. The railway no longer hired men, and in December on reaching the state line of Colorado it ran out of funds. The long railway boom in the United States was ending, and a bank crash in the Eastern states was to have drastic repercussions. All appeared now to be engaged in the same search for any employment as was Tom himself only to find that there were no jobs to be had in Kansas City, Lawrence, or Topeka. He moved on to Dodge City. Two months earlier, in September, the railway had reached Fort Dodge, which promptly changed its name, bringing with it merchants who opened hotels and stores for the multitude of soldiers, railway workers, and buffalo hunters already on the scene.

The soldiers had come at the end of the Civil War to keep the Plains Indians in check when settlement pushed west, and here the Plains Indians still attacked, resentful of westward settlement that robbed them of their birthright, for hunters and settlers disregarded the treaty that had set aside Indian territory south of the Arkansas. The construction workers of the Atchison, Topeka and Santa Fe had only just been thrown out of work in the month that Tom arrived. The great occupation was and had been buffalo hunting; the railway camps had required the meat; tongues and hides were shipped eastward, and when in the previous year a method was devised of tanning the hide into commercial leather, the mass extermination of the last great herds had begun.

Dodge City stood on the banks of the Arkansas River, which separated the northern and southern herds; the slaughter accelerated relentlessly. Passengers on the train bearing Tom westwards had shot them with ease, and he was soon to join in the hunt: 'The train before us,' he told his parents, 'had been thrown off the track, a noble bull indignant at the invasion of his domain by a monster more terrible than himself charged the engine between the driving wheels and soon he lay in one ditch, the engine in the other. This we were informed happens frequently.'

With his skill as a marksman learned from Indians on the circuits, and taught to ride by them and his father, who in younger days had once lived in the saddle, Tom took up buffalo hunting, but this was a dangerous sport for amateurs, many a hunter coming to grief through accidents, and in this coldest of all Decembers many froze to death. 'I have made two excursions out about twenty miles once north & again N.W.,' he wrote home on Christmas Eve. 'We slept on the Plain most of the time but had a dug-out the last four days as it was very stormy & cold. Many got lost, the storms come up so suddenly, and were frozen to death or lost a limb or two.' He survived one deadly storm during which over a hundred hunters perished. His anxious father wrote: 'We are delighted to have a letter from you yesterday, it being a full month since we had received anything from you before. I hope you will, now that you have seen so much of the romance of the West, make your way home at once.' But return to home and college had to wait; he was hired as a carpenter at three dollars a day and began work immediately.

Dodge City boasted fifty houses – frame, dobie, and sod – as well as dug-outs and tents, accommodating five hundred inhabitants, nearly all of them men: 'Your Western man is almost of necessity an exaggerator,' Tom told his parents. 'He lives say in a small town and with an eye to business desires to see it prosper, and to induce manufacturers and others to settle in it and as nothing is so successful as success he gives out that his village is a city.' The village lived up to the American West's reputation for lawlessness. 'Hardly a night passes without someone being seriously hurt; pistol practice is the prevailing epidemic here. At the upper end of the street a large barnlike structure strikes your notice; it is the Hotel. As you enter upon the right is the bar with its tumultuous uproar, on the left the office in which you are requested to deposit your valuables. In one corner with a blanket over him lies a man in a semi-conscious state, a night or two before he received a ball in the head & there he will have to lie till he dies or recovers as there is not a bed to be had in the town. Every man is supposed to have his own bed with him in the shape of a couple of double blankets and a buffalo robe. The town consists of saloons, restaurants, gambling houses, stores and dance houses.' The Reverend W.S.B. replied: 'Time is precious and I feel anxious that you should be back again at your studies with the least possible delay. Come therefore at once.' He came home loaded with buffalo skins but without the fortune he had set out to win.

Several of the old generation had already slipped away. Thomas Gibbs's brothers, John, Benjamin, and Philip, had all three died with the eccentricity that had always characterized them. In the United States at John's funeral, the preacher used a text from the Book of Job that Caroline found puzzling for such a firm upholder of the faith: 'For Thou writest bitter things against me, and makest me to possess the iniquities of my youth.' In Oshawa the bachelor's hall that Benjamin inhabited defied description when it was at last breached by his worried relations. Caroline reported: 'We did try to sweep a little path to the bed. He said, "don't sweep that out of doors, put it in the corner with the rest."' T.N. thought it not half so bad as he expected, but Caroline answered: 'I asked him how it could be much worse. Uncle Philip would not stop there five minutes, the atmosphere of the room was so bad.' Or at least until Almira, T.N.'s wife, took matters in hand.

Benjamin died in October of 1868, to be followed in November by Philip, whose remains were laid beside Ben's in the Union Burial Ground: 'a good many, mostly old people met at the house,' said Caroline. Only William was absent, attending Missionary Society meetings in Guelph, which was reeling from the effects of an epidemic: 'He said they were so crowded with business they hardly had time to bury their dead.' In Oshawa, Thomas Gibbs, old and ailing, said: 'It will be very easy to tell which of my father's sons will go next.' Two years later, Mary hastened from Goderich to his bedside, but his great deafness made it annoyingly difficult to question him on his prospects for eternity, which wife and daughters so ardently wished to do during the long vigil. Mary reported to the parsonage: 'It will not be the same degree of blessedness that it might have been, but it is a great & unspeakable blessing if it be only salvation from sin & eternal death.' Worn down by wife and daughters, Thomas talked at last about his imminent death and the future life, readily quoting from the Scriptures.

The Reverend W.S.B., not one to dwell on another's faults or omissions unless they proved a means to repentance and conversion, replied that there was much consolation in remembering that her father's old age had been a happy one and now he was going home to God. The patient suffered almost unbearable pain without complaint, and onlookers marvelled at a constitution that underwent powerful and futile medicines; even so it was reported that his wit came bubbling up; this had sustained him in many trials. Of his being a Christian there had never been any doubt; it was his reserve on such matters that could not be tolerated. He died on February 11th, 1871, and Mary told her husband: 'The house you may suppose is desolate enough & poor dear Mama is heavily stricken although she bears up wonderfully considering everything.' She had forgiven him long ago.

In the summer of 1872 and now a widow, Caroline travelled once more to England, this time with her daughter Sarah, Sarah's husband, James, and a party of Gooderhams (including our grandmother, Hattie, who was seventeen and would one day marry Tom) on the first lap of their long-extended tour of Britain and Europe. She spoke more firmly than ever as a citizen of her adopted country, admiring Quebec City's magnificent setting and the beauty of the St Lawrence. No sooner landed in Liverpool than she began to compare the land of her birth unfavourably with Canada, encountering an England that had passed through the Industrial Revolution so as to be almost unrecognizable: 'The smoke of the different furnaces passing through Wolverhampton and Birmingham is fearful, the atmosphere filled with dense smoke.'

She saw much that shocked her, the grime and poverty of the large cities, the failure to relieve the poor, and this was the time that she returned to her childhood home, St Mary's House in Chalford, sat down and wept at the memory of earlier, unhappy days and found her father's name, Monkhouse Tate, quite forgotten. She visited her sister-in-law Elizabeth Gibbs, now Mrs Blake, who had never contemplated emigration, whose parents had once feared that she and her young husband might beget a race of paupers, whose son now prospered in the medical profession, and who herself lived surrounded by every comfort, coach and coachman, garden and gardener, and maids.

Six months later, on March 3rd, 1873, at the Goderich parsonage, Mary wrote in her diary: 'My darling Mother entered into Life.' Walking briskly along the street in Toronto on her way to her daughter Amelia's house, Caroline had suffered a heart attack; all was over in a minute. The *Vindicator* praised her Christian virtues and ended: 'none ever sought her support or aid in vain.' It noted her birth in the City of London, the daughter of Monkhouse Tate, Esq., and so the question of her birth is as puzzling as ever. Long afterwards, by way of epitaph, Mary said: 'God gave us such a mother who amid the poverty, wretchedness and sorrow she passed through never lost hope, never lost faith in Him whom she had been taught to trust.' Her letters to this daughter begin 'Dearest Mary,' or 'My beloved Mary'; they were very close.

T.N. had once said: 'Poor old Body,' by which he meant no disrespect to his mother. 'She only lives to do good to others.' She was always on errands of mercy to the sick and the poor in the town in which he himself felt a prisoner and which he would have left on several occasions, if only he could. She had said a few years earlier that her last days were the best in every sense of the word (barring her husband's failure to speak out on religion), while just before her grandson Tom came to live in Oshawa and looking back on a long life of decidedly mixed blessings she had written to her daughter in Newmarket: 'How wisely is the future hidden from our view. Could I have seen all that was before me when you came into the world, I should have sunk into the earth at the prospect before me; so we find it, bitter and sweet – sweet and bitter all the journey through – and much mercy mingled in the cup we have to drink.' This too is her epitaph.

Oshawa, except as the scene of political frays to which this tale will return, largely recedes from view, while parsonages pass in sequence until Toronto, where this tale began, is our home. Tom had taken up his studies once more at university, boarding at a dollar a week, and living on a diet consisting chiefly of bread, butter, potatoes, and milk. 'I have had the blues myself and feel as if everything was going wrong and inclined to quarrel with everyone, myself included,' he said.

The dread hand of unemployment continued to grip the town of Goderich, so that minister and wife, living on credit until the circuit could fulfil its obligations, wondered more than ever what the future would bring. Tom wrote to his mother: 'I should think you would have a good excuse to leave Goderich before the end of the year,' and if the minutes of the District Meeting in May of 1873 noted that all the circuits were healthy and prosperous, the statement referred more to the soul than the purse. But Mary said: 'I shall feel very sad to leave Goderich. To tell the truth I feel I have had quite enough of change and would, if spared, like something a little more permanent but there is not much probability of that.'

Then how sorely was she tried in the summer of 1873 when Conference disposed of her husband and self to Clinton. A long depression, lasting until 1880, descended on the whole continent, affecting in Canada both agriculture and manufacture, and the Clinton Methodists had already warned the Church some months before, during the previous minister's time, of their inability to support a minister at all and had emphasized the decision by selling the parsonage under him. Once having made an appointment, Conference, which would not have considered Clinton a demotion, had no intention of changing its mind, but here was a challenge the Reverend W.S.B., in poor health, was increasingly unwilling to meet. Many ministers experienced these disappointments; moreover, the Wesleyan Methodist Church thought well of both pastor and wife, appeared to count on him to build up this wayward circuit, and knew nothing of the warring emotions rising up within him, nor of the increasing anxiety and weariness that were to culminate in his disenchantment with the Church Temporal in Canada.

There being no parsonage, and aware too of the new circuit's refusal to accept a minister and its treatment of the previous incumbent, he went alone: 'He was so depressed when I left Goderich,' Mary told Tom, 'that contrary to his usual placidity I began to feel that he might cut himself loose at any moment, his feelings were so outraged & that you know is not like him at all.' Once more her husband, who usually began his circuits with faith and optimism, even now counselled: 'Continue instant in prayer, my dear Wife, and cultivate a cheerful trust in God. Be assured I will not forget you. The Lord is leading us by a way that we know not and in paths that we had not known.'

These paths scattered his family to any relative who could take them in, with no end in sight, but he would not give up the education of his sons. Mary said: 'The fact is we must get out of debt. I don't see any other way.' The Reverend W.S.B. replied: 'As I have struggled so far to get them to a point where they can take a respectable place in their professions I would, if need be, rather suffer a little than be turned aside from my purpose, which I may say I have cherished all my life.'

Months passed, and the minister moved from week to week to different houses, unable to find any lodgings for his family in the town; there seemed to be little or nothing for rent. He conscientiously visited every member of the congregation. He wrote to his wife: 'I do not know what to say. At present my duty appears to be to labour and to wait. How soon the whole thing will be over, and though this life has been a failure the life to come may not.' T.N. advised him to go to the United States; Mary sent bulletins on her own poor health, which reacted as usual to parsonage crises, with every indication that she did not wish to face Clinton.

When at last the circuit decided on a house, it was in such a state of disrepair as to be almost open to the elements and requiring months of work: 'Don't let any money be spent on papering,' she said, 'for all the home it will be to me.' The search for temporary lodgings continued; she wrote again: '... Let Millie settle it and not go visiting anywhere as it is only spending money,' but Millie pursued a merry-go-round of visits until at length her mother observed: 'Millie thinks she may have outstayed her welcome.'

The Reverend W.S.B. bade his wife be constant in prayer and place her trust in God; he visited most of the town and talked to all he met about their souls: 'I do want to see one widespread and thorough work of grace before I go hence to be no more.' But summer faded without prospect of uniting his family or his belongings and, lacking even a warm coat as late autumn nights grew cold – it remained packed up in Goderich – he made up his mind: 'I will do nothing rashly,' he assured her, 'except I can decidedly better myself.' Armed with recommendations from his brother ministers and buoyed up with false hopes, he crossed the border only to find that ministers there fared little better than himself: 'I went to Buffalo,' he said, 'but found things in such a state that I did not say anything.' He returned home almost reconciled to his lot until the desperation of his situation struck him again: 'Imagine my feelings when I found nothing whatever had been done.'

By the end of November, the house not yet plastered, and still unable to find any rooms for rent, he reported himself entirely in the dark, altogether at sea, without compass or helm, and it waṣ madness to remain in the Wesleyan Methodist Church: 'My affection is strangely alienated from the whole thing and I fear that my connexion with the church will be a mere artificial and mechanical thing in which the heart will have very little place. I am sorry it is so. It was not easy as you know to produce this alienation, but I am afraid it has been effectually done. Unfortunately my views of Christian doctrine are in the main in harmony with the teaching of Wesley. If I could be a Calvinist I would not be a Methodist minister twenty-four hours. I suppose you will think me insane in writing so and I rather expect you are correct. I think the pressure has been a little too much for my brain. But you have been the good angel of my life.' This outburst thoroughly alarmed his wife: 'Has anything occurred to make you feel so dissatisfied with your church relationships, that is, anything more than I know? I fear all sorts of things.'

The Church viewed this six-month separation from his family as no different from the lot of any missionary and all their men were missionaries. Nor would it have felt itself responsible financially for his family when relatives were available to care for them, although Mary would have taken a different view, even then writing to her husband from Oshawa: 'Everyone is very kind here but I feel it is an imposition to stay longer ... *Something must be done.*' At the same time, she hastened to assure Tom that he must finish his studies: 'We shall live in a primitive way and save all we can so as not to go into debt and yet finish your education. Providence has helped us beyond all we could expect so far ...' A month later, her husband said: 'Don't let Tom live on two dollars a week. He will run down and not be able to study. And see that he is not getting too shabby. Things are not so far gone that we can't keep him somewhat decently. Encourage him to look up and look up yourself.' After getting his undergraduate degree, he had begun the study of law, at first earning a pittance and still leaning on his parents.

The Reverend W.S.B. soon had to admit: 'I am trying to look up, but it is very hard to do so.' Then Mary too said: 'I am trying to believe that God is our Father & friend & will guide us to the end.' Still, in the depths of her discouragement, she assured him of her love and support and he answered: 'The Lord bless you my dear, dear wife, the Lord reward you for all the undeserved kindness which you have bestowed upon your most unworthy husband, W.S. Blackstock.' Of his shortcomings she was quite well aware, but always in her estimation he possessed superior qualities of mind, so far unrecognized. Years earlier, when his first attempt at having articles published met with rejection, she had consoled him: 'You are not the first great man that has had to wait.'

In mid-December, when at last the parsonage was ready, Mary wrote to George that she had arrived safely in Clinton and found Papa ready to take her to her new home. Money as usual was scarce: 'I have none at all,' she told Tom, 'as your Papa keeps the purse now and buys everything for the house. I would like to have a little pin money but it cannot be had.' By this and other means, the spectre of debt was laid to rest. This was just as well for between living on credit and getting into debt a firm moral line was drawn, and for its part the Methodist Church would have looked askance had it known that Upper Canada College or the University of Toronto had been to blame for some at least of its minister's difficulties. Yet nothing had deterred him, neither prospect of debt nor risk of censure, and more often than not Mary's judgment was more balanced than her husband's in his emotional crises: 'I sometimes have the impression,' she had told him in November during his darkest hours, 'that the quiet place you are in, all things considered, affords as good an opportunity for soul saving as any other.'

Contrary to expectation, minister and wife left Clinton in the following June with the same regret they felt at leaving any circuit. They moved on to Napanee, where over fifty years earlier John Gibbs had stopped as miller on his way up from Lower Canada, and here the Reverend W.S.B. applied himself with his customary vigour to the welfare of his new flock. T.N. well knew the vicissitudes of ministers' lives, having observed their treatment over the years by members of Oshawa's temple of Methodism, which one minister had just left, a victim of undeserved vindictiveness. Another had just arrived, and T.N. wrote to Mary: 'His wife was the observed of all observers & she seemed to feel it scarcely deigning to lift her eyes up thro' the service. Next to the minister is his wife in Methodist churches and you will have the experience anew in Napanee shortly. Your husband having passed thro' the ordeal before you arrived there.' He pitied ministers and their wives with all his heart. But head high and conscious of whose banner she was privileged to bear, Mary was unlikely ever to have sat downcast in any church pew.

The second stage in the union of Methodists was taking place in that year, 1874, when the Wesleyan Methodist Church in Canada, to which the Reverend W.S.B. belonged, united with two other bodies to form the Methodist Church of Canada, the amalgamation being partly in answer to the federation of the British North American provinces of 1867. This had opened up the North and West for settlement, which in turn required concerted missionary action, and the Conference in 1874 included ninety-four laymen, amongst them Mary's brother William and her brother-in-law James Gooderham, indefatigable supporters of missionary work, as too was her sister Sarah. It appointed the Reverend W.S.B. one of the delegates to the Primitive Methodists, without success, however, for that body did not join until the third great round-up ten years hence.

The Church's Kingston District, in which lay the circuit of Napanee, delegated him to attend a conference of distinguished theologians, many coming from abroad, in New York. He reported home on the outstanding papers he had had the privilege to hear, and as usual he kept his wife posted on proceedings; after all, she was his partner in the great work of ministering. He went on to Washington, where he was introduced to the Speaker of the House of Representatives: 'The moment I mentioned Kingston he immediately connected it with the name of Sir John [A. Macdonald] and spoke in the warmest terms of admiration of him.'

Throughout his life, 'to have a large dish of conversation' constituted one of the Reverend W.S.B.'s great pleasures, whether with high or low, and he never missed an opportunity in the street or on any conveyance to approach strangers. He held strong views, but these never altered his genuine love of people. All prejudice vanished when he walked up a Toronto street one day, on his return from the Methodist Book Room, conversing with a Roman Catholic brother in the habit of his order, who filled him with admiration and respect. Conferences, usually evangelical, brought him in contact with men of learning, varied experience, and intellectual ability; travel to American cities opened vistas of museums, art galleries, and churches, mental and spiritual stimulation, which, as usual, Mary could only experience vicariously in her husband's retelling. At Baltimore and elsewhere, he was invited to preach; in Philadelphia he heard a fine sermon at the Methodist Episcopal Church and it was given by a woman.

With a railway pass from William Gooderham, Jr, he had visited Chicago in 1872, a year after the fire, and while praising the inhabitants' energy and self-confidence, but viewing them with the preacher's eye, he had written home to his wife: 'In the eager and almost insane pursuit of wealth lies their danger. There must be an inner life of the people which conceals itself from the stranger ...' What was not concealed was the lawlessness and violence, and this theme of the United States as a violent and volatile society at times, although at other times seen as a land of great opportunity and promise, recurs in family correspondence. On this occasion, a nervous householder, wife of a Methodist minister, had slammed the door in his face, having mistaken his umbrella for a weapon.

Over the years, at Mary's urgings, he had paid brief visits to his father, that unsatisfactory figure who after his wife's death went to live in Port Huron in Michigan with his daughter. Some years previously, it too had come in for uncomplimentary remarks by Caroline Gibbs when her cook Eliza had gone there to keep house for her brothers: 'She says she walked thirty miles and blistered her feet. The beautiful Huron city she was going to has six houses, chairs without backs, no potatoes to be had for money or love, flour $12. per bbl ... No place for worship.'

On one holiday during the happy, carefree early years at Goderich, minister and wife had set out together on a trip across Lake Huron, but the ferry impaled itself on a rocky ledge, suspending its passengers over sixty feet of water for three days until they were rescued. However, Mary's holidays usually depended on excursion tickets to the houses of relations, where, far from repining, she enjoyed herself. She knew her place, it seems, in the scheme of things, although she longed now for a church in Toronto where the family could all be together, a dream abetted by hints and assurances from her husband's colleagues as to the editorship of the *Guardian*, but, as dreams do, it died: 'It is hardly likely that we shall ever know what it is to have a home of our own in this world,' she told her sister Sarah.

In their second winter on the Napanee circuit, the deep snows and storms of February made her husband's pastoral rounds exhausting; the horse had long since disappeared from the accounts: 'Stormed all day, could not get out,' he entered in his diary and a few weeks later added: 'Thoroughly worn out. Went after service to Bro. James' and scarcely felt able to go home.' Napanee had bowed to the depression that affected all North America, so that the Quarterly Returns in the spring of 1876 could not pay the minister's salary, and on May 8th Mary wrote to Sarah: 'I am weary and must close. Mr B. is poorly & feels like sitting down if poverty did not stare him in the face.' One month later, she sent her husband at Conference an ultimatum: 'No money yet. I don't intend asking for it if I never get it, but if you don't do business on better principles another year, I will not promise to be as enduring as I have been.' As the November Quarterly Meeting approached, she returned to the theme: 'I hope you get what was due, but have my fears.'

Deeply as she sympathized with her husband, she could no longer run the parsonage if this state of affairs continued: 'I say this in no wrong spirit. God only knows what I have endured to be compelled to see anarchy and disorder rampant during the last three years.' It was all too much for her, but some weeks later, as if compunction seized her when she thought of his unrewarded labour and their precarious living, she told him: 'You were never so dear to me as now, and I never loved or admired you for your intrinsic worth as I do at this moment.'

Late at night, writing furiously, he fired off articles on politics, current events, and matters spiritual, 'Nothing So Cheap as Men' and 'What Can Be Done for Our Poor' appearing in December. He had always held that no man could love his neighbour unless he were prepared to make this world a better place for his presence in it. This meant striking off the fetters of every slave on earth, waging ceaseless war on war itself, intemperance, sensuality, and lock, stock, and barrel, on sin. 'I am going to make a bid for the reviewing of the books of Harper & Bros. In the meantime I keep hard at work at the sermons. I am very tired,' he said, and an ever increasing number of town meetings on education, temperance, and other issues as well as meetings at working men's clubs claimed his attention as the Church confronted the growing social problems of the day. But as these issues occupied more of the local mind, it proved harder to interest men or the young in prayer, worship, and revival meetings.

In the domestic sphere, the autumn of 1876 had already delivered a great shock that had brought Mary post-haste to Toronto, where Carrie, their second daughter, now attended school. She had been placed in the care of a widow, a relative of the Reverend W.S.B. In earlier correspondence, this Carrie appeared as a lively affectionate child; she now confronts the reader as headstrong and unmanageable: 'I concluded to let her go where she would have no girls of her own age inviting her out,' Mary had informed Sarah Gooderham, but, unknown to her parents, Carrie had secretly engaged herself in the previous May, one month before her sixteenth birthday, to Donald Downey of Napanee. In November, ostensibly settled in for the school year, she had agreed to elope with him. Eventually, after much argument, heart searching, and final admission that she was beyond their control, her parents gave grudging consent, but the Reverend W.S.B. either could not or would not attend the wedding, which was performed by the Church of England, Donald being adamant on that score.

Donald had some means and assured his mother-in-law that he took all responsibility for Carrie's incompetence as a housekeeper, which must have confirmed any view that he had married a child. She was handed over like a parcel: 'I never remember to have felt such resignation in great trial,' Mary wrote in her diary. 'God forgive all my sins and mistakes in reference to her. She appears different to the rest of my children, less disposed to be governed and no disposition to acquire an education, the consequence is that she is ignorant of even a common school education, can scarcely read or write intelligently. This has been a great grief to me.' No hint of such behaviour has hitherto been breathed, and this Carrie, who now begins her triumphant march through life, sweeping everything before her, has made her escape from the restrictions of poverty, bursting like a butterfly from the chrysalis of the parsonage. Her bewildered parents soon heard that, dressed in the finery Donald lavished upon her, she delighted in being the belle of Napanee balls.

Two years later, taking stock of her deficiencies, she announced her intention to go to school in

England, late in the day as it obviously was, which provoked her brother George to say: 'Donald too might much improve himself by reading closely a couple of hours per day. He should first of all master the English grammar,' and her anxious mother travelled rapidly west from St John's near Montreal, the circuit that followed three years in Napanee. 'These expensive whims must not be cherished. They are all wrong,' said her father, who delivered a lecture on husbands and wives remaining together (without mention that his own wife was frequently absent). He doubted too that Donald could afford this indulgence. Indeed, businesses everywhere were collapsing like a house of cards.

Thwarted in her plans for self-advancement, Carrie refused to eat, lost weight, and afforded her mother an excuse to remain in Napanee far from the circuit of St John's, her present home, if it could be called a home. The visit lasted six months. If Mary failed in her duty to St John's by her ever lengthening visit to Napanee, here she assiduously attended church services and class meetings, often acting as class leader, sending candid appraisals of church, ministers, and local worship home to her husband. One preacher, in particular, a tract distributor on the Welland Canal, earned her severe displeasure: 'On Tuesday afternoon he read extracts from some author that he did not name about shouting, responding, *etc.*, & then lectured about the want of it here ...'

She had some satisfaction in causing Donald's father, a successful grain dealer, to dwell on High and Holy things, or so she thought. Here there was scope for he was known to indulge in liquor, but then he had not the advantage of being Methodist; he was Church of England and he sometimes swore, but the two got on well together and he was heard to say that Mary was no ordinary woman. She basked in this reflected glory, although she reported home with satisfaction that Carrie had stood firm when Donald's father endeavoured to draw her into the arms of the 'Episcopal.'

The circuit Mary was so obviously intent on escaping, St John's on the Richelieu River in the Montreal District, had at first suggested some advantages. 'You will have more time for writing & can be more regular in your habits & perhaps that will improve your health,' she had told her husband, and in this optimistic mood she had arrived there in July of 1877: 'I am struck with the universal politeness of the people, so natural and easy.' This included the large French-speaking population, who erred, however, in other ways: 'Romanism is felt here. Just fancy, croquet playing right under our church windows on Sabbath evening while your Papa was preaching, and Protestants must grin and bear it.' But more to the point, the town soon flagged deep in the depression's grip, and this had followed hard on the heels of a disastrous fire that had destroyed a large number of factories and left many without work.

As the weeks passed, little dispelled either the gloom she soon felt at the distance from friends and family or the loneliness in this small Methodist isle set in a French-speaking Roman Catholic sea. She unburdened herself to Tom: 'I don't know whether it will ever seem much like home to me. I feel terribly homesick at times, have had hard work to keep down the tears, but do not tell all that I feel for fear that I make the others say what is in their hearts.' She could scarcely bring herself to unpack: 'But I suppose we shall be here a year at any rate, unless someone dies and an opening is made in that way ... We are lost here, no newspapers. I tell your Papa we must have the *Mail*.'

No longer viewing life from the vantage point of soul-saving, she said outright that the Church had made a great blunder in this appointment, and although she did not say so, her husband had worked long and hard in the ministry, satisfied his fellow clergy, sat on committees, attended conferences and meetings, served as delegate, reported proceedings to the *Guardian*, written articles for it, and now was appointed to the St John's circuit, which at the time of his arrival had only seventy members. The Methodist Church would have viewed the matter quite differently; he was the right man for the job.

Mary, waiting in Napanee, had seen the advance postings and could not conceal her disappointment: 'Of course, the Kingstonians don't want us or you would have gone there instead of G.' Arrived at St John's, as her husband's first and frankest critic, she said to George: 'As I listened to one of your Papa's best efforts I thought what a pity it was that it should be lost on so few hearers ... I could not help saying to Millie after I came in the house that it was a masterly sermon.' But he was cheerful, as he always was with each new circuit, mindful of God's mercy on them all and occupied in the constant demands of services, sermons, meetings, and visits, scarcely even noticing the general despondency around him; for Millie, too, seemed to wither on the vine. Her mother said: 'It will be desolate enough in the winter for her if she stays.' In spite of the advantages to French, there were no kindred spirits. At Napanee, Millie had spoken vaguely of looking for some way to earn money: 'I don't see how it can be done,' said her mother, 'as there are only a few things open to girls,' no longer alluding to schoolteaching or anything else.

'I begin to have a liking for this place,' Mary admitted as she settled down in St John's, but real or imagined, casting shadows over their time there, her failing constitution and depressed state of mind sent her, on the remains of an inheritance from her father, most of which had gone towards the boys' education, to Caledonia Springs, a spa on the Ottawa, during the whole of August, 'this monotonous place.' She delegated Millie to run the parsonage, but the latter's hard work in the kitchen for a parsonage tea had meagre results; baking was not her forte.

This training at home and at church might be supposed to qualify ministers' daughters as perfect parsonage wives, but no eligible young ministers appeared on the scene or anyone else. Instead Millie kept up her French and began to call herself Amélie. To the end of their days, her parents considered her the cleverest of their children: 'My dear, clever daughter,' said her father, and by now their youngest daughter, Mary, sometimes called Mollie and at others May, at fifteen had begun to have a life of her own on the outer edges of art and poetry.

'It is a very dark day,' the Reverend W.S.B. wrote to Caledonia Springs, although he had just returned from the happiest of outings on Lake Memphramagog with May and Millie, for once released from the coils of duty, he ever showed an infinite capacity for enjoyment. 'I scarcely know one of our people except Mrs Dewar, Mrs Ramsey, who is solvent. My heart is burdened with the thought of them. I feel that it would be selfish and mean in me to think much about my own affairs surrounded by so much suffering.'

As summer flowed into autumn, he returned to the theme: 'It is, I am afraid, likely to be a very hard season in this place, but I hope with the blessing of God by what I can get for my labour here and the little I can earn by writing, we will get through.' He forgot his own troubles in producing articles and editorials on politics and social issues; one entitled 'Left Handed Loyalty,' published in the *Montreal Gazette*, roused the *Globe* to reply in two and a half columns. 'Your father,' Mary told George, 'has sources of comfort and strength within himself, by which he resists the temptation to dwell upon what is despressing, which I have not. The more his spirit is tried by adverse influences, the more does the fortitude of the Christian and the patience of the philosopher display itself.'

In this darkest of backwaters, the minister worked hard at his sermons and in the late hours of night read, as he had for so long, widely and deeply. He had always placed a high premium on education and scholarship, always regretting his own deficiency in this regard. History and philosophy helped to buttress his arguments in the pulpit against what he held to be insidious and pernicious doctrines from earlier free-thinkers now flowing belatedly through the circuits. But while he acknowledged the intimate connection between philosophy and theology, as a minister he strove to render an account of God and never indulged in intellectual entertainment; he was first and foremost a preacher; he expounded the Gospel.

He attacked those who would get rid of the idea of a creator; he held that science and religion are not necessarily antagonistic, that the apparent conflict stems more from a defectiveness in human knowledge, and apropos of Darwin's theory he told the flocks that it mattered little if man came from frog spawn or the dust of the earth: 'It is what we are rather than how we came to be what we are, in which we are most deeply concerned.' In this way, he struggled to keep abreast of new ideas while never wavering from the essential transcendence of his faith, never watering down the message to accommodate the growing latitude of some at least of his listeners. He did not think of himself as a popular preacher telling his congregations what they wanted to hear. His wife believed their present situation a calamity, indeed an insult, but if he had earlier spoken of trying to better himself by crossing the border to the United States, it was for reasons of health or the need to provide adequately for his family that had goaded him on, not the lure of a more fashionable church.

'We have been in the tightest place we were ever in, having neither money or credit,' Mary told Tom. Every minister's proverbial stand-by, living on credit until salaries were paid, proved unavailable in French-speaking St John's with the two English grocers in receivership and no credit available from the French-speaking. Only the aid of the Missionary Society together with a cheque for forty dollars from the Toronto *Mail* belatedly saved them. By March of 1879, six weeks after the Quarterly Meeting, the circuit still owed her husband over a hundred dollars, while assurances or well-intended promises only postponed the reckoning and increased the humiliation of having to remind them. In turn, he could not pay his bills: 'I feel a good deal discouraged,' he wrote to Napanee, 'but I know in whom I have believed and am trying to look to Him.'

This was his reply to Mary, lingering still in Napanee, when she asked for a little money to buy a new bonnet; she had received nothing from him in four months; nothing was forthcoming now. Had it not been for Carrie and Donald's generosity in plying her now with much-needed new shawl, bonnet, and black silk dress, her self-esteem might have suffered more. At last, her husband had to pursue the circuit member on whom such matters as his salary devolved, but from day to day he was put off with excuses: 'Last night he was at a prayer meeting and apologized that he had been so busy during the day that he had not had time to attend to it, but I should have it today, but it is six o'clock and he has not come yet.'

Faith was the talisman to his survival, the constant theme in his sermons; saving souls was still his purpose in life. To increase the little congregation, he introduced Gospel hymns, 'not quite so heavy as our own hymns,' alas to little effect, but he never gave up: 'And I hope, my dear wife, that you are dwelling in the Secret place of the Most High and abiding under the Almighty.' But corporeally she dwelt in Napanee with little inclination to return to St John's, so that her absence as the months passed by gave rise to enquiries in the circuit and surely with a rebuke implied for a minister's wife had a decided role to play, which Mary no longer fulfilled. For who was to lead the ladies' meetings on prayer or fulfil a host of other roles?

On April 28th the minister told his wife that he had received no money at all except five borrowed dollars and a couple of small marriage fees. He had fallen in the winter on icy steps in Montreal and hurt his arm; a visit to the dentist had cost him several teeth; he brooded over his failure as a father, at least so far as Carrie was concerned; and now suddenly the news from Donald in Napanee that Mary bordered on a nervous breakdown, which the latest tidings of their financial situation provoked, galvanized him into action: 'My anxiety as you may suppose was very great about you, and other matters touching our future weighed very heavily upon me. I found it difficult to sleep at night and I felt to the degree that I have never felt before that I was really an old man.' With more determination than was usual with him, he made up his mind to ask for a transfer to Toronto, where George and Tom now invited their parents to live. The Transfer Committee was to meet in Montreal on May 1st. Deliverance was at hand.

Tom said: '... certainly, if you are not worth more to the cause than one may judge from the amount of consideration you get you need not feel anxious about its suffering when you leave.' Mary knew her husband better: 'Your Papa,' she had said earlier, 'would never be happy unless he had ministerial work to do.' Then, in June, prayer and the good offices of James and William Gooderham combined to persuade the people of the Berkeley Street Church in Toronto to call him *nem. con.* to their pulpit. One cloud darkened the welcome tidings; this church still owed the previous minister the large sum of two hundred dollars, but the Reverend W.S.B. could move to Toronto and both sons had been called to the bar, Tom in 1877 and George two years later, the star to which their father had so long hitched his waggon and which had meant such penny pinching. George said: 'I often wonder why it is that I have been so fortunate in having such parents as I have.' Long gone was any talk of the United States.

CHAPTER NINE

THE MORE HER SON GEORGE talked of entering politics, the more Mary attempted to dissuade him, and as his uncles' history unravelled in Oshawa the easier it is to see her point of view. Dearly as she loved her brother T.N., she had cast an increasingly disapproving eye on the machinations of government and politicians of either party, and when the closing of the salt mines at Goderich threw the town into a downward spiral in 1871, she had written to him then: 'I feel thankful for the position you occupy before the public, and earnestly pray that you may be found faithful to those high and holy principles which alone can save you from the blighting and withering influences of political life.' To be sure, high and holy were not words to describe the politics of the day.

'Money is being made by your uncles,' she had informed Tom in January of 1871; Gibbs & Bro. thrived and was to rank as one of the largest mills in the country, producing in time, according to newspaper accounts, one hundred thousand barrels a year. On the other hand, T.N. made frequent references to the heavy cost of grain purchases; moreover, the mid-seventies required considerable capital to equip mills with new machinery in keeping with the technological advances, and by 1875 a select committee of the House of Commons spoke of a depression in the flour-milling industry. Along the way, however, T.N. amassed numerous company directorships and presidencies of financial institutions all over the country. Already vice-president of one bank, after Confederation, when banks expanded considerably, he founded and became first president of another; he was also organizer of a mortgage company and, with the Prime Minister, a founder and director of the country's second insurance company, all these activities being an extension of local business and trade. The men who engaged in producing the country's raw materials, in this case the milling of flour, became financiers as a matter of course.

'I see,' wrote Sir John A. on March 31st, 1871, 'you are getting on very well in Parliament and hope you will continue to do so during the remainder of the Session.' He framed much of the new Bank Act of 1871. His name was well known, the more so as the *Globe* pursued him relentlessly, and some said that George Brown had never forgiven him the defeat in South Ontario. The *Vindicator* was kept busy refuting accusations or counter-attacking.

On March 23rd, 1872, as preparations got under way for the general election of that year, the Prime Minister, alarmed at the extent of annexationist sentiment alive and well at the time, summed up the rationale for his party's continuance in office in a letter to William, who had agreed to run in the North Riding: 'It has been truly said that a party, like a snake, is moved by its tail. The tail of the Grit party is the Annexation section, hence my great anxiety that the Canadian Constitutional party should triumph next summer. With five years more over our heads I think that Confederation will have hardened from gristle into bone, and that no attempts, external or internal, to destroy it would be successful.'

Unfortunately, some of Oshawa's voters, disgruntled workers at the Oshawa Cabinet Factory, were busy condemning William, its president, as an enemy of the working man and of keeping their wages low. Adding further insult to injury, they said that while T.N. treated employees with courtesy, 'such however cannot be said of the President of the [Cabinet] Company, W.H. Gibbs.' Worse still, they were to claim that he released his workers one hour earlier every Saturday prior to the election only to revert to the longer day immediately afterwards.

On August 12th, 1872, Macdonald sent this message to T.N.: 'I understand that the R.C.s [Roman Catholics] in Mara and Rama are not [the word is difficult to read but appears to be "not"] right. Take my advice in my last letter and buy them up like sheep.' On March 22nd, 1872, the Prime Minister had considered this expediency to help William: 'We must take the opportunity,' he told T.N., 'of so readjusting the constituencies as to help our friends.' By these means and *vox populi*, the party won the ridings, their victories celebrated in Oshawa with three torchlight processions, one each for T.N. and William and another for the Prime Minister, who came down in person. Rumblings from the loser in the South Riding had little effect. 'The Grits threaten me with all sorts of things,' T.N. told his sister Mary, '& if the law did not keep them in check w^d do something desperate.'

In the by-election of 1873 that followed T.N.'s appointment to the Cabinet, religious sectarianism played havoc with the hitherto politically faithful, seduced alas by the Liberals at fifty dollars each: 'but the bargain is generally for so much not to vote. Many who were friends of mine when they came to town, left it resolved not to vote.' One week earlier, Macdonald had had a word with the Archbishop, explaining that this was the most Catholic government Canada had ever had or would have. The problem was how to use such information in a constituency with so many Orangemen in it.

To say the least, the government's position was shaky during the Pacific scandal, and, on June 19th, 1873, the Prime Minister impressed upon the candidate the absolute necessity to win, that he must not be beaten, that he should throw in two or three years salary if necessary: 'I know that you will do this as you do not take office for the sake of the emoluments ...' But Gibbs & Bro. had required large infusions of capital, so that T.N. replied he could not afford to spend any money and that too much had been done in that way already, an ambiguous phrase. Ontario millers had incurred losses to American competitors in the Maritimes market; the depression of 1873 in both Canada and the United States had begun; and the cost of T.N.'s Ellesmere Hall still weighed upon him. Railing against the surliness of R.C. voters, complaining of free-spending Liberals steeped in bribery, in which the Conservatives must have been close behind, and labelling Whitby as rotten to the core, he rushed from one corner of the riding to the next.

Hardly had that by-election been won than the loser accused him of tampering with the Whitby voters list and threatened to take him to court, but he seemed unperturbed, sailing on to become Minister of Inland Revenue, and no trial took place for want of evidence. The party suffered a staggering defeat in 1874, and in Oshawa political antipathies plumbed the depths: 'It enters into everything, social, political, financial, municipal. The religious is about the quietest now.' Five weeks later, he was writing to Mary: 'Now it is my house & surroundings that fasten me tightly down. If I had their cost in cash I fancy Oshawa w^d not contain me long, at least so I think now, but then if not that it w^d be something else.'

The party's eclipse in 1874 and its revival in 1876 saw himself and William out and in again, but all was not well in South Ontario in the general election of 1878; local Conservatives were at sixes and sevens questioning the cost of the huge political picnics, said to have been an invention of the Gibbs brothers. 'I think,' said their nephew George, 'Uncle T.N. is pretty safe, but Uncle W.H. is a gone goose.' Their sister

Mary at the parsonage said: 'The fact is the country is being demoralized and both parties are contributing towards it.'

The electorate pronounced both brothers gone geese. Convinced of the justice of their cause, T.N. and William took their opponents to court on charges of bribery and, failing to win their case, proceeded to the Supreme Court on innumerable, and they thought, well-substantiated charges. Only the divided opinion of the Court and the support of Mr Justice Taschereau did something to assuage the disappointment of losing the case. T.N. was never to understand why the R.C.'s had singled himself and William out especially: 'The same sinister influences were at work North and South,' he told Macdonald; 'money and the Catholics did the work.'

The Reverend W.S.B. heard that when T.N. was asked to estimate his expenses in the elections (it is by no means clear how many were implied), he answered that it was in the neighbourhood of thirty-thousand dollars, a sum which would have included the enormous political picnics. The revelation came as a shock to the parsonage: 'What a fool he was to spend so much over the miserable things,' wrote the minister to his wife, 'and what has he to show for it today but the ill will of scores of people by whom he might have been respected and loved?' To which Mary replied she was trying to divert George, under pressure from his uncles, from entering politics: 'I hope no one belonging to me will spend money such a way again. It might have been devoted to much nobler purposes,' she said.

Macdonald repaid his debt to T.N. by making him a senator, but disasters hailed fury-like upon him: a daughter lay mortally ill; his son Charlie in Montreal was declared bankrupt, unable to pay five cents on the dollar; and the economic stagnation that so affected the circuits that they had difficulty in paying their ministers' salaries sapped T.N. and William's fortune. Even a good harvest failed to stimulate business, and the prospect of almost certain profit induced them to invest a quarter of a million dollars (so it was said) in barley: 'I suppose,' Tom wrote to his mother, 'if the season is late this year in closing up they will get it all off their hands at good figures?' The season changed abruptly, and winter came early, freezing the barges in on the Erie Canal, by which the barley had been shipped to New York; the barley was ruined and had to go as ballast to England, a total and disastrous loss without even proper insurance. The firm never recovered: 'If only,' said Tom, 'they had gone out of business a year earlier they would have been wealthy men.'

The debacle in Oshawa was almost complete: Gibbs & Bro. had vanished; the Oshawa Cabinet Company survived, but family fortunes suffered a resounding crash. The brothers' financial entanglements, especially T.N.'s in large land-holdings, mortgaged to the hilt, can only be described as so labyrinthine as to defy unravelling. A few years later, T.N. suffered a stroke and never recovered; rumour had even Ellesmere Hall mortgaged. William moved to Toronto; the sons and daughters to Montreal, Toronto, or the West; one made and lost a fortune in New York. All left the town which T.N. and William had done so much to build, and nothing remains as a reminder of the past but Gibbs Street misspelt as 'Gibb' and the graves in the Union Burial Ground.

T.N. died in April, 1883. The *Vindicator* devoted its entire editorial page to him and said, as obituaries do and without reference to sums spent on elections or the mortgage mess, 'Through adversity and prosperity he maintained a character for unbending integrity, and his word was always as good as his bond.' The mayor ordered all places of business closed on the afternoon of the funeral, the largest ever seen in that part of the country; the sidewalks were crowded with people and the sidestreets filled with carriages as the town and surrounding countryside gathered to pay their respects. The cortège left the church to the last strains of that favourite valedictory, the 'Dead March' in *Saul*; the town council with mourning badges took its place at the head of the procession, which stretched for a mile and a half, and the town bell tolled for his passing. His sister Mary thought of all that was owed to him from the time he had come home as a boy of fourteen from Uncle Philip's school in Devon, steered them all to safety, and never complained of the heavy burdens cast upon him.

Floating like a cork on a troubled sea, William set out to salvage his own unenviable situation. With his eyes on the West, and westward was after all the century's cry, he was on his way to Regina, where the Qu'Appelle and Long Lake Colonization Co., his own and T.N.'s last venture, demanded his attention. They had both jumped at the government's offer of land on fair terms to private companies, with profits based on the number of settlers each succeeded in placing on it. The opening up of land for settlement by the building of the C.P.R. and the misgivings aroused by an expansionist United States gave these undertakings a patriotic cachet.

Loud and cogent objections met the scheme, but applications came from societies, churches, businessmen, senators, and members of Parliament, especially Conservatives. At first the public clamoured for the Qu'Appelle Company's stock, but soon all the companies ran into trouble. William spent a great deal on the venture, introducing every amenity only to discover belatedly, as did other companies, that the land was arid, and on July 19th, 1887, he wrote to Macdonald asking for compensation for himself and his son Willie, who had acted as manager: 'This means almost ruin to us two ... This (confidentially entre nous) is all we have left in the world.' Eventually, the government came to terms with all the land companies, including the Qu'Appelle, but William had lost a great deal of money.

From Toronto as alderman, a position not to be compared with his former elevation to Parliament, but with dreams of returning to Ottawa, William asked the Prime Minister for a place in the Senate as his due, each letter more importunate than the last, to which he received no reply: 'To say that I was greatly disappointed in not finding my name amongst the lately appointed senators would but faintly express all I felt,' he told Macdonald on February 2nd, 1884. On March 23rd, 1885, he wrote again: 'If not too much trouble kindly drop me a telegram confirming my appointment when I shall proceed at once to Ottawa to take my seat.' He mustered arguments in his favour, the chief being what it had cost Gibbs & Bro. over the years to devote so much time and money to enter politics, referring on February 2nd, 1884, to his own and T.N.'s 'unswerving devotion to yourself and party.'

Losing hope for himself, he proposed his son Willie as senator in his place and added pointedly that Willie declined to be a candidate for the Commons, having both the fear and experience of his uncle's and his father's political life before him. On this note of grievance, regret, and disillusionment, William ended his political career; in Toronto, his business acumen restored some wealth and self-esteem.

Oshawa receded into the past. James Lobb, husband of Mary's sister Amelia, had long forsaken it when William's department store succumbed to the general drift of business to Toronto, and here he too had turned alderman, as well as Lloyds agent and commission merchant, until the conviction seized him that he was a sinful and God-dishonouring man, which drove him to melancholia and suspected suicide (the reader will notice the number of such deaths and there are more to follow). 'Poor man,' said Mary, 'he felt the vanity of everything that this world offered him and how vain his pursuits had been.' And Mr Holt, widower now of her sister Emily, as if in fulfilment of William's indictment, appeared in directories as builder, well driller, contractor, and even carpenter until he too disappears from view. But his son, James, immediately climbed back up the social ladder.

Toronto bloomed in the last decades of the century; adventurous young men came up from the country, Tom and George amongst them. The former, having passed his final law examinations well, now hung around the town Micawberlike, said George, waiting for something to turn up but finding few chances in the city, which was already overcrowded with lawyers. He opened an office and then entered a partnership in a firm that did a good business: 'Everyone seems to think that I made a good move in forming this alliance for the time at least.'

Mary had once expressed the hope of seeing both her sons follow in their father's footsteps as Methodist ministers 'standing,' she said in appropriate language, 'before men as ambassadors from the Court of Heaven.' But it was in the courts of law in Toronto that they now stood, bent on the pursuit of justice (and incidentally of wealth), and since the course of parenthood never has run smooth, some of Tom's views caused consternation.

Though fairly constant, his attendance at church in Toronto while his parents were still at Napanee had failed to satisfy his mother: 'He appears to think reason is guide enough for him.' His father had echoed the sentiment: 'One thing thou lackest. You have not, I am afraid, given your heart fully to God.' George proved more amenable, until the strain of concentrated study took its toll. 'Poor fellow, he has sadly over done himself,' said his father. Indeed George, who showed for the first time his Achilles' heel, readily admitted: 'I was in such a terrible state that I actually rose and prayed for death.' He lapsed into a religious mania which Tom, lodging with him, found hard to bear and which was to return even more forcefully later on.

'Now, as you hope for the mercy of God yourself, do not say one word driving him from his moorings,' their father warned Tom angrily. '... From your sentiments in your letter to your mother, I differ in toto. Religion makes no one insane, but it saves countless thousands from insanity. It is the devil that wrecks people.' A statement that brooked no argument.

Religion was becoming a private affair, and Tom had entered into a sphere very different from the concerns of circuits and small towns. His independent stand dismayed his parents, especially as the partnership he had joined did not meet with their approval: 'The business is not the kind to make a first rate man such as he is well able with a fair chance to become,' said his father, but others had congratulated him on this step up the ladder. He explained to his mother: 'I find in matters of business the one thing that pleases friends is success and one is generally the best judge of how that is to be obtained for himself.'

A year later he boasted: 'Business goes well with me,' but rumour, fanned by Aunt Sarah, said that Tom smoked and drank; someone else reported him the worse for wear after a cousin's wedding. Mary wrote to George: 'It is so distressing to refer to a matter that I did hope no child of mine would ever give me an hour's anxiety about.' The partnership was to blame;

he must have been led astray, and his mother now remembered sundry remarks he had made long ago about his liberty and not being dictated to; she worked herself up into the nervous state that helped to end her visit to Napanee.

The hateful partnership soon terminated. Tom joined Beatty, Chadwick & Biggar: 'For this,' said Mary, 'he is indebted to his Uncle Gooderham and of course is greatly pleased.' She knelt down and thanked God: 'I can't understand how it is that he so readily takes up with a certain class of people.' His Aunt Sarah Gooderham, whose favourite he was, expressed shock when she heard him say that he would be quite satisfied with the rewards of this life: 'Don't indulge in it,' said his mother, 'as it has a bad influence upon yourself and leaves wrong impressions upon others.' George expressed no such disturbing views and in the world beyond the circuits of Napanee and St John's, restored now in health, he was making his mark, already a member of the firm of Rose, Macdonald & Merrit, lionized by hostesses for his handsome looks, quick wit, and skill as a speaker. He told his parents: 'I am invited to Senator McMaster's tonight.'

The large Gooderham clan had welcomed Tom into their homes ever since his arrival in the city as a schoolboy. Aunt Sarah had early seen that he admired Hattie, the eldest daughter of George Gooderham, and now as his reputation and law practice grew, she saw nothing to hinder a match. Mary informed her husband: 'Sarah says she told Tom he might as well get some of the nice girls with money as anybody else and added there is H.G.' But Tom told his mother: 'I should have endeavoured to make an impression long ago but that takes all confidence away from me.' Aunt Sarah pooh-poohed this reticence, saying he had a profession, rich and respectable relations, and moreover was the son of a minister. His father said: 'Tom is a goose if he does not go in and win that nice girl.'

In the autumn of 1879, at the news of their engagement, Mary said: 'The best part of it is that she is a treasure in herself. I doubt if anyone could be found that would please me as well. I suppose she must have faults for all have them but no one seems to know what hers are. Universal testimony is that those who know her best, love her the most.' A quarter of a century later, she had not changed this view: 'I love her more and more as the years go by, so conscientious in everything.' Sarah, whose intellectual purview was narrow, said that Hattie had a good mind but had spoiled herself reading novels, a description no one else would have recognized.

The wedding took place in January of 1880 at the bride's home on Trinity Street, and although still in mourning for a sister who had died recently in childbirth, Hattie wore a scarlet taffeta wedding dress. The honeymoon was spent at Niagara Falls. An allowance from her father enabled the young couple to begin married life at Gerrard and Berkeley Streets, and within a few years, as Tom's practice expanded, they moved around the corner to the more elegant world of Sherbourne Street.

George's nuptials, however, caused quite a stir. He had been courting a young lady of whom his Aunt

Sarah spoke most highly. His mother thought she showed intelligence, good common sense, discriminating thought, and piety, altogether a most desirable daughter-in-law. Such was not to be. Without forewarning came the announcement of George's engagement to Emma Moulton Fraser, stepdaughter of Senator McMaster and daughter of a late Bay City, Michigan, tycoon. After this whirlwind courtship, but who whirled whom it is difficult to say, their wedding took place in Bay City, but scarcely had it done so when a long poem entitled 'The Mysterious Wedding' appeared in the Toronto *Grip*:

> Have you heard the latest sensation?
> The astounding event of the day?
> No! – You don't even look interested;
> Miss Fitzmillion was married today.

The poem was exceedingly apt and the sixth verse ran:

> The bridegroom, you say? Why young Rackbrain
> Good-looking, but poor as a rat:
> Though a lawyer, and highly connected;
> With cleverness, brains and all that.

In this vein it continued for eight more verses, taking care to note that young Rackbrain 'not three weeks ago was engaged to Miss Anna Melrose.' Three days later, an apology appeared in the *Mail*, explaining that the publisher of the *Grip* had not known that this poem was based on actual circumstances, thus drawing even more attention to it. This courtship had not reached the stage of an engagement, but nevertheless it had been unceremoniously terminated. Hardly a day passed without Mary's prayers that the young lady in question, whose name was indeed Annie, might find a good husband and suffer no loss from being so embarrassingly and publicly jilted.

Emma's stepfather, Senator McMaster, eminently successful as banker and trader, a Baptist and a Liberal, offered George no political support, in which direction lay George's aspirations, but he must have opened innumerable doors for him through social and business contacts. Still, George hoped to inherit his Uncle T.N.'s mantle, and by 1884 he was asked to contest the provincial by-election in Lennox for the Conservatives. His mother said: 'If you had consulted me before consenting, I should have said "don't accept it," very decidedly. I hope that you will go into this contest with faith in God believing that He takes cognizance of what is done at elections as well as what is done at church conferences and synods and that He will hold you to strict account for the manner in which you influence people morally.' George lost, but only by forty-two votes, established his reputation as a speaker, and caught the local imagination sufficiently to have a hamlet named after him.

In 1887 in the Parliamentary riding of West Durham, traditionally Liberal, he ran against Edward Blake, the leader of the party, and lost again but with a fairly good showing. If in the country as a whole the Conservatives won a small majority, they were still in trouble over Riel, the continued depression, and the failure to attract settlers to the West. From now on, George was sufficiently in the public eye to be lampooned as 'Pompey,' appearing in a caustic poem, 'Pomp de Scallawag, His Temptation and Fall,' which began:

> In Blackstock town there dwelt in state a darkey known to fame,
> Who bore, with lardy-dardy grace, the fascinating name
> Of Pompey Pushcart Blackamoor de Scallawag Esquire,
> An unsophisticated black, a most atrocious liar,
> A lowly born philanthropist, who often came to grief,
> 'Bekase de white trash swar I hab de mohals ob a tief.'

This continued for twelve inspired verses.

Lovely, wealthy Emma entertained on a lavish scale in their Jarvis Street house; a talented pianist, she spent her days practising (later the piano was to drive George out of the house), but for the present the range of George's acquaintances grew as did his law practice by leaps and bounds and so too his fame. Suddenly, in 1887 after the briefest of illnesses, their eldest child, a little boy of six, died of diphtheria, from the shock of which Emma never recovered. Two months later, the same epidemic caused the death of Tommie, whose portrait we knew so well in the nursery of '79.' He was four years old, the second of Tom and Hattie's children. At first the doctor wrongly diagnosed the case and too late performed a tracheotomy.

The parents, banished from the sick room, waited through the sad night: 'Dear Hattie lies on the library lounge beside me,' Tom wrote to his father, 'while upstairs is our darling Tommie in a death struggle with the dread diphtheria and not expected to last till morning ... He was a typical boy, a regular Hotspur, loving and beloved. On Sunday he asked me several times: "Pa, won't you take me where the oranges blossom?" Dear Soul, he will go where they are ever in bloom.' Hattie added a paragraph which Mary felt few mothers could have penned in the circumstances, but the Reverend W.S.B. wrote in his diary that it would be hard work to comfort the parents: 'What can one say in such terrible circumstances? The Lord bind up the broken hearts.' The house on Sherbourne Street was closed, and two years later Hattie took the children, Billy, Lizzie, and the newborn baby, to England, where she remained for two years, and Tom crossed the Atlantic back and forth.

The Reverend W.S.B.'s itinerant life had already ended with the move to Toronto, where, with the help of his sons, he had a home and an adequate income. The last seven years of his ministry, active and happy, were spent in city churches until a bout of typhoid fever forced his superannuation. From Berkeley Street Church, he moved to Riverside, and from there to King Street, each representing a very different section of society: the first, prosperous; the second, of modest means; and the third, working-class poor. By this time, Toronto was known as the city of churches, 'Toronto, the Good,' but in the world beyond, the Church was being assaulted on all sides.

His active duties ceased as a movement took hold of the Methodist Church embracing new social and political solutions in the face of the increasing poverty of industrialized cities; the social gospel predominated. If he adhered still to the old Wesleyan outlook, the essential conservatism of Irish Methodists, he denounced conditions in Toronto slums, the poverty of her unemployed and of her immigrants. He flailed un-Christian racial discrimination, especially as he saw it operating in the United States. He lamented the abandonment of religion in the public schools, which he feared would lead in the end to mayhem in the young of a country that no longer feared God or kept His commandments.

He turned his attention to such movements as the final union of the Methodists. He wrote on the theological, political, and social issues of the day. He crossed swords in whatever party with theorists, visionaries, and men of doctrinaire views; he waged war at times with Goldwin Smith, dubbing him 'notre grand littérateur' whenever the latter preached that Canada's destiny was to join the United States. Patriotism, love of country, and allegiance to the Crown were not badges publicly displayed, but deeply felt though seldom spoken, and if at one time ill health and poverty had made the Reverend W.S.B. contemplate a move to the United States, his mother's country, his heart was Canadian and therefore British. He wrote with pride of the Union Jack, which had braved the battle and the breeze for a thousand years, even if this was somewhat of an exaggeration, and in extolling the bravery of those Canadians of an earlier generation than his own who had fought in the War of 1812, he made the point, as he always did, that they fought for King and Country.

Mary's respect for Macdonald never dimmed. In Philadelphia, which she was visiting in 1891, she heard of his imminent death: 'I don't feel like sightseeing under the shadow of such a national sorrow,' she said. 'I have just bought an evening paper,' she told her husband next day, 'and see that Sir John is worse. I am sure that there will be grieving and weeping throughout the country and many prayers offered for him.' He died on that day, and she was overwhelmed with sadness.

The Reverend W.S.B. fired off articles on temperance and Sabbath observance, as Sabbatarian as ever. He had long entered into sectarian disputes, aiming his darts at new papal claims or High Anglican pretensions, and he never outgrew his early Irish Protestant origins. He reviewed books for a number of newspapers and journals as well as producing articles on theology, politics, philosophy, history, and travel, which, if not exceptional, were thoughtful and at times provocative, and although unequal now to pastoral work, his first love, he was happy. Mary enjoyed a tranquillity she had never known.

He loved London: 'I observed,' he wrote there one day, 'that it sits astride the Thames as usual, that it is as full of contrasts as formerly, the rich and the poor ... here are the highest style of people on the earth, and the very lowest, and they separate from each other by the thickness of an egg-shell. There is much food for thought in this.' He travelled through France, then Italy and Greece, with his store of poetry in mind; he described at length the contents of museums and galleries, his letters testifying to a lifetime of reading; and as an indefatigable tourist in Egypt and the Holy Land, his outlook was scarcely to be reconciled with the provincialism of his early days. He missed no opportunity to mingle with Egyptians, and when a Copt merchant invited him into his home, he found a world he could enjoy. But if the unhappy lot of Egypt's poor and of its women aroused his sympathy and disapproval, at the same time he was vigorously denouncing any attempts at women's entry into politics at home.

At shrines and archaeological sites in the Holy Land and in Greece when he fell in with foreign clergy or scholars, he frequently turned to the ancient Greek that he had studied in lonely vigils at the parsonages. The hours of reading he had devoted late at night to the furtherance of the Heavenly Kingdom and his own secret pleasure bore rich fruit now as he toured the ancient world. For these happy years, he had Tom to thank: 'Our dear, generous, unselfish and noble son.'

Mary accompanied him on several trips to England and found her Aunt Elizabeth Blake, the last member of her father's family, still vigorous at eighty-three. She saw once more poor Carrie Dixon, the daughter of Mary and Silvanus Gillard of Kingsbridge, who had lived in Oshawa with her aunt and uncle calling them Ma and Pa: 'She is the same good creature that ever she was.' Wan and careworn, she lived in fear of ending her days in the workhouse, for Mr Dixon had ventured into farming until seven years of bad harvest had ruined him, history continually repeating itself in his affairs until one last and different glimpse has him, now a widower, comfortably ensconced in a small country cottage where he conducted experiments in science, his life-long passion, and lived with his daughters, who had taken courses at the National School of Cooking to fit them as instructors.

Once more, how far this is from the royal schoolroom where Thomas Gibbs's second cousin had been tutor to the Prince of Wales. Mary and the Reverend W.S.B. learned that Mr Dixon's elder daughter Minnie regularly attended revival meetings by Welsh ministers, and had just paid a visit to the grave at Saltash in Cornwall of her grandfather, Silvanus Gillard, who had once been a Baptist minister there long ago. And so, all things have a beginning and an end.

At home the Reverend W.S.B., as president of the Theological Union of Victoria College, a director of the *Canadian Methodist Quarterly*, and member of several historical societies, found himself much in demand as a public speaker, so that Mary said to one of her daughters: 'I never see any one but members of my own family and your father is busy writing from morning till night and consequently sees few people too.' She visited health spas and Holiness Meetings, attended the Woman's Missionary Society, never ceased to attribute the dullness of life and lack of opportunity to discrimination against women, and spent most of her time digesting newspapers for their social, political, and religious content.

She welcomed the Doukhobors to Canada as the best kind of settlers and observed that the religious press in the United States had made no protest against the Cuban-American War: '... they are being deluded with the idea that humanitarian considerations influence them, when sugar trusts and commercial interests have been and are at the bottom of the whole thing.' And just as in the darkest days of the past when her two brothers had come to her aid, her elder son looked after his parents now. She said to her husband: 'Dear Thomas's kindness has made it very different from what it might have been.'

Nevertheless, she wrote in her diary: 'The ambitions of my dear children have been limited too much to this world; wealth, fame and pleasure having been the main objects of pursuit ... I see and hear of others combining both the temporal and the spiritual interests of their fellows but mine are not in it. They do not consider the poor, or stretch out their hands to the erring and fallen, as I desire to see them do, or as I believe God intended them to do.' And the Reverend W.S.B. looked with alarm at the ever widening gap in the United States between a few immensely rich men and the poor, but he is silent on the steady accumulation of wealth, albeit on a Lilliputian scale in comparison, by his sons; he kept no regular diary now into which he could pour his private thoughts. Tom had already slipped quietly over to the Church of England as being more congenial than Methodism, attending St Peter's Church on Carlton Street. Behind him sat the Mohawk, Oronhyatekha, whom Father well remembered.

Mary viewed the world from Homewood Avenue, a home – thanks to Tom – she could call her own now that the musical chairs of ever changing parsonages receded into the past, and she could enjoy occasional travels to alleviate boredom. If the *Missionary*

Outlook was to call her intellectually highly gifted, it also was to say that she suffered much from ill health, which as I review her life seems to have served her well at times.

Nearby in town her sister Sarah Gooderham, who had so often provided sanctuary for Mary and the children at both Meadowvale and Streetsville, delved deeply into church activity and good causes. James Gooderham's untimely and unfortunate end on the Credit Valley Railway had indirectly promoted his widow to a higher sphere on earth, although Sarah reminded others: 'the light has gone out of my heart and home.' She devoted herself to the Methodist Church as the first president of the Woman's Missionary Society, an office she held for fifteen years, and she sat on the boards of the Girls Home, the Boys Home, The Haven, and the YWCA. When the University of Toronto refused to grant professional degrees to women, she was one of the founders of the Toronto Women's Medical College, and ten years later in 1893 for a brief time, one of the founders of the National Council of Women of Canada. But while she expressed sympathy for women, 'downtrodden women' she frequently said, she was no suffragette. The goal was to serve God and the Church.

Sarah spent her life alleviating the distress and poverty she saw around her; she also saw, as did all the churches, greater scope for conversion in far-flung fields. In 1882 she pressed for the Woman's Missionary Society to found a girl's school in Japan, saying: 'I will contribute even to the lessening of my principal in the bank.' For Great-Great-Grandfather

Gooderham's will still rankled within her; she had not inherited James's share of the estate, and as she carefully explained in the following year to the young woman sent out by the Society to take charge of the school, her resources were limited: '... you know that the death of my beloved husband before his father has disappointed any dreams I had in doing much in that way except by self-denial, but like yourself I have been trained to that.' Sarah was quite well off.

The school, situated in Tokyo, was attended by the daughters of upper- and middle-class parents, as well as some poor non-fee-paying students, and it achieved instant success. It also grew into a centre of evangelism, as was to be hoped, and while conversion was not obligatory, the record shows that many pupils embraced Christianity. Five years later, at the invitation of the Japanese government, the Methodist Church of Canada decided to found a girls' school at Shidzuoka. In 1892, during a visit to Japan at their own expense, Sarah and another member of the Woman's Missionary Society, Elizabeth Strachan, made their way to Shidzuoka, leaving Tokyo by train and proceeding in springless carriages by jolts and lurches up a mountain, passing the night at a country inn, and by day viewing exciting scenery.

Here two young women missionaries had been planted: '... the only foreigners,' wrote Mrs Strachan, 'living in this province of four hundred thousand inhabitants, which speaks well for their courage and devotion to duty and is no less creditable to the law-abiding friendly attitude of the people.' The trip was a complete success, and at home the members of the

Society congratulated themselves, but trouble was in the air. Not unexpectedly, such proselytizing began to rouse the ire of Buddhists, for whom it had a tinge of *lèse-majesté*. Moreover, anti-foreign sentiment was on the increase in Japan.

Sarah's zeal to emancipate Asian women from their all too obvious physical and spiritual bondage, from the cruelties and hardships they bore, was of a piece with her outspoken condemnation of discriminatory legislation against Asians in Canada and the United States, which, she said, so falsified the teachings of Christ. She described the plight of women in the East in forceful language: 'She is usually unwelcomed at birth, uneducated in childhood, neglected in sickness, compelled to marry, divorced for trifles, accursed in widowhood, unlamented at death, and despised as unworthy of immortality.' But in her address to the Society in 1892, Sarah stated emphatically that women everywhere (and surely this included Canada, too, where Sarah's sister Mary talked of discrimination against women) had to be taught that they were more than chattels wholly at the disposal of their male relations. The theme is constant.

On their return journey from Japan, the two women made a detour into the back reaches of British Columbia to view Indian schools under the aegis of the Methodist Church. They visited three Christian Indian villages, which they held to be the very model of neatness and prosperity in contrast with any other native village with its confusion, disorder, and poverty (according to the Missionary Society report for that year). One can visualize them on their tour of inspection. If the Society with all the churches contributed to the destruction of native culture, it by no means follows that Aunt Sarah or her ilk had any firm idea of our own culture, and if she went so far as to further her niece May's ambitions to appear on the stage, I doubt if drama or the arts were high in her list of priorities.

In defence of the churches, let it be said that they attempted to open for the native peoples the door to equality where there is no distinction of race or colour, to arrest their decline in the face of ever more aggressive white settlement, and by arming them with education to protect them from the ever more grasping white commercial interests. But chiefly the churches were obeying the Gospel command to go into all the world and preach the Gospel to the poor.

When Sarah was old but still undaunted, the Methodist Church sent her as its representative to London in 1899 to attend the British Women's Temperance Association, albeit she bore the name of a very large distillery. But at home she felt rather lonely; one of her nieces said that her seventieth birthday had come and gone: 'she had no word from anyone.' When she died, her will was contested (I think it was by her sister Amelia's family) on the grounds that in her last years, while of unsound mind, she had been unduly influenced by the beneficiaries, which of course was soon noised about the town.

For all her selfless courage and hard work, one scene remains in my mind, her nephew George's remarks as a schoolboy about his Aunt Sarah's sitting in a corner cogitating over her aches and pains while his Uncle James danced attention on her. And later on, Mary had admonished George: 'I would not, if I were in your place, make any remarks about Aunt Sarah,' reminding him that there were plenty of people ready to comment on her peculiarities without family doing it too. What they were is left unsaid, but there is one happy if tenuous link with this great-great-aunt; at 79 Prince Arthur Avenue as children, we used to turn over with great care the cloth pages of the illustrated children's stories in Japanese that she had once brought home for our parents.

As for Mary's sister Amelia Lobb, her large family spread over the continent; one son left for a career in Ceylon and another, according to old Cousin Marion, who after all was Amelia's daughter, dispatched his wife in a drunken brawl in British Columbia at the end of the last century. I think he got off on the extraordinary plea of provocation or self-defence. In Newmarket, Joseph Collins died, loaded with local honours as a patriarch in spite of the idiosyncracies that had annoyed his brothers-in-law in Oshawa, and everyone said how old and wrinkled Caroline Collins looked. But they had made the same remark thirty years earlier at the death of her dear son John; the black border on her bonnet then had made her look so old, and she was only forty-one at the time. Children loved her, and in the nineties Tom, our grandfather, used to take his children, my father amongst them, to Newmarket to visit the aunt who had been so kind to him in his childhood when his mother was ill or there was no parsonage ready to house him.

CHAPTER TEN

With plenty of time to ponder the mysteries of existence, Mary became ever more introspective. She lamented her own failure as a mother, or so she thought, as Millie's indispositions grew more frequent: 'Millie is better again,' she said, 'that is better for her ... she is very averse to being the subject of conversation.' But in the privacy of Homewood Avenue this daughter held court to her own thoughts. There are different kinds of freedom. To many it seemed that Millie had retreated into the servitude of family and domesticity. On the contrary, she had defeated any attempts to channel her into hated schoolteaching, although others said she was a born teacher. She had likewise turned a blind eye to any other possible career and enjoyed the freedom to create her own intellectual world. The parsonage had always set a high priority on learning and the art of conversation.

Much later on, no longer interested in matrimony, if ever she had been, Millie had an admirer, a professor of German at the Berlitz School. As for her sister Carrie, whom anonymous letters in the 1880s informed of Donald's infidelities, she made her escape from Napanee, but in spite of drink and debts his promises to reform lured her back again until the pattern repeated itself and she fled to California, always blessed throughout her life with innumerable friends of either sex who flocked to her aid.

With Tom's help, Carrie made for London, where she left no stone unturned for her own advancement, introducing herself immediately to the relation who had been tutor to the Prince of Wales. He treated her with much kindness and without a trace of condescension. And then, against all the laws of probability, she returned once more to Donald, revelations of whose behaviour had thoroughly shocked his mother-in-law. Mary said, however: '... I have never forgotten the uniform kindness and consideration with which you have treated me. I shall never forget it no matter what the future shall be.'

The future, however, brought his broken pledges, and he seduced a girl in Napanee, who was now with child, a story in everybody's mouth. People turned their backs on him in the street. Carrie's mortification was great. At last her deliverance came by his sudden, mysterious, and complete disappearance, never to be seen or heard of again. Seven years later, at her brothers' insistence, she rid herself of him by divorce, which in those days could be secured only by means of a bill through the Senate in Ottawa.

Sketching and music drew Mary and the Reverend W.S.B.'s youngest daughter, May, into a circle of young artists and writers attracted to a burgeoning Toronto, which had begun to show an interest in English Canada's literary and artistic growth. She soon made the acquaintance of the poet Archibald Lampman, a life-long friend. Her ambition fixed on the stage; she studied elocution. 'Who knows,' she confided to a brief diary, 'when the time comes they may even be willing for me to be an actress. I live in hopes.' George's wife, Emma, invited her to give recitations at evening parties, and May went through a Pre-Raphaelite phase, arriving at dinner parties with her long hair entwined with flowers and flowing loose, which raised local eyebrows. But no career resulted from her study of drama in New York at Aunt Sarah's expense in 1887, and in the following year, on the Island of Jersey, where her sisters and her parents spent the winter – 'Thank God for a dear kind Tom,' said Mary – May announced her engagement to Herbert McKeggie of Barrie, Ontario. 'I hope that he has a good record in the past,' her mother entered in a diary. 'I have had such a relation from dear Carrie of Donald's vileness as has made me feel that too much care cannot be taken.'

With her friend Elinor Sutherland, whom she had known at home in Canada and whom the world was later to know as the daring (for those days) novelist Elinor Glyn, May left for a tour of England and parts of Europe, where the two young women knocked with some success on the doors of writers or the celebrated. Elinor's romantic, passionate novels soon earned her this well-known jingle:

> Would you like to sin with Elinor Glyn
> On a tiger skin?
> Or would you prefer to err with her
> on some other fur?

May's wedding, attended by the royal tutor, took place in London, and May made her home in Barrie, now a small town of considerable pretensions, an outpost of respectability: 'I shall have a good plain home and a kind loving husband,' she said. Well off, the owner of a bank with branches in nearby towns, and reputed to be the most successful private banker in the province, Herbert like Mr Holt was a staunch Reformer. At Inglenook, May devoted her time to painting and the entertainment of artistic and literary friends. Here music, poetry, and art orbited in her little salon, where all were travellers in the mind, but these leanings gave her a slightly bohemian reputation, which did not sit well with Herbert's family. They were later to accuse her of stealing their family Bible, which all the while reposed in their family vault, and, so Mary said, of 'other things too mean to mention.'

Writers, artists, and poets found a welcome at Inglenook, amongst them Archie's sister, Annie Lampman, to whose training in Germany in the early nineties as a concert pianist Herbert McKeggie was handsomely contributing until a letter arrived in which Annie's mother told of other plans. After years of study, Annie was engaged to marry, but the gentleman's refusal to countenance any career dashed Mrs Lampman's hopes of seeing Annie become an ornament to Canada 'in the divine art we both love,' by which she meant May. The mother also cautioned May to say nothing about the engagement, which was by no means secure; there had already been several others that had evaporated: '... she has been most unfortunate in these affairs before and the publicity was most unpleasant to say the least.'

This engagment also came to nothing until the final one to another gentleman. The Reverend W.S.B. attended the wedding, which took place at a lakeside country church, and before the service began the bride and groom locked its doors in order to achieve the maximum privacy. Immediately after the ceremony, dispensing with any reception and already dressed for the occasion, they descended the church steps to enter a canoe laden with tent and baggage, sailing off on a wilderness honeymoon. 'I hope,' said the Reverend W.S.B., 'the husband is not altogether too ethereal as Mr J. is of a highly nervous and artistic temperament, a disciple of Count Tolstoi withal. I should imagine that their style of living will be one of severe simplicity.' It was also noisy; they returned to settle down to a life of music and two pianos in the house. But Annie was greatly talented and in the face of many obstacles had shown perseverance and courage; had she remained longer in Germany, she might indeed have become an ornament to Canada.

In her growing circle of interesting friends, May reached out and touched the stirrings of a national culture, which in her own way she tried to foster, but fate intervened now to disrupt the rhythm of her days. Father's older sister, Lizzie, could remember being sent as a child to Barrie in the nineties to keep her

Aunt May company when Uncle Herbert would meet the train with his cutter, and on the rapid ride to Inglenook the clinking sound of bottles beneath the great buffalo robes could be distinctly heard. They told a tale, and Lizzie needed no second bidding to enter into a complicity of silence with her uncle.

In time May's visits to Toronto grew more frequent, at seeming odds with her idyllic life: 'My dear little Wife,' said Herbert, all the while caught up in stock fever and losing heavily on the New York Exchange. He sold the bank and died suddenly; the local paper praised him, rumours of bankruptcy and suicide circulated, and an impossible will so entangled what was left of his estate that when bequests had been made, there was nothing left for May. Without Tom's help, she would have been destitute, and while she had long followed the contemporary craze for photography, in which she seems to have excelled – she had her own darkroom at Inglenook – she lacked the drive and ambition that characterized her sister Carrie ever since her departure from Donald and Napanee. May turned down an invitation to join a New York firm specializing in society portraits. Still, her work appeared in salons and exhibitions, and many thought her quite talented.

George's wife, Emma, had sufficient talent as a pianist to be invited, although the date is not certain, by John Philip Sousa to join his band, but this it seems was quickly squelched by her mother, Mrs McMaster. As her marriage began to founder, and in order to annoy George, Emma often arranged musical evenings if she knew he had a big law case on the following day. She now wandered far, in the hope of assuaging her grief after her little boy's death, to New York, Newport, and Newburg, where her mother moved on the edges of American society, and to Britain, France, Norway, and Russia: 'Pray for me, dear George,' she wrote, 'that the bitterness of our loss may be taken away.' And although she wrote 'dearest George' and signed herself his truly loving Emma, 'I miss you so much,' her plans made no mention of a return to home or children. 'My dear, dear George, only He who seeth in secret, knows how I regret my foolish, frivolous, ill spent life.'

George's career advanced at a dizzying rate as barrister at court, where few could rival him. Briefs came pouring in, and as lawyer for the C.P.R. (both he and Tom were Q.C.'s now), engaged in 1889 in the British Columbia boundary case and in the following year in the Birchall case as defending counsel, he established himself as one of the country's best-known criminal lawyers, with a reputation as a spellbinding orator. All this may have owed something to his father's talent as a preacher. George's fame spread far, and in spite of his record of electoral defeats Conservative ridings pursued him eagerly as candidate; one more defeat lay in store. West Durham again nominated him in the election of 1891, a meeting, so the newspapers observed, attended by an unusually large number of females. His mother said: 'I quite expect that in a moment of weakness you will say yes to them. Your weak point, George, is that you are too susceptible to flattery.' He fully expected victory; many old-time Liberals like Edward Blake declined to support the Liberal party's position on unrestricted reciprocity, but Conservatives had not counted on free-trade farmers prevailing over tariff manufacturers. Macdonald said: 'I am greatly grieved at Blackstock's defeat but we must find a seat for him.'

The death of Sir John A. Macdonald and the Conservative party's decline into oblivion after five prime ministers in as many years put an end to George's aspirations. Simultaneously, from his pinnacle of professional and social acclaim, he fell quickly into limbo, obsessed with imaginary illnesses, for which his earlier breakdown when his newly acquired religious mania had so irritated Tom was but a dress rehearsal. He abandoned his career in order to visit one specialist after another. All said there was nothing whatever the matter with him, and Emma continued her travels, taking large quantities of opium to relieve agonizing and unspecified pain. Only the Reverend W.S.B. had a kind word to say for her, and as for his son he said: 'My heart bleeds for him when I think of his own weaknesses and of his sad surroundings.'

Unable or unwilling to work, George took to spending his days in bed, neglecting his profession, while the women of the family censured Emma: 'If George could be made to see her as she really is, he would break with her forever and that would be his salvation.' Emma instituted divorce proceedings at Newport on the grounds of non-support, which gained a good deal of notoriety in Toronto when newspapers reported the judge's scathing remarks about George's failure for many years to support her, but then it was she who had flown the nest. In less than a year, Emma married a man fifteen years her junior, whose constant presence in the wings had earlier raised all sorts of suspicions. The coupled settled for a time in Montreal, where, according to welcome gossip that reached Toronto, no one called upon them.

Far from feeling bitter, George said: 'I love her still in the best sense of the word and believe no serious ill of her,' and now he turned against his own family. He warned Tom, his long-suffering benefactor: 'Loose irreligious notions of both of us are responsible for my downfall ... You are living utterly away from God and some terrible thing will happen unless you alter your ways.' Specialists in Toronto and New York advised commital to an institution, and Dr Daniel Clark of the Provincial Lunatic Asylum said: 'He has travelled hither and thither as his fancy dictated in the vain hope that he could get away from himself, humoured and coddled by his friends, a person of senseless impulses with no discretion or judgment in spite of his natural shrewdness and cunning.'

At last Tom refused to spend another cent until George was lodged in a hospital: 'out of which he cannot come for a term of years unless cured and until then I do not wish to hear more about him for I am wearied beyond expression by the whole business.' And at Tom's expense, George took up residence in one American institution after another, generally complaining of his luxurious quarters as the Black Hole of Calcutta and longing for Wiesbaden or some other spa with its more exciting clientele. His friends thought he resisted all attempts at help in his desire not to get well; he passed from one physician to another, including Dr Osler, all of whom diagnosed him as a chronic, hysterical hypochondriac, but at home to his sisters he was still 'dear George' and it was still 'poor Tom.' 'Your sister Millie,' his father wrote to George, 'loves you with a love stronger than death.'

Released at last from medical care, George got into his old stride again. Active in his law practice, which rapidly expanded, he headed for New York and the Waldorf Astoria, sending the bills to Tom, and settled down as legal adviser to hopeful entrepreneurs in various schemes, coal in Pennsylvania, railways in Mexico, an air-brake invention, the Trans-Canada Railway. Wealthy and influential friends introduced him to New York society, in which he revelled: 'Between business and social engagements I am full of occupation all the time,' he said. Robert Erskine Ely, a New York friend of Carrie's, said: 'I do not know his like anywhere.'

In 1903, at home his name a household word throughout the land, he was in New York again: 'Our business affairs go well.' He had appointments with Pierpont Morgan and other financiers, the railway magnate James Hill, the British ambassador, and members of the United States Cabinet. He received a flow of invitations from New York society, where his reputation as a brilliant lawyer, orator, and conversationalist burned bright; taken to the opera, guest of honour at dinner parties, he was in his element: 'I am feted everywhere, dinners and luncheons all the time. The houses [at Newport] are beautiful and the money they all spend simply fabulous ... They all say

I am the best known private foreigner in the U.S.' None of this was due to his imagination, and in April he reported: '"Blackstock" is a name in everybody's mouth and in all the papers yesterday as Mr Whitney's horse of that name, named after me of course, won the great race, the suburban handicap on Monday. The papers have great headlines "Blackstock wins."' At Quebec the same social pleasures awaited him, dinner with Sir Wilfrid Laurier, or lunch in George's honour at the Garrison Club or another at the St James's in Montreal.

In June he crossed over to London to be picked up just as quickly by the rich and titled. He had immediately sought out the one Gibbs baron: 'Dined with Aldenham family en famille. Everybody so sweet and simple and such charming manners. They have a beautiful place in Regent's Park, just like the country, a grand old mansion.' Lord Strathcona called on him at the Hotel Cecil with pressing invitations to stay, but after the first visit George wrote home: 'I should be glad to avoid it as the cold terrifies me. You can't believe how dismal the place is.' Lord Mountstephen called and sent invitations as did Lord Thring, James Bryce, the editor of the *Times*, and countless others. No letter reached Toronto without mention of the prominent people who courted George. Society hostesses were equally anxious to capture him: 'They are all very kind and nice to me.'

He had caught the imagination of the Unionist (i.e., the Conservative) party, who invited him to stump the countryside on their behalf; George needed no second bidding, and they invited him to stand for

Parliament: 'I mean in a general way it was urged upon me.' The party, unaware of his strange behaviour in the past or the verdict of such men as Dr Daniel Clark or Dr Osler, but greatly impressed by his oratory, asked him to stand in the Forest of Dean against Sir Charles Dilke and offered to pay all his election expenses. 'Life here agrees with me wonderfully,' said George, but there were difficulties: 'If one knocks about in society, pays visits to country houses expenses are enormous.' On subsequent yearly trips to the United Kingdom, George kept up his contacts with British politics, declined requests to run for Parliament, and in 1910 found himself in much demand as a speaker during the general election. His reputation was prodigious: 'I am having invitations right and left, far more than I want.' The excitement proved too much.

Carrie's adventures proceeded at a slower pace. In the winter of 1888, which she had spent with her parents and sisters on the Island of Jersey, she had buckled down to study in an effort to repair the breach in her schooling, and Mary reported: 'Poor child she is working very hard to improve herself in every way.' After Donald's disappearance, she went to New York in the early nineties, where at first she was badly off and lonely; then George came to her aid. Determined to be independent, working during the day and attending lectures at night, she began to meet men and women of original and stimulating minds who were interested in the social and political problems of the day, and she soon made many friends, one of whom was Robert Erskine Ely, geographer and early pioneer in the field of adult education, director of Harvard's Prospect Union.

She changed direction to become an assistant to a well-known American neurologist (after all, she had had some experience in looking after George), and he appears to have had wonderful faith in her ability to handle his wealthy neurotic female patients, whose very wealth and idleness had brought them to nervous collapse. It was her duty to accompany them on long curative tours of Europe and the Far East, but not all the tours ended amicably; on one at least, the two ladies had reached such an acrimonious impasse that George threatened the heiress with a lawsuit. Brash and ambitious, by all accounts captivating and clever, Carrie now had a career and an assured income. At the end of every tour, she submitted a bill to the patient in the best medical tradition, a fine distinction which raised her in her own mind to a professional level.

In New York her range of acquaintances increased, and in London, by the kindness of the erstwhile royal tutor, she was introduced to several well-known names. She knew Prince Peter Kropotkin, émigré and anarchist, who admired her intelligence and wit, and when Father's sister Lizzie went to school in England in 1901, Prince Kropotkin came down to take Lizzie out to lunch. George pleaded with Carrie: 'I hope you will not throw aside any offers of marriage you may receive.' Mr Ely, her devoted admirer, had proposed a great number of times without success; then suddenly on one of her round-the-world voyages, she met and engaged herself to a British Army doctor at

Rangoon. She had fallen in love with Burma and India; here was scope indeed for her ambition. As for Major Duer, Father used to say he could hardly have known what had hit him. In October of 1904 George saw her off at New York on her way to marriage and the subcontinent; she sailed well armed with letters of introduction from Lord Strathcona to governors and viceroy.

She thrived. On visits to Simla, that hill-station of Raj respite, she and her compatriot Sara Jeannette Duncan, Mrs Everard Cotes, rivalled each other in their minor coteries of friends and admirers. She travelled extensively and, never a typical memsahib, cultivated friendships with Indians. In 1911 she sent for her nieces, Tom's daughters, Lizzie, now known as Elizabeth, and Barbara; it was the year of the great Durbar, and after presenting them to an imposing array of acquaintances during the social season at Delhi and succeeding in having her tent placed as advantageously as possible at the Durbar itself, she took them on a motor tour from one side of India to the other. They were, in fact, the first people ever to make the complete journey across the vast subcontinent by car; the Grand Trunk Road had existed since ancient times from Calcutta to the northwest, but it had only just been opened up in its entirety to motor traffic. They set off with a competent driver and Carrie's black short-haired chow, named Jack, the gift of a Chinese mandarin friend.

Welcomed and entertained at the palaces of Carrie's maharaja acquaintances, they stayed also in Salvation Army hostels, for her greatest friend in India headed the organization and Carrie was not one to worry about such a dichotomy. From Barrackpore, north of Calcutta, they travelled to the North-West Frontier Province: to Attock, Peshawar, and beyond, where no accommodation was available and the Army was engaged in keeping an uneasy peace. They slept at Army cantonments, where they were unwelcome, unpopular, and had no right to be. 'Where in the name of ... is that ... American woman?' one colonel was overheard to say.

At Barrackpore, Carrie had begun to teach her nieces how to shoot, and in the car she always sat with a box of loaded pistols on her lap, but the unlicensed ownership of pistols or guns in British India was a crime that could be punished by death; she had quietly removed her husband's firearms from his mess. Back in Peshawar or Rawalpindi, when the police arrested her driver, Carrie offered some resistance. Yes, she knew he was an escaped convict, but he was the only reliable mechanic available; this was why she had insisted on her nieces learning how to use the pistols. The man was wanted on a murder charge in Calcutta. The replacement driver proved not to be so reliable for on their return the car somersaulted at night – they always drove by night and rested by day – into a waterless canal. They were injured, Carrie seriously, but lucky to escape with their lives; Barbara succeeded in climbing out of the pit to make her way to a railway track, where she flagged down a train by signalling with her white petticoat.

Carrie had developed a keen interest in the stock market, taken to gambling on it, and made frequent visits to Toronto and New York with this in view. Then just before the War, in her fifties, in an even greater gamble, she adopted a baby in England, passing him off as her own, so that many an eyebrow lifted in New York, London, and Toronto at the announcement in the birth columns of the newspapers. Later on, unsubstantiated rumour had it that by persuading her husband to sign a false birth certificate she exposed him to blackmail for the rest of his life by a black-sheep of his own family. She named the baby Jackie, the same name, it will be noted, as her beloved chow which had earlier accompanied her to India's northwest frontier.

The trio, parents and adopted baby, were on their way back to Burma and India when war broke out, putting Major, now Colonel, Duer in charge of one of the two military hospitals in Malta, but presumably not the one from which Vera Brittain was to flee. His hospital cared only for troops from India, so many of whom fought side by side with ours in that war. On their return to Rangoon in 1919, Carrie died of cholera, but more of the effect of the injuries received in the car accident several years earlier; while, in time, her husband ended his days in the south of France, where the climate was mild and the living cheap, the announcement of his death arriving in a cable at lunch time at '79' when I was about thirteen, and although I had scarcely taken note of him before, the exotic setting of the Riviera made an impression on me.

In the nineties Mary had said of Tom, our grandfather: 'We often fear that his burdens may make him old before his time.' At the turn of the century, she said again: 'It does seem terrible that so many are dependent on him but there is no use dwelling on that.' He had long taken on all responsibility for his parents and sisters. In the larger world, the mines swallowed time, health, and fortune, while by involving himself in the James Bay Railway and the Central Ontario Railway in an unsuccessful attempt to establish Toronto more firmly as a railhead in competition with Montreal, the headquarters of two freight-carrying lines, only an immensity of trouble ensued. But as a corporation lawyer, he was well known and eminently successful, and as manager for his father-in-law's business affairs he had overseen the construction and furnishing of the King Edward, the city's first large luxury hotel. Three months after its opening, he could say: 'The Hotel is crowded and is a huge success.'

The pursuit of *objets d'art* for the hotel had taken him on many trips to Italy, a land he loved. Always a happy traveller, he made frequent trips to London with Hattie, and he had visited Egypt; it was the age of tourism on the grand scale. At home, '79' rang with the lively talk and laughter of guests; he had many friends and liked to entertain. Vestiges of this convivial past endured for many years during our childhood in the calling-cards that appeared in the hall on silver trays or the sight of elderly gentlemen on New Year's Day, when they came to see our grandmother after they had paid their respects to the Lieutenant-Governor and the Bishop. By 1904 Grandfather was seriously ill and the end was not far off.

In his turn, the Reverend W.S.B. approached death, saying in characteristic vein: 'My own life has been made up of such a degree of imperfections and faults that I am astonished that the goodness and mercy of God has been so conspicuous in His dealings with me.' He died in September of 1905, and Mary wrote in her diary that he had been her companion for over fifty years and now had gone to his heavenly home. As if in atonement for the years of poverty and neglect, tributes flowed in and newspapers printed columns on his life. Already, in 1896, Victoria University had conferred an honorary Doctorate of Divinity on him, and the Church spoke of him now as one of its most widely known ministers.

Mary said: 'His last audible prayers were for Tom,' and on July 25th, 1906, the front pages of the papers carried news of Tom's death and long laudatory accounts of his life; they noted his huge losses in connection with mines, which later were to puzzle me for never had this been mentioned in my hearing before, but memory tells me that family were divided between those who closed their eyes to reality and those who had grasped the facts.

Some foreboding must have clouded Grandfather's last years: a son and heir, on whom such hopes had rested, the reverse of his father's coin; but on the credit side ranged a happy marriage, children who idolized him, and the capacity throughout life to enjoy the moment. Then, when Bright's incurable disease brought blindness and unrecognizably bloated and transformed his stocky frame, he bore the suffering well, and now it was the Gospels, Isaiah, and favourite hymns that he wanted to hear. On the day of his death, his mother entered in her diary: 'My dear precious son Thomas passed away about 6:15 this evening to be forever with the Lord I hope.' Four years later, she followed him, surely to those mansions above which had ever been in her thoughts.

∽

The blinds came down at '79' and Hattie, our Grandmother Blackstock, took some of the family on the first of those tours of Britain and Europe. On another tour eight years later, the War broke out. Immediately, our grandmother's large touring-car was converted into an ambulance and sent off to France. Father's older brother Billy, unable to join up but anxious to do his bit, had another car converted for himself to drive. In February of 1915 a convoy of Red Cross vehicles assembled in Belgrave Square, and seated at the controls of the large white van with the enormous red crosses painted on its sides he passed Constitution Hill, rounded the Victoria Monument, entered the grounds of Buckingham Palace to be reviewed by the King, drove on to Southampton, crossed over to France, and continued until he reached the Vosges Mountains, which overlook the Marne. Six months earlier, the British and French armies, the latter reinforced by the taxi-brigade, had beaten off the Germans in the War's first battle. Then, all too soon, Billy was sent home by the Red Cross, a casualty of peace not war.

In Canada a generation answered the call of King and Country. In England, Father's younger brother,

George (not to be confused with Grandfather's brother), joined up immediately and then transferred to the Canadian Army's First Division to become in time a lieutenant-colonel before he was twenty-five (which was exceptional in that War); he was mentioned twice in dispatches and awarded the Military Cross. But my father's war service bore a different stamp. He had gone to England to do post-graduate work in chemistry in 1911, first at Oxford and then at Manchester under Charlie (later Chaim) Weizmann, who was to become Israel's first president. He enlisted, as soon as war was declared, in that strange force in the British Army the UPS, the University and Public Schools Brigade, where all had to come from the great public (i.e., private) schools or the universities and nearly all were privates.

Transferred to some regiment (I forget which, but I think it was the Royal Fusiliers) as a private, Father awaited the call to France that never came, dressed in one of Mr Selfridge's ill-fitting uniforms, with which this particular department-store owner had been selected to supply the British Army. According to Father, the uniform fitted only as long as he remembered to hunch his shoulders. By the following May, he was no closer to the Front: 'The officers have given up the idea of military training ...' Now twenty-seven, with poor sight in one eye, he could hardly have fired a reliable shot, nor was he officer material, constitutionally unable to make a sudden decision, always examining everything from every point of view, and all the while trying without success to transfer to the Canadian Army, writing letter after letter to anyone who might help him get to the Front.

Week in and week out, digging trenches in Croydon or Epsom, then marching the many miles to the opposite trench, usually in foul weather, to fill it in, all in the name of military training, while the real war by August of 1915 in France took its terrible toll, he was released at last through the efforts of Weizmann and others to spend the War in Birmingham in charge of research units at one of Britain's largest munitions factories. Here, at least, he received rapid promotion. In the last desperate year of the War, when almost every man who could march was sent to France, he made another attempt to reach the Front and was just as successfully foiled, being sent off on one training scheme after another. He arrived in France in the last months of the War.

As for Father's sisters, Barbara joined the Red Cross V.A.D. (Voluntary Aid Detachment) in a group that contained a good many titled young women, and then, because she had shown some talent in nursing, the physician in charge suggested she train at the London Hospital, exceedingly hard work in hard conditions but to her a sort of manumission; hitherto, our grandmother would not entertain the thought of any career. Two younger sisters, Hat and Dot, at twenty and eighteen, were also Red Cross V.A.D.'s, the former as a cook (without any acquaintance with kitchens except a five-weeks course), the latter as a nurse. Both spent four years in Walmer on the Kent coast of southeast England at St Anselm's, a small hospital which was soon taken over by the Canadian Army, and into which streamed casualties from France. Here at dawn they could hear the early morning boom of guns across the Channel when it heralded new battles.

As cook, Hat showed some initiative when she bicycled off to Walmer Castle, one of the famous Cinque Ports, of which the seventh Earl Beauchamp was Lord Warden – the honour had been held by Wellington and was to be held by Churchill – to ask if she could borrow his butler once a week, for she could not manage to cook legs of lamb or joints of beef for a hundred on Saturday night and then carve the meat for Sunday dinner; the request was granted.

Father's sister Elizabeth, now married and living in Scotland on her husband's large sheep farm, invited scores of Canadian servicemen to spend their leaves in peace and comparative plenty, while her husband drove a Red Cross ambulance at the Front. He was put in charge of evacuating casualties from Boulogne. During one of the greatest battles of the war, the Second Battle of Ypres, when the Germans used chlorine gas on British and Canadian soldiers, for which the battle is justly famous, a staff-car with three officers and driver passed by him just as a shell decapitated the four occupants, and still the car continued on its crazy death-ride. This scene he described on his next leave home, laughing uncontrollably, which horrified Elizabeth until she realized that the shock had been too much for him.

The War did not end at Armistice Day; a year later, two of Father's Gooderham cousins killed themselves. Lyman, a young officer in the trenches, gassed and taken prisoner-of-war, could not overcome the horror he had seen. He went over to Buffalo and shot himself. Grant, a pilot in the Royal Flying Corps, where life expectancy was said to be three weeks at the most, had survived but was so badly affected that once home again he began to tell his friends that he just could not face returning to France. They assured him repeatedly that the War was over; he would not believe them nor could he escape the feeling of dread that he must have had all during the War, and so he went down to Toronto's waterfront and drowned himself.

By a coincidence that rounds off this tale, when the family – my grandmother, Father, my mother, and the aunts (for their brother George had returned as part of the Army with his men) – came home in 1919, landed at Quebec, and boarded the train for Toronto, a head-on collision with another train caused a fire that destroyed all their belongings at Terrebonne, where one hundred years earlier their great-grandparents, Caroline and Thomas Gibbs, had begun life in the New World on the seigniory of Roderick Mackenzie. At the Union Station in Toronto, a large group of relatives welcomed them, although one of Grandmother's sisters remarked that they were dressed like Belgian refugees; tact was not one of the strong points of some of our relations.

Outwardly the Great War did not alter life significantly; it went on as before until the mounting effects of the Depression and the changes brought about by the Second World War swept away this particular world. But inwardly the country carried for years to come the sense of loss and grief. If Canada won her spurs on those battlefields, it also lost a generation, from which perhaps it never recovered.

Women, however, gained something, for they had played such a part that their role changed. Hat said that her war work gave her a sense of freedom: 'You had something to do and you put your whole heart into it.'

Just before the outbreak of war, George Tate Blackstock (Grandfather's brother) had fallen once more into his old disequilibrium, this time in England, but no amount of persuasion induced him to leave the country. Nieces and nephews failed in every strategy, and when at last they succeeded in placing him aboard ship at Southampton and returned to London congratulating themselves, he was there before them by an earlier train. Eventually he sailed for Canada to be cared for by his adoring sisters, Millie and May, and Colonel Duer said: 'Surely, there can be no physician in the whole country who thinks that rest can do George any good now.'

After the war, he removed himself to Buffalo for several years, probably as an economy; failing eyesight had forced him to give up his profession and he had always spent lavishly. There it appears he assumed the name G.T. Atwood, under which he sent out violently anti-American letters to newspapers. 'I have duly noted your remarks about your failure to find culture and breeding in the United States,' replied one angry reader, unless, of course, it was George himself who had written the reply, 'and I feel it would not be out of place to say here that there is at least one sailing a week to your rotten little Island, so why further endure the agonies of a second class America?'

In 1921 on December 27th, he died at home in Toronto, greatly mourned by his sisters: 'No words can tell what his dear, delightful companionship meant to us.' The *Globe*, describing him as a leading criminal lawyer in the country, observed that he had had a remarkable knowledge of the English language (which surely came from his father and the parsonage): 'He was wonderfully good society and was known over the Continent as a fine entertainer and a great conversationalist.'

George's daughter, who lived with her mother and not with her father, inherited his 'speechifying.' In the late 1890s, when she was about fifteen, she visited Washington and attended Congress one day; a Congressman rose to say that Canadians were only waiting to join the United States, whose cry of Manifest Destiny had long sounded in Canadian ears. George's daughter leapt to her feet and cried: 'Never, never, never,' and, with all the ardour that consumed her, she went on to tell why this should be so. Ushers escorted her from the premises, but not before some of the members stood up and applauded and all this was apparently recorded in newspapers. On the following day, her American grandmother, Emma's mother, abruptly placed her on the train for Montreal (or possibly it was Kingston, I am not sure which) but there, as it pulled into the station, she was met by an enthusiastic crowd and a brass band. If, as a nation, we seldom expressed our innermost feelings, or wore our hearts on our sleeves, we felt a deep and passionate love of country nonetheless.

The Methodist parsonage had bound its children

together even if the miles were to separate; it gave them a sense of who they were. It provided our grandfather, Tom, his brother George, and his sister Carrie with the impetus to go out and challenge the world, and opened a quieter one to his sisters Millie and May, who, with the self-assurance that the parsonage had also given them, were oblivious to what the world thought. In 1924 when Dot, their youngest niece, married and the wedding reception took place on a warm May day in the garden of '79,' the bridegroom saw the gate open and two elderly women walk in. He said: 'Whoever can that be?' Dot replied: 'It is the aunts.' Her Aunt May had come strangely gowned in crimson silk, with the last twelve inches or so of the dress, and a stole to match, of heavy crimson beaded work with large squat white cross-legged figures (surely they were buddhas, or is my imagination playing tricks on me?) all around, which Carrie had once sent home from India.

This, like so much else, is part of my inheritance, and it raises in my mind the thought that our family from the beginning has had a fair share of eccentrics. Indeed, if I have a regret now as I look backwards, it is the fading away in our thoroughly different city, not of the pomps of yesteryear but of an independent spirit which produced the eccentrics; in our youth, they abounded in the town. Today it is disaffected strata of society that do not conform, and all in a thoroughly predictable manner, but rarely does the individual in his or her own unique way; a blandness has fallen upon us. And there are other regrets now that the old Canada has gone forever, although I would not want to turn back the clock. As though a flood had washed it away, it has gone; a new and uncertain country forever trying to define itself has taken its place. But the old Canada knew who we were, Canadian: North American but not American, and with roots deep in the past of Britain and France. We were distinct and different from all three.

May died in 1924. Nieces and nephews made every effort to watch over Millie but in vain, for she remained aloof, proud, independent, and smartly attired; she had always shown a flair for fashion. Then, surrounded by her many cats and kittens, and living on alone, she secluded herself in the house on Homewood Avenue, conversing with visitors from an attic window, until she too died. But as old Cousin Marion observed several years later: 'She lived in a world of her own and always her family in her estimation stood head and shoulders above the rest of the world, so she wasn't unhappy in her memories.'

Now, as I close this rambling tale, in my mind's eye I see Millie pouring over the contents of the letters, reading them evening after evening, just as I have done too, until her sight failed; we are alike in some ways, though I have Carrie's love of foreign lands. And although Millie put 'destroy everything' on those bundles, it was she who preserved them, and they have thrown light into dark and hidden corners of my past, and told me something of what my country is that these men and women, with their faults and failures, speaking to each other down the years as its history unfolded, had a share in building.